Southern Echoes

SOUTHERN ECHOES

Meritez

The Wright Family from the Delaware to the Rio Grande

George W. Wright

HERITAGE BOOKS
2019

HERITAGE BOOKS
AN IMPRINT OF HERITAGE BOOKS, INC.

Books, CDs, and more—Worldwide

For our listing of thousands of titles see our website
at
www.HeritageBooks.com

Published 2019 by
HERITAGE BOOKS, INC.
Publishing Division
5810 Ruatan Street
Berwyn Heights, Md. 20740

International Standard Book Number
Paperbound: 978-0-7884-5885-9

For Melissa, Jonathan and
the future generations...

"It is the province of history to tell the biography,
not only of men, but of Man;
to present the long procession of generations
as but the passing thoughts of one continuous life;
to transcend their blindness and brevity
in the slow unfolding of the tremendous drama
in which all play their part."

BERTRAND RUSSELL

Contents

Acknowledgments

There are many whose contributions have made this book a reality. I am especially beholden to Chuck Parsons whose article on Linton and Lawrence Wright in *Old West* magazine set my work in motion.

Many thanks are also due to Donaly E. Brice at the Texas State Archives, Patricia Harmon in Georgia, Victoria P. Young in North Carolina, Anne M. Norton in South Carolina, Richard L. Lindberg in Pennsylvania and Michael Trenchard in the United Kingdom. I am also grateful to William Angresano for his artwork featured in this book and Joel Mitnick for his graphic design assistance. Quotes from *Taming the Nueces Strip: The Story of McNelly's Rangers* by George Durham as told to Clyde Wantland, (c) 1962, are used by permission of the University of Texas Press.

Numerous family members have furnished materials and recollections including my father Robert F. Wright, uncle Edwin D. Wright, Jr. and cousins Philip T. Wright, Jr., Helen Frances Boomgarden, Evelyn White, John T. Wright, Jr., Tommy and Susan Wright, John T. Wright, IV, Eric Nikolai and Edward R. Stanford, Jr. Special thanks to our cousin David T. Dixon for sharing his invaluable research materials and ideas.

Lastly, affectionate gratitude is due my wife, Susan, for her patience with my absorption in this project.

Preface

The Wright family narrative that follows is mostly derived from original archive records and published sources.

The ubiquity of the Wright name made tracing our lineage a laborious task. After years of researching the wrong Wrights and convinced our forebears came from England to Virginia, I was about to publish another version of this book several years ago. Fortunately, at that moment I stumbled onto new DNA-based scholarship proving I had strayed far afield. That painful epiphany prompted me to return to the Georgia archives where I picked up our real ancestors' trail leading back to South Carolina and Pennsylvania. I was rewarded with the discovery that our family's true story is far more interesting than the one I had to abandon.

My love of the past is lifelong but the notion of a book about the Wrights was many years in the making. The stories I heard at my grandfather's knee about his father's life as a Texas Ranger and frontier doctor first sparked my fascination with that era. Later, as a father, I wanted to know more about our earlier ancestors, how they lived and what they thought. As those generations recede further into the distant past these pages remind us they were once as vibrant in their days as we are now in ours. More importantly, this is the story of our nation as it was experienced by the first ten American generations of our family.

George W. Wright

April, 2019
Edgewater, New Jersey

Disembarking on the Delaware River

1 Philadelphia Freedom

In the late 16th century the English and Dutch eyed the continents beyond the Atlantic Ocean where their Iberian rivals had a century-long head start in the race for overseas conquest and wealth. In the 1580s Sir Walter Raleigh led three failed attempts to establish a permanent colony in North America. In 1606 a fourth expedition was assembled by the London Company. Its royal charter described the territories England claimed as all lands "along the Sea Coasts between four and thirty degrees of Northerly Latitude from the Equinoctial Line and five and forty degrees of the same Latitude." In other words the new colony stretched from the Atlantic to the Pacific encompassing most of the present United States. Raleigh christened it Virginia for Elizabeth I, the virgin Tudor queen.

Thirteen years later Puritan settlers aboard the *MAYFLOWER* bound for the Dutch enclave at New Amsterdam, now New York City, strayed off course and landed at Cape Cod. They founded the Massachusetts Bay Colony as the first community of Protestant dissenters in the New World. Aside from its main commercial purposes, colonization became an effective way for England to export its religious dissidents. The Crown chartered eleven more colonies. The last one, Georgia, was established to resettle British debtors prison inmates as a human barrier between South Carolina and Spanish Florida.

As the settlement of North America got underway English society was experiencing profound upheaval and division. That process was crucial in the making of America and a prime reason why Britons left their homes on perilous voyages to the New World. Under Queen Elizabeth's Stuart successors, King James I and his son Charles I, relations between the aristocracy and subordinate classes steadily deteriorated.

The Parliament that evolved from Magna Carta of 1215 was still subordinate to the Crown which retained all real authority, particularly the power to tax. By the early 1600s the demands of governing a diverse, populous society had outgrown England's autocratic feudal traditions. The Stuarts inherited and abused a system that rewarded courtiers and royal favorites from the nobility at the expense of the lower gentry, manufacturers, merchants and artisans. The latter were stifled by a corrupt government that parted them from their wealth and gave them no real voice in the nation's affairs. Politically, the conflict was reflected in a struggle between the monarchy and Parliament over the right to rule.

The frustration of the underclasses spawned radical Protestant sects, including the Baptists, Puritans and Quakers. They preached equality of all men before God and on earth but their gospel was heresy to the Church of England. Mainstream and sectarian Protestants alike increasingly saw the monarchy and Anglican officialdom as secretly Roman Catholic. King Charles I's marriage to a Catholic Spaniard, repression of the Presbyterian Church of Scotland and wars against the Calvinist Dutch aroused his subjects' worst fears. A massacre of Protestants in Ireland in 1641 raised the anti-Catholic furor in England to a fever pitch. Rumors of "popish" plots in the royal court and High Church abounded.

Worse still England suffered from a severe depression in its textile industry and massive unemployment. The poverty and despair of the urban populace completed the explosive mix. In early 1642 a botched attempt by Charles I to arrest members of the House of Commons prompted Parliament to form a Committee of Safety and its own New Model Army. Charles fled from London to Nottingham to summon volunteers and the men of York, Wales and Cornwall swore allegiance to their King. Most of southern and eastern England rose to defend Parliament. The English Civil War was on.

The Parliamentarians found their leader in Oliver Cromwell, a wealthy member of the House of Commons. His revolutionary forces defeated the Royalists after a seven-year war that ended in the capture and beheading of Charles I in 1649. Over the following decade England experienced the zealous influence of the Protestant radicals, especially the Puritans. Absolute power was concentrated in Cromwell, who assumed the title of "Lord Protector." Only his demise in 1658 kept him from crowning himself King of England. A year and a half later the dead king's son Charles II returned from abroad and the House of Stuart was restored to the throne.

Like their martyred father, Charles II and his brother James II had Papal sympathies that led to the final overthrow of their line in the Glorious Revolution of 1688. Charles II also shared with his father a debt to Sir William Penn. Sir Penn was an opportunistic navy admiral who supported Charles I at first, switched loyalty to Parliament during the Civil War and then sided with Charles II after Cromwell's death. To repay a loan from Sir Penn, Charles II made a large land grant in 1681 to his Quaker son William Penn, Jr.

William Penn, II

The grant was part of the colonial province known as Upland on the western shore of the Delaware River. William named the colony Pennsylvania in honor of his father and was designated its Proprietary and Governor. Pennsylvania was a haven for Penn's fellow Quakers in England, but he declared it open to all faiths. The Society of Friends, as the

Quakers called themselves, spoke of their new community as a "Holy Experiment" where the kind of persecution and repression they had suffered elsewhere would not prevail. In Penn's colony, freedom of worship and speech flourished to a degree that was unknown in the Old or New Worlds. Until the Revolutionary War large areas of the colony remained under the Penn Proprietorship which William's sons John, Richard and Thomas inherited after his death in 1718.

As word of Penn's charter spread among the Quakers already living in the other colonies, a group of them in Burlington, New Jersey elected to join the hamlet of about 500 settlers downstream on the west bank of the Delaware River. The village became Philadelphia. The Jersey Quakers included a bricklayer from Birmingham, England named George Guest and his wife Alice (nee Bailyes) who had recently settled in Burlington in 1680. Their children were George, John, Elizabeth and Phoebe.[1]

The Guests temporarily encamped in a cave on the Delaware at the foot of present-day Chestnut Street in Philadelphia. Nearby they built a permanent house on the site now located at the northwest corner of Front and Dock Streets. It became the city's first inn, the Blue Anchor Tavern. Before the Guests finished constructing their home, William Penn, Jr. visited the Blue Anchor when he sailed into Philadelphia aboard the ship *WELCOME* on his first visit to the new colony in 1682.[2] Several years later the pirates Edward Teach ("Blackbeard") and Captain William Kidd were said to frequent the Blue Anchor.[3]

The Blue Anchor Tavern

After establishing themselves as innkeepers, the Guests increased their wealth by acquiring Philadelphia city lots. During 1682 to 1702, George and Alice Guest bought eight lots in Philadelphia. Alice held title to three of the lots in her own name reflecting the measure of legal equality women enjoyed under Penn's administration. During 1701 to 1706, their son John purchased several city lots and lands in Chester and Newcastle Counties south of the city.

On June 26, 1701 John Guest married Mary Signy in a ceremony approved by the Philadelphia Society of Friends Monthly Meeting House.[4] John and Mary produced four children, Richard, Mary, Priscilla and Hannah who was born on February 6, 1705.[5] At age 25 Hannah Guest married out of her Quaker faith on March 15, 1730 to an Anglican lad named William Wright in St. Paul's Church in Old Chester fifteen miles below Philadelphia.[6]

St. Paul's Church, Old Chester, Pennsylvania (c.1705)

William Wright lived in Glasgow, Scotland and worked as a postilion rider ("post boy") before he came to America as a bound servant at age 18. British law required William to make the 400-mile trip from Glasgow to London to register with the Lord Mayor and General Sessions Court for overseas work. He signed up in London on May 8, 1725 for a five-year indenture and embarked to Philadelphia. The British archive records suggest that William worked for a Quaker farmer and businessman named John Cooke after he arrived in Pennsylvania.[7]

An 18th century postilion rider

The Cooke family owned extensive properties in Chester County between New London and West Caln, near East Caln where William later settled. Through an apparent connection to the London emigration authorities, Cooke also acted as a middleman who brokered the shipment of dozens of servants from England to Pennsylvania, Maryland, Virginia, South Carolina and Jamaica. Of the many workers Cooke brought to the colonies to trade to other masters, it is interesting that he chose to employ William on his own plantation. The Cookes were associated with the Philadelphia Society of Friends which may explain how William met Hannah Guest. Their marriage in 1730 occurred around the time William finished his five-year stint with the Cookes.

Within three years after marrying William and Hannah saved enough money to petition for a license to operate a tavern in West Caln, Chester County some forty miles southwest of Philadelphia. In starting their country inn, the young couple may have benefitted from Hannah's experience in her family's business, the Blue Anchor Tavern.

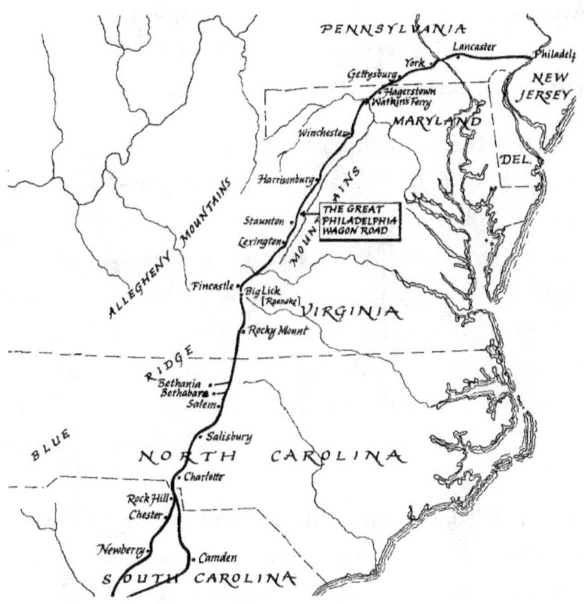

The Old Conestoga Road

West Caln was an ideal site for a tavern being situated midway between Philadelphia and Lancaster, a day's travel from either city. In the early 1700s settlers streamed along the Old Conestoga Road that stretched from Philadelphia west for about a hundred miles to the Susquehanna River and thence south along the Appalachian Mountains through Virginia, the Carolinas and down to Georgia. Like all travelers through history, they needed overnight accommodations for their families and animals.

William's and Hannah's August 29, 1732 petition submitted to the Chester County Justices of the Peace identified their tavern as previously operated by James Swaffer from 1721 to 1731. They described the house as lying along the Old Conestoga Road which was the "Great Road leading from Philadelphia to Conestoga [Lancaster]." They cited the "necessity of a public house for the accommodating of travelers and others and also to ease several of the poor inhabitants of this Township who are often oppressed with travelers upon that road."

Accompanying the Wrights' petition was a 20-pound bond payable to provincial Governor Patrick Gordon and naming James MacMath as a co-guarantor. The bond provides:

> The condition of this obligation is such that if the above bounden William Wright on obtaining his lycense to keep a publick house of entertainment for the selling of wine, beer, cyder, ale, brandy, rum and other strong liquors & if therefore the said William Wright shall not during the continuance of the said lycense suffer any unlawfull games to be housed in his house nor shall make use of mollasses or other meterials in brewing of beer or ale, but shall during the said time use & maintain good order & rule therein & observe all the laws & ordinances which are or shall be made relating to Innkeepers or Taverns within this Province then this obligation to be void of effect or else to stand in full force & virtue.

The Wagontown Inn

MacMath occupied the land as a tenant of the Penn Proprietors while awaiting his patent which he received in 1739.

West Caln tax records show William and Hannah Wright operated their tavern from 1732 to 1735 as MacMath's subtenants. The tax records for East Caln just across the Brandywine Creek first record the Wrights living there in 1735. That may be when they conveyed their interest in the tavern to James Way who eventually bought the land and house from MacMath in 1742.

The Way family operated the impressive stone house as the Sign of the Waggon until the mid-1800s. It was later known as the Wagontown Inn and still stands at 401 West Kings Highway in Coatesville.

Soon after their marriage William and Hannah Wright began building a family of five children who reached adulthood. They were Anne (Walker); William, Jr.; our direct ancestor James; George and Moses. The inclusion of Hannah's name in the Wrights' 1732 tavern petition and bond suggests she played a major role in managing the inn. If so, the increasing demands of child rearing on Hannah may account for the short three-year life span of the Wrights' inn.

Chester County records list William Wright as an East Caln landholder, but not a deed owner, in the late 1730s and early 1740s. His status during that interval is explained by the 1739 survey of James MacMath's 100-acre patent where the tavern was located on the west side of the West Brandywine Creek. MacMath's survey describes William as being "seated" on the adjoining lot across the Brandywine along the opposite bank. William was occupying that land in anticipation of receiving his own patent from the Penn sons which came five years later.

Under a July 25, 1744 deed John, Richard and Thomas Penn granted to William Wright for fifteen pounds and ten shillings a 150-acre patent in a part of East Caln that is now located in West Brandywine Township. The lot was surveyed by Samuel Lightfoot on December 6, 1745 and measured out to 156 acres. William's land included over half a mile of frontage along the east bank of the West Brandywine. The land was about three hundred yards north of the Sign of the Waggon, so the Wrights must have kept a close connection to their former tavern after the Ways took it over.

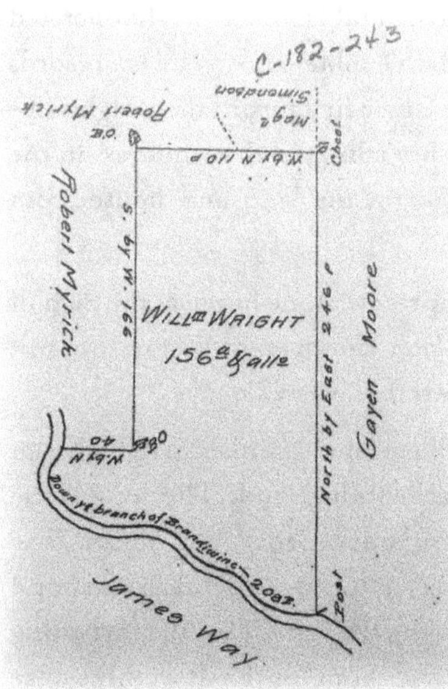

Survey of William Wright's East Caln land (1745)

William's patent was good farming land and the Brandywine's steady flow made it a suitable place to build a mill. During the next dozen years, William prospered as a farmer and fulling miller. A fulling mill captured falling water to turn a wheel, axle and gear box that operated reciprocating wooden paddles to agitate water in a holding tank. The process was used to clean and fluff wool clothing. In short, the Wright mill was a colonial laundromat.

By the late 1740s Pennsylvania was the most populous colony with about 250,000 citizens.[8] Chester County saw healthy economic and population growth in the mid-1700s as the frontier pushed westward. It had more than a thousand farms producing horses, cattle, sheep, corn, oats, wheat and rye. Its orchards yielded apples and peaches for eating and making whiskey and brandy. The mills and forges along the Brandywine and other streams hummed with manufacturing activity.[9]

By the early 1750s the Wright children were beginning to reach adulthood. William and Hannah foresaw the day when their sons would need more land to support themselves and families. The Wrights must have heard talk from passing travelers on the Old Conestoga Road about the abundant free land down south. Several hundred miles away, North Carolina's royal governors were doling out land patents to entice settlers to their colony. Like many Pennsylvanians, William took advantage of the grants to acquire lots totaling three and a half square miles on North Carolina's border with South Carolina. William sent his second son James to settle on his new land and the others soon followed.

As James Wright prepared to leave for the Carolina territory, Great Britain was moving toward a war with France that would be fought on three continents. It was known as the Seven Years War in Europe and the French and Indian War in America. Britain claimed all lands east of the Mississippi River but the French had a lucrative fur trade in some of those territories and were naturally loath to hand them over to their enemies. In 1753 King George II granted a charter to the Ohio Company that included 600,000 acres in western Pennsylvania occupied by the French and their Indian allies.

To enforce British interests, Virginia Governor Robert Dinwiddie dispatched his 22-year-old colonial militia commander Major George Washington to expel the French from Ohio Company territory and take their stronghold at Fort Duquesne near the fork of the Allegheny and Monongahela Rivers. Washington's troops defeated the smaller French force they first encountered, but had to withdraw in the face of the large garrison that held Fort Duquesne. While the Virginians were building their own makeshift fort the French captured them and sent them home. Before releasing their prisoners, though, the captors forced Washington at gunpoint to confess to the murder of a French officer. In response, the colonial governors met with delegates from the Iroquois Confederacy in Albany, New York to plan war against the French and their allies, the Delawares, Ottawas and Shawnees.[10]

In the spring of 1755, British General Edward Braddock arrived in Virginia and marched through Maryland with several British regular and colonial militia regiments to seize Fort Duquesne. He was joined by Major Washington who was familiar with the Pennsylvania back country. The young major was also anxious to redeem his honor and finish the mission he had begun the year before. As Braddock's large column forded the Monongahela River about seven miles from Fort Duquesne, they were ambushed by French troops and Indians throwing the British into confusion and a headlong route. Braddock was mortally wounded and his force suffered nearly 900 killed and wounded. Washington miraculously escaped unharmed despite all the other officers in his regiment being killed or wounded.[11]

The catastrophe on the Monongahela only steeled the British will to have the Ohio country. They sent more regular and colonial regiments from Philadelphia to guard the frontier settlements and wrest Fort Duquesne from the French. The troops often marched through Chester County along the Old Conestoga Road past the Wrights' farm and their former tavern. On September 16, 1757 the Second Battalion of the Royal American (60th) Regiment was en route to join General John Stanwix at Carlisle when it stopped in West Caln at the Sign of the Waggon after covering 14 miles that day.[12]

Braddock's Defeat at the Monongahela River

Fort Duquesne was finally captured by General John Forbes in late 1758. The next spring another expedition under General Stanwix was sent to rebuild and hold the fort renamed Pittsburgh for Prime Minister William Pitt, the Elder. Stanwix began requisitioning civilian materiel for the war effort and issued a directive to local authorities to fill wagon quotas. He ordered Chester County to furnish 66 wagons and teamsters for his army:

> A number of waggons will be wanted for His Majesty's Service and, in order to *avoid Impressing, and all other severe Methods,* I have thought proper to make the following very advantageous Proposals...Each Waggon to load at the Grand Magazine at Carlisle; and for every Gross Hundred Weight, carried from thence to Pittsburgh (formerly Fort Du Quesne) to receive forty-two shillings and Sixpence...(emphasis added).[13]

General Stanwix was not at all pleased with the colonists' tepid response to his offer of "very advantageous" rates for the grueling 400-mile round trip between Carlisle and Pittsburgh. Stanwix carried out his threat to impress wagons, including one belonging to the Sign of the Waggon's owner James Way.[14] The general complained, "Bucks and Chester have given us only Nominal Assistance by sending us Impressed Waggons unfit for this Service by the Weakness of the Horses and Carriages. The Managers meet with more opposition in these two Counties than in any others..."[15]

General Stanwix demanded the fines be dramatically increased from 40 shillings to 20 pounds on those who failed to comply with his orders. The Pennsylvania Assembly was unintimidated and refused to enact higher penalties against their electors. Instead, the Assembly politely suggested to the general that he "pay off old contracts" and give the drivers more money for the "Risque and service expected from them."[16]

The colonists' reaction to the British army decrees was a harbinger. Their passive resistance to King George II's appropriations of labor and property during the French and Indian War foretold more robust defiance of the taxes and "other severe Methods" that would soon be imposed by his son, George III, to force the Americans to pay for that long, costly conflict after it was over.

William Wright took ill in the fall of 1757. Aware of his impending death, he signed his last will and testament on October 4 in the presence of his attorney William Clingan and friends Alexander Rogers and John Walton.[17] William left to his eldest son William, Jr. "his choice of any one of places in Carolina James excepted." James received the lands "he now lives on." His will provided for "son George next choice & Moses of others" and further specified:

> The plantation in Caln to be sold with movables and debts paid & money arising from said sale to be in manner following. To my wife fifty pounds, to daughter Anne fifty pounds, the remainder left to be

> divided to son James one sixth part & if remaining parts in three equal divisions between my sons William, George and Moses
>
> William Wright

William died within the next several weeks. His estate was inventoried on November 28, 1757 and his will was probated on January 10, 1758. The inventory suggests he was fairly wealthy by the standards of his day with personal assets valued at over 672 pounds. Besides the 156-acre farm, his other property included the fulling mill and tools, household furniture, utensils, apparel, a wagon, saddles, bridles, a strawberry roan mare, a white mare and her tail colt, a black colt, nine cattle, sixteen sheep, geese and caches of harvested grain, hay, oats and flax.

The next summer William Wright, Jr., placed a notice for the sale of his father's land and mill in Ben Franklin's Pennsylvania Gazette published in Philadelphia:

> To be sold by Way of publick Vendue, on the 18th Instant, at the House late of William Wright, deceased, a Plantation, containing 150 Acres of Land, 60 of which is cleared, with 15 Acres of Meadow, and more may be made; there is on said Plantation, a good new Fulling mill, with all the Utensils fit for carrying on the Business, situate on Brandiwine, in East Caln Township, Chester County. The Vendue to begin at Ten o'Clock. The Title and Conditions will be made known at the Time and Place of Sale, by William Wright.[18]

A year later Hannah Wright was in failing health too. She dictated her will and made her mark on it in the presence of her half sister Ann Davis, wife of Hugh Davis, and Robert Withrow. The preamble reflects Hannah's deep religious faith at the end of her life:

> In the Name of God Amen this 7th of July 1759—I Hannah Wright of East Caln in Chester County being sick and weak in body but of perfect mind and memory thanks be to God and calling to mind the mortality of my body and knowing it is appointed once for all to die do make and ordain this my last will and testament and principally and first of all I give and recommend my Soul into the Hands of God who gave it and my body I recommend to the earth to be buried in a Christian like and decent manner at the discretion of my friend nothing doubting but at the general resurrection I shall receive the same again by the mighty power of God and as touching such worldly estate wherewith it hath pleased God to bless me within this life I give and dispose of the same in the following manner...

Hannah left to her son Moses twenty pounds and her "rideing mares," to her sister Ann Davis ten pounds, to her daughter Anne Walker "wearing apparel and cow" with the remainder of her effects to be divided equally between her three eldest sons William, James and George. She named her "trusty friend" William Clingan as executor. Hannah's March 22, 1760 estate inventory records her modest belongings as a rug, blanket, side table, spinning wheel, iron pot, pewter dish, pail, strainer, cow and 50 pounds in cash held by her son William.

Hannah's daughter Anne lived out her life in East Caln with her husband John Walker. Within a few years after his mother's death William, Jr. joined the exodus from Chester County to the Carolinas where his younger brothers were waiting for him.

Heading south on the Old Conestoga Road

2 Carolina Bound

William Wright, Sr. was among the many Pennsylvanians who received land patents in Anson County, North Carolina from royal governor Matthew Rowan. In the early 1750s he was granted four lots comprising about 2,250 acres on a Broad River tributary he named Wright's Creek. It was later renamed Bullock's Creek. William's lands straddled both sides of the Creek just above Tryon County's old border with South Carolina about twenty miles west of the Catawba Nation's territory.[1]

Guyan Moore was another Tryon County patentee whose land abutted William's property. Guyan was also William's adjacent neighbor in East Caln, Pennsylvania. The border region between North and South Carolina was a magnet for Pennsylvanians. In just thirty years from 1750 to 1780 the Carolina back country's settler population increased from almost nothing to a quarter of a million souls.[2]

When the Carolinas' boundaries were re-surveyed in 1772 William's properties became part of South Carolina's New Acquisition District that was bounded on the east and west, respectively, by the Catawba and Broad Rivers and now includes upper York County. William's former lands are about five miles west of the town of York and three miles north of Sharon, South Carolina.

Soon after William Wright, Sr.'s second son, our direct ancestor James, arrived in North Carolina he married a woman named Hannah whose maiden name and birthplace are unknown. No record of their marriage was found in Pennsylvania or the Carolinas. Thus,

Hannah was probably from the sparsely populated frontier region where James settled. Based on their eight children's ages James and Hannah were likely married in the mid to late 1750s.

Hannah Wright's last will and testament filed fifty years later in Clarke County, Georgia in 1808 identifies her daughters as Sarah Clark, Hannah Walker and Nancy Stokes and her sons as William, John, our direct ancestor James, Jr., Richard and George Wright. As James, Jr. died before his mother, her will also names his children and her grandchildren, Mary Ann, William, Elizabeth, our next direct ancestor James III, John and Moses as beneficiaries.[3] Hannah's will is a crucial link connecting our Pennsylvania, South Carolina and Georgia lineage. Her signature on other Georgia records proves she was literate which was true of less than half of American women in the late eighteenth century.[4]

Within a few years after their parents died in Pennsylvania, William, Jr., George and Moses Wright followed James down the Old Conestoga Road to settle on the Carolina lands their father willed to them. When they arrived at the end of their 600-mile trek they must have been awed by the rich land, flora and wildlife they found along the Broad River. The upcountry's hills, plains and valleys teemed with elk, buffalo, bear, deer, wolves, panthers, beavers, otters and wild turkey in the mid-1700s.[5]

South Carolina's eminent eighteenth-century historian Dr. David Ramsay wrote:

> In the year 1750, when the settlement of the upper country began, there were so many buffaloes, which have long since disappeared, that three or four men with their dogs could kill from ten to twenty in a day...Deer were so numerous that a rifleman with a little powder and shot could easily kill four or five in a day. A common hunter could kill in the autumnal season as many bears as would make from two to three thousand weight of bear bacon.[6]

Cherokee Chiefs Oconostota (L.) and Attakullakulla (R.)

When James Wright set out for North Carolina about the time the French and Indian War began in the spring of 1754 he could not have known he would soon find himself in the war's vortex. On September 16, 1754 seventeen settlers were massacred at Buffalo Creek only ten miles north of the Wright lands. It was reported to South Carolina's royal governor that the attack was carried out by "French or Northward Indians...where the People were making Forts and thirty familys left their Crops."[7] In 1758 several hundred Cherokees were returning to their towns in present-day eastern Tennessee after volunteering as British allies at the siege of Fort Duquesne. As the Cherokees passed through Virginia they were fired on by settlers resulting in the deaths of many warriors. The Cherokees were enraged by the attack after serving British and colonial troops as scouts and guerrilla warfare trainers. The survivors went home to plot revenge against the nearby Carolina settlers.

After two years of frontier warfare the South Carolina authorities and Cherokee leaders began to parlay for peace. Talks were aborted when royal governor William H. Lyttleton ordered the seizure of fourteen Cherokee emissaries at Fort Prince George forty miles west of Wright's Creek. Chief Oconostota led a failed attempt to rescue the hostages resulting in their deaths. The Cherokees next attacked Fort Loudoun in eastern Tennessee. After negotiating the Fort's surrender they ambushed the retreating garrison at Cane Creek with heavy British losses. General James Grant responded to the Cane Creek incident with overwhelming military force that destroyed most of the

Illustration of Cherokees ambushing retreating Fort Loudoun garrison at Cane Creek by Ernest C. Peixotto (1869-1940)

Cherokees' lower towns. Chief Attakullakulla had no choice but to accept peace with Great Britain and South Carolina at the cost of surrendering half his Nation's territory.

The Treaty of Paris ended the war in 1763. However, the fragile truce with the Cherokees was followed by civil unrest caused by the royal authorities' oppressive taxation and neglect of public safety. The backwoods became infested with roving bands of thieves, highwaymen and worse. Even before the war the respectable citizens of Craven County, South Carolina living between the Pedee River and Lynch's Creek petitioned the colony's Upper House of Assembly demanding action against the criminals:

> We find the frontier here to be a place of refuge for many evil-disposed people and those of the meanest principles, crowding in amongst us—such as Horse Stealers and other Felons, having made their escape from North Carolina, and other parts—others cohabiting with their neighbors' wives, and living in a most lascivious manner, while we have no way or means to suppress them.[8]

The civil authorities were unwilling or unable to control the outlaw gangs that were often powerful enough to corrupt and intimidate the King's men. Dr. Ramsay describes the lawlessness on the Carolina frontier:

> Till the year 1770, there were no courts of justice held beyond the limits of the capital. The only legal authority in this infancy of the back country was that of justices of the peace, authorized by the Governor, who always resided near the sea coast. With his scanty means of information, to select proper persons for that office was no easy matter. The greatest villains generally had the most money, and often the most friends. Instead of exerting their authority to suppress horse-stealing and other crimes, some of these justices were sharers in the profits of this infamous business.[9]

In that social vacuum the settlers organized all able-bodied men into companies that drilled in military tactics and ranged the countryside hunting for brigands.[10] As North Carolina's law-abiding citizens took justice into their own hands, the "Regulator" movement arose in the mid-1760s Granville, Orange and Anson Counties. The movement spread to York and Chester Counties in South Carolina which were in a similar state of anarchy.[11] The Regulators acted out of righteous self-defense but were an intolerable threat to royal power. In North Carolina they were crushed by British regulars and colonial troops under Governor William Tryon in a major engagement at Great Alamance Creek in 1771. Some consider Alamance as the first battle of the Revolutionary War which began in earnest four years later.

The Crown's agents suppressed the remnants of the Regulator movement with military force, criminal prosecutions and death sentences. South Carolina's Regulators refrained from open defiance and avoided the harsh fates suffered by their neighbors. The uprising prompted limited reforms. The South Carolina legislature established justice courts in 1769 at Ninety-Six (now Cambridge), Orangeburgh and Camden which helped restore some order in the interior.[12]

North Carolina Governor William Tryon addresses the Regulators

Contrasted with the serenity they knew back in East Caln, the Wright brothers had to be constantly armed and watchful to protect their families and property in the Carolinas. The records of their land transactions, however, suggest they not only survived but prospered. Farming in the upcountry was mostly for subsistence and generated little cash. The settlers relied instead on land sales to newer immigrants and the brisk trade in animal skins for hard currency.[13] During the years the Wrights lived on the Broad River they were well-positioned to profit from the traffic in hides that began in the Cherokee country and flowed downstream to the port of Charleston. There the furs were loaded on British ships to meet the heavy demand for taxidermy and buckskin garments in Europe.

The Wrights acquired their original lands in North and South Carolina at low prices through inheritance and royal grants and sold them high, often to one another. Under a 1765 deed William Wright, Jr. "of East Caln Township in Chester County in the Province of Pennsylvania" sold to his brother James 600 acres on the Mecklenburg County side of Wright's Creek that William received from his father's will. The deed was witnessed by their brother Moses and recites James was living in Anson County across "Wright's Creek on the North side of the Broad River." James paid William "fifty pounds Lawful money of Pennsylvania" for the Mecklenburg land.

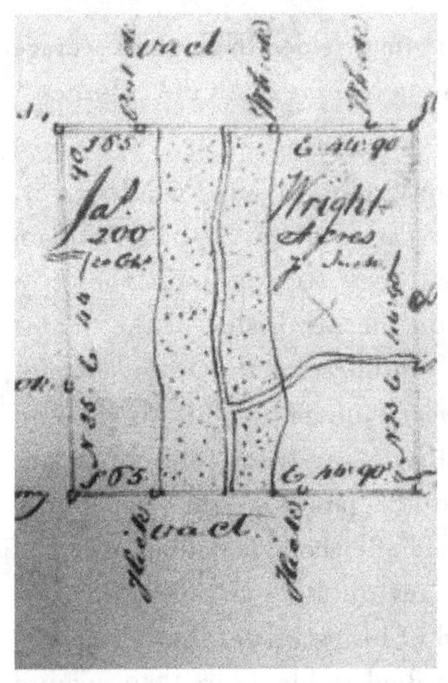

Plat for James Wright's 200-acre Turkey Creek patent (1763)

In 1763 and 1767 James Wright received royal patents for 100-acre and 200-acre lots in South Carolina on the Turkey Creek branch of the Broad River in upper Craven County about twenty miles below Wright's Creek. A few years later James and Hannah sold their Turkey Creek lots for 1,500 pounds to Isaac Sadler of Lancaster County, Pennsylvania. William Wright, Jr. left Pennsylvania and settled in Tryon County, North Carolina before 1770 when he sold to his brother Moses for 55 pounds a 600-acre lot on Turkey Creek that William received as a royal patent from South Carolina.

George was the first of the Wright brothers to move to lower Craven County, South Carolina in 1766 where he acquired 200 acres in St. David's Parish, Cheraw District. A 1770 mortgage records that George was also a planter in St. Mark's Parish, Camden District, where he loaned 95 pounds and 11 shillings to Jean Ross. The same year George sold to Moses for 200 pounds his 600-acre share of their father's legacy. Five years later Moses and his wife Agnes deeded that land to John Steen for 1,000 pounds.

During 1771 to 1774 William, Jr., James and Moses Wright sold most their Broad River properties that became part of the New Acquisition District when South Carolina's northern boundary was extended. They planned to follow George and settle in St. Mark's and St. David's Parishes east of the Santee River near the High Hills of Santee. The rich lands in that region offered the Wrights a greater share of the immense agricultural wealth of South Carolina's lower

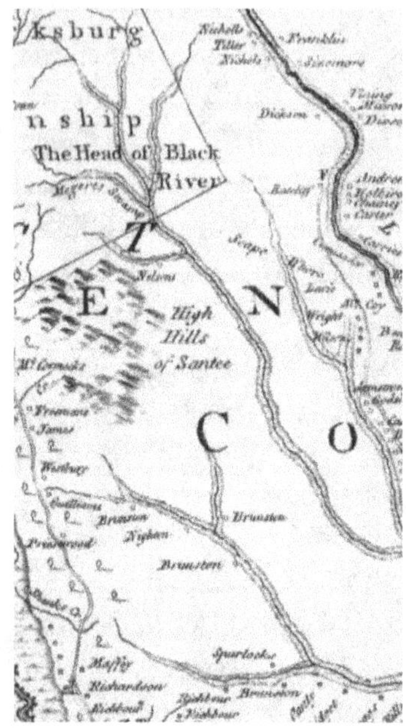

Detail from a South Carolina map showing the Wright and Wilson lands east of the Santee High Hills between the Scape Whore Swamp and Lynch's Creek (1773)

country that yielded the highest average per capita income of all the colonies.[14]

According to a 1771 deed William Wright, Jr. was a saddler in St. Mark's Parish when he paid William Carpenter 2,100 pounds for 300 acres on the north side of the Santee River southwest of the River Swamp. That year William bought 150 acres on the Little River from John Brennan. In late 1771 James Wright's paper trail vanished after he and William, Jr. sold 535 acres on Bullock's Creek. No record of his estate was found suggesting he died suddenly in 1772 around the age of forty. Hannah was left alone to raise their three daughters and five sons. But she did not lack financial means as shown by substantial land purchases in her own name after James's death.

In 1772 Hannah Wright followed her brothers-in-law to the Camden District. There she purchased from the above-mentioned John Brennan a 500-acre lot on the Beaver Dam Branch and a 250-acre lot on McGirt's Branch of the Scape Whore Swamp a few miles south of present-day Bishopville.[15] Hannah's tenant John Belton was recorded as paying two years of quitrent to her son John Wright in 1775. Hannah's close neighbors to the south were the Wilsons who also hailed from York County's New Acquisition District.

The fertile river and swamp banks where the Wrights settled produced a bounty of rice, indigo, corn, flax, rye, wheat, oats, barley and tobacco. The Santee's waters were laden with trout, catfish, rockfish and sturgeon. East of the river the High Hills of Santee rise 300

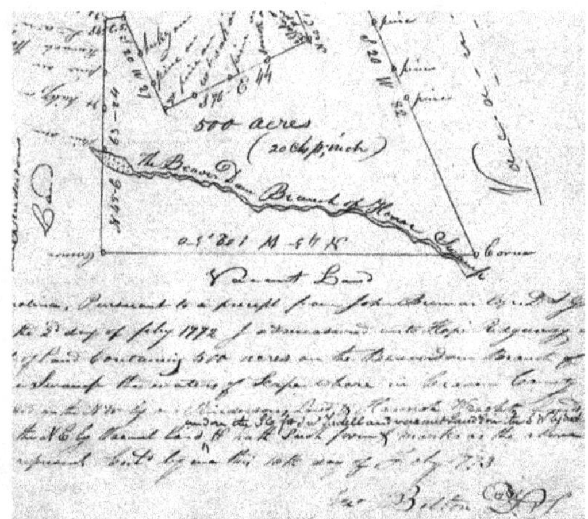

Plat for Hannah Wright's land on the Beaver Dam Branch of the Scape Whore Swamp (1772)

feet above the surrounding plains. In the 1700s the Hills' orchards yielded superior cherries, peaches and apples.[16] The Wrights lived well in the Santee territory during the few short years before the specter of war returned to haunt their world.

In the summer of 1774 a General Provincial Meeting was held in Charleston to address the dire conditions in Boston where the British had closed the port, confiscated private arms and declared martial law as collective punishment for the "Tea Party" harbor raid. The Charleston assembly passed a resolution declaring, "That while the oppressive acts relative to Boston are enforced, we will cheerfully, from time to time, contribute towards the relief of those poor persons there, whose unfortunate circumstances may be thought to stand in need of most assistance."[17]

On June 24 the people of South Carolina defied the British blockade and shipped 200 barrels of rice to the people of Boston. Charitable money collections were held across the province. In the winter of 1774 to 1775 the citizens of St. David's Parish donated cash totaling 125 pounds and eleven shillings. George Wright gave a pound and twelve shillings to Boston's relief.[18]

South Carolina's aid to Boston was matched by the other colonies and expressed Americans' growing conviction that they shared a noble cause transcending local self-interest. From New England to Georgia they were uniting in common defense and hatred of tyranny.

William Wright takes custody of a captured British officer after the Battle of Stono Ferry

The Spirit of '76

A dark pall hung over the colonies when Hannah Wright and her eight children settled on their new land in the Camden District. Two years earlier British troops shot down five citizens in Boston. The Crown tightened its grip on the city after the Sons of Liberty boarded ships one night and dumped their tea cargos into the harbor to protest import taxes. On September 5, 1774 the First Continental Congress met in Philadelphia to present a list of grievances to Parliament. Most Americans, though, still considered themselves loyal Englishmen.

The Revolutionary War began in the north and ended with victory in the south. The first "shot heard round the world" was fired on April 19, 1775 when a British regiment sent out from Boston to seize more colonial arms scattered a small militia force at Lexington Green. But the Redcoats were checked at Concord Bridge and driven headlong back to Boston by a much bigger Patriot contingent. Along with two and a half million other Americans the Wrights were about to be swept up in an epic conflict.

With the fate of the North Carolina Regulators still fresh in their minds Mecklenburg County's citizens published a Declaration of Independence on May 20, 1775 more than a year before the new nation did so. In June the Second Continental Congress appointed General George Washington as commander of its armed forces. Initially the Patriots won a string of small victories and controlled most of the countryside. With vastly superior naval power the British held Boston for a while and later seized Newport, New York City,

Philadelphia, Charleston and Savannah from which they lashed out at their unruly subjects.

The Lexington Minuteman

For a time, life in the southern colonies was unvexed by the war in the north but the Carolina frontier reignited when the Cherokee Nation sided with Great Britain against the Revolution. South Carolina would soon endure a British invasion and more than 200 battles on her soil. James and Hannah Wright's sons William, John, James, Jr., Richard and George collectively fought in a dozen or more of those engagements. All of them survived the war.

Enlisting in the Patriot Cause

A Revolutionary War pension application filed in 1854 with the U.S. War Department by John Wright's daughter Martha Wright Blackstock in the name of her mother Alcea ("Alsey") Langston Wright gives us a few bits of information about her father's and uncle William's service.[1] Yet, Martha's papers reflect she knew very little about their remarkable war records. Perhaps they rarely spoke about their experiences.

Taken together, Martha Blackstock's pension affidavit and other historical records give us a rich narrative of John and William Wright's service to the Patriot cause. Martha offers the following: (1) her father John and uncle William each had two tours of duty; (2) her uncle William once told her that he and her father fought in a battle together; (3) as a child she saw her father's discharge certificate and Continental paper money in their home and (4) John's last tour was under Captain Robert Ellison with whom her father scouted for the legendary General Francis Marion ("The Swamp Fox").[2]

A Continental six dollar bill

Martha Blackstock's pension papers were submitted to Secretary of War Jefferson Davis with a copy of indent number 857 from the South Carolina Treasurer's files. The indent records a payment of 28 pounds sterling to John Wright in 1786 for service in the state's First Regiment of the Continental Line.[3] Martha further attests that her parents John and Alsey were married in Columbia County, Georgia in 1788, they lived in Jackson County, Georgia until her father's death in 1806 and her mother died in 1852. Secretary Davis denied Martha's pension request because her mother Alsey was no longer alive to receive payments.

South Carolina's Continental Army muster rolls show John and William Wright enlisted early in the war. John signed up on August 20, 1777 for a standard 16-month tour in Captain John Buchanan's company of the Sixth Regiment (Rifle) commanded by Colonel Thomas Sumter and later Colonel William Henderson.[4] William also joined the Sixth on March 9, 1778 for a four-month tour until July 26, 1778. As privates, John and William were each paid ten dollars a month in Continental currency that would be nearly worthless by the end of the war.

Shortly before John Wright enlisted, his neighbor John Wilson also joined the Sixth Regiment. Like the Wrights, the Wilsons moved south from York County before the war and lived just below Hannah Wright's homestead on the Scape Whore Swamp. Wilson served in the Continental Army and South Carolina militia from 1777 to 1782 in some of the same units with the Wright brothers. While a militiaman Wilson received extra pay to furnish his wagon for regimental use.[5]

Mustering into Captain John Buchanan's company

After William Wright left the Sixth Regiment in mid-1778 he re-enlisted in early 1779 in Captain John Carraway Smith's company of the Third Regiment of light horse rangers.[6] The Third Rangers were led by Pennsylvania-born Colonel William ("Old Danger") Thomson who had a plantation near Stateburg in the High Hills of Santee.[7] William's enlistment was supposed to expire on November 1, 1779. But when he and John joined the fledgling American army they could not foresee events that would extend their tours well beyond their expectations.

There is good reason to believe Hannah Wright's middle son, James, Jr., kept close ties to his birthplace on Bullock's Creek in York County's New Acquisition District after the family moved down to the Scape Whore. This thesis is supported by James's enlistment in the New Acquisition District militia, a published Wright family history account that his wife Mary Ray Wright bore their first child Mary Ann in North Carolina around 1780 and James's appearance as a witness to a 1782 deed for property on the Catawba River in northeastern York County.[8]

Around 1779 or 1780 James Wright, Jr. joined Captain John Lindsay's company of the New Acquisition District Regiment led by Lieutenant Colonel Thomas Neel before Neel was killed in action.[9] For a year after Neel's death his regiment was commanded by Lieutenant Colonel Samuel Watson and Major William Bratton.[10] The New Acquisition Regiment was so named because most of its troops were recruited from South Carolina's border territory in York County that was acquired from North Carolina in 1772.[11]

James Wright, Jr. joined Neel's militia not long after his neighbor John Wilson mustered out of the Sixth Continental Regiment in February, 1779 and re-enlisted with Neel.[12] James and John served together for much of the rest of the war. Some of John's militia pay indents reflect his unit affiliations, but James appears to have used his pay to buy land bounties after the war.[13] James's indents were not found in the South Carolina archives, making the details of his military service more challenging to reconstruct.

The New Acquisition Regiment was reorganized in June, 1780 by Thomas Neel's son, Lieutenant Colonel Andrew Neel, and Lieutenant Colonels William Hill and John Lisle.[14] The regiment was assigned to General Thomas Sumter's First Brigade of South Carolina Militia after he left the Continental service. Sumter's Brigade included an independent cavalry force of New Acquisition militiamen commanded by Colonel Hill and known as Hill's Regiment of Light

Dragoons. Like light horse rangers, dragoons conducted reconnaissance and screened infantry movements. Unlike rangers, dragoons did not usually dismount to engage the enemy. Instead, they fought on horseback with sabers using full-on charges to break up British and Tory infantry formations.

General Thomas Sumter

Colonel Hill owned an iron works on Allison Creek about ten miles east of Bullock's Creek. Given Hill's proximity to the Wrights before the war, he likely did business with James, Sr. and his three brothers. Original evidence that John Wilson and James Wright, Jr. were serving together in 1781, when Wilson is known to have been with Hill's Light Dragoons, leads to the conclusion that James was also one of Hill's troopers.[15] James's post-war commission in the Wilkes County, Georgia mounted militia further suggests his cavalry service in the Revolution.[16]

After mid-1780 some New Acquisition troops stayed with Major Bratton and others joined the Turkey Creek Regiment led by Lieutenant Colonel Edward Lacey. Like the Wrights and others who settled on Turkey Creek before the war Bratton and Lacey were Pennsylvanians.[17] New Acquisition and Turkey Creek militiamen sometimes fought together and re-enlisted with three other Pennsylvanian officers. They were Colonel Andrew Pickens of the Upper Ninety-Six Regiment and Colonel John Thomas and Lieutenant Colonel Thomas Brandon of the First and Second Spartan Regiments, respectively.[18] The latter units were mustered in the adjacent Ninety-Six District on the west side of the Broad River dividing the Ninety-Six and New Acquisition Districts. When militia enlistments expired, soldiers were usually free to join other units led by officers they liked and trusted.

During 1781 and 1782 Hannah Wright's youngest sons Richard and George joined Camden and Cheraw District militia units near their home on the Scape Whore.[19] George was paid for supplies furnished and 220 days served in Lieutenant Colonel Jacob Baxter's Upper Craven County and Lieutenant Colonel Lemuel Benton's Cheraw District Regiments.[20] Richard spent 378 days in those regiments.[21] Baxter's and Benton's light horsemen were part of General Marion's Second Brigade of South Carolina Militia.[22]

Near the end of the war Richard and George Wright served under General Marion with their elder brothers John and William after the latter left the Continental Army. Following William's discharge from Thomson's Rangers he rendered 120 days of militia service in 1782.[23] According to Martha Wright Blackstock's pension papers, her father John's final tour that year was with Captain Ellison's company in Baxter's regiment of Marion's Brigade.[24] Martha's hearsay account of her father's last service with Ellison, written more than 70 years after independence, is corroborated by the detailed orderly book Marion kept throughout the war.[25]

THE 1778 FLORIDA EXPEDITION

Before the British invaded South Carolina its Revolutionary forces conducted operations against local Loyalists and their Cherokee allies. In 1776 and 1777 the Patriots launched two failed campaigns against British forces in Florida which the United Kingdom acquired from Spain in the 1763 Treaty of Paris. In the spring of 1778 the Patriots mounted yet a third ill-fated invasion of Florida with a loose coalition of Georgia and South Carolina Continental Army and militia regiments.

They were placed under a divided command with General Robert Howe in charge of the Continentals whose South Carolina contingent was led by Colonel Charles Cotesworth Pinckney. The Georgia militiamen were led by their militarily inexperienced Governor John Houstoun. The South Carolina militiamen, including Neel's New Acquisition Regiment, were headed by the popular veteran General Andrew Williamson. The combined Patriot force counted 3,000 men with 1,200 Continentals plus 950 South Carolina and 750 Georgia militia troops.[26]

Colonel Charles Cotesworth Pinckney, by James Earl (1761-1796)

Colonel Pinckney's South Carolina Continentals included Sumter's Sixth Regiment.[27] John Wilson and John Wright had spent months training with the Sixth Riflemen. In March, William Wright and hundreds of other young men responded to the call for more volunteers to go to Florida and he joined Sumter's outfit with his brother John and friend Wilson. The Scape Whore lads were surely itching for their first fight knowing 400 South Carolina Loyalists were already on the way to join the British at St. Augustine.

General Williamson's South Carolina militia left Sunbury, Georgia in April and crossed the Altamaha River at Reid's Bluff. Meanwhile, a fleet of Georgia navy row galleys ferried Howe's Continentals from Savannah down the coast and put them ashore in Florida to link up with the militia. Howe and Williamson timely rendezvoused, but they had to wait several weeks for Governor Houstoun to catch up with them.[28] Houstoun finally crossed the St. Mary's River from Georgia into Florida in late June but, by then, the idle Continentals were wracked with sickness and reduced to only 300 men fit for duty.[29]

As the Patriots marched down the Florida coast, they were stalked by Tory snipers using Cherokee tactics. Houstoun, though, pushed his Georgians miles ahead of the rest of the army. On June 30 Houstoun stumbled into an ambush by British regulars and Tories at Alligator Bridge but luckily his men sustained only a few casualties. At that point the expedition became paralyzed by Houstoun's and Williamson's refusal to put their militia under Howe's command for a coordinated attack on their weaker enemy.

Fearing a debacle Colonel Pinckney wrote to General William Moultrie in Charleston, "If we do not retreat soon, we shall not be able to retreat at all, and may crown this expedition with another Saratoga affair, in reverse."[30] Howe wisely withdrew from Florida and declared victory by expelling the British and Tories from Georgia. A nineteenth century historian took a dimmer view of the 1778 Florida campaign:

> Thus ended this expedition, conceived in ambition and jealousy, planned without due caution, marred in its execution, and utterly without benefit in its results.[31]

Revolutionary War row galleys

Howe loaded his men back on their galleys for the return voyage to Savannah. John Wilson and the Wright brothers ended their round-trip cruise to Florida dispirited and denied glory. William left the Sixth Regiment in late July and returned home. John Wilson's and John Wright's tours continued until early 1779. Despite the Patriot advantage in numbers, and suffering no major reversal in the field, the Third Florida Expedition was defeated by its own dysfunctional leadership.

SAVANNAH AND STONO FERRY

By late 1778 the war in the northern colonies was in a stalemate. To break the impasse the British opened a southern front by landing a large force near Savannah on December 28. The next day they surprised the Americans and routed Savannah's defenders, including the Sixth Riflemen now led by Colonel Henderson. A few days later command of the Continental Army's Southern Department passed to Major General Benjamin Lincoln who was highly regarded by General Washington.

Soon after capturing Savannah the British increased their strength in Georgia to 4,000 troops and marched up the Savannah River to take Augusta on January 31, 1779. John Wilson and John Wright were discharged from the Sixth Regiment a week later on February 7. Wilson joined Neel's New Acquisition militia in March and Wright took leave until the end of the year. In the spring William Wright re-enlisted in the Continental Army as a private in "Old Danger" Thomson's Third Rangers.

With Savannah firmly in British hands its commander, General Augustine Prevost, took advantage of Lincoln's deployment near Augusta to make a bold thrust against Charleston. When General Moultrie refused to surrender the city, Prevost retreated as Lincoln returned to give chase. Prevost had well planned his counter-march to Savannah and built a fort at the ferry crossing on the Stono River where he placed a strong rearguard force. Stono Ferry was manned by 500 Scots from Lieutenant Colonel John Maitland's 71st Regiment of Foot (Fraser's Highlanders) along with 300 Hessians and Carolina Loyalists. The 71st Highlanders were a scrappy lot. After enlisting in Glasgow, Scotland they mutinied on the way to the colonies when told they would not be led by their favorite officer.

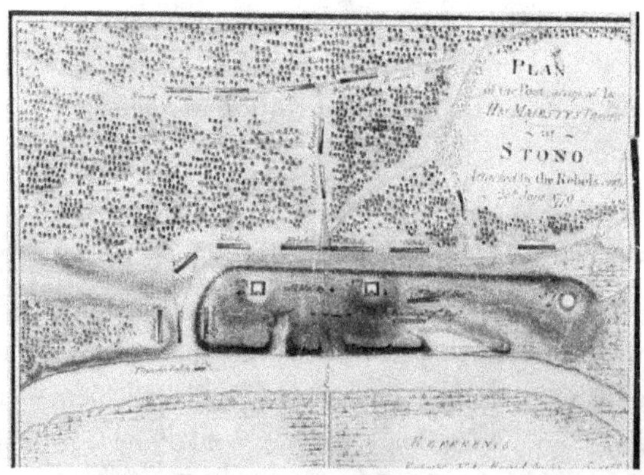

A British map of the Stono Ferry battlefield

For the assault on Stono Ferry, Lincoln deployed the South Carolina Continentals and militia on his left wing. They included Thomson's Third Rangers, Henderson's Sixth Riflemen and Neel's New Acquisition militiamen. William Wright was a private in Captain John Carraway Smith's Third Ranger company. John Wilson and his wagon were part of Neel's regiment.[32]

Maitland posted two Highlander companies as pickets outside the fort to discourage rebel raids and sniping. On the morning of June 20 the Scots awoke to find themselves trapped in the open between the fort's stockade walls and 1,200 Patriots. Lincoln ordered an all-out attack hoping to seize the garrison with superior numbers. The Americans fixed bayonets and quickly overwhelmed the exposed enemy pickets killing, wounding and capturing all but nine who made it back inside the fort.[33]

The Americans advancing on the left were blocked by a marsh but remained steady under heavy fire poured into them by the Hessians behind the walls. Lincoln pulled his men back when he saw a large body of reinforcements crossing the Stono to rescue Maitland.[34] In less than an hour thirty Americans were dead. They included Lieutenant Colonel Thomas Neel, struck in the head by a ball, and Private Hugh Jackson, an older brother of future President Andrew Jackson, who died of heat stroke.

In July the Third Rangers issued a payroll sheet with an intriguing note next to William Wright's name: "Left [June] 20th at Stono Ferry with a British officer." Colonel Thomson gave William custody of a 71st Highlander officer captured in the bayonet attack on the pickets. The prisoner was brought to a secure location to await exchange for an American officer of equal rank. The next month's payroll denotes "Delivered" on William's line indicating his mission was completed. "Old Danger" must have had implicit personal confidence in William to entrust him with such a valuable captive.

"Attack on Savannah" by A.I. Keller (1866-1924)

During September and October Lincoln's army and an allied French force attacked the British garrison at Savannah but Prevost repelled them. Thomson's Third and Henderson's Sixth Regiments participated in the action. William Wright was with Thomson's Rangers during the siege while John was still on leave from the Sixth.

CHARLESTON UNDER SIEGE

John Wright returned to duty with Captain Buchanan's company by December, 1779. A few weeks later, the Sixth Continental Regiment was disbanded because of low enlistment and attrition. Its troops were transferred to the First and Second Regiments and John was among those re-assigned to the First under Colonel Pinckney's command. John is listed on the First's muster roll for February, 1780 showing its troops were "in garrison" at Charleston. February was the last month they were paid. The March payroll for Thomson's Rangers records William Wright was also "in garrison" at Charleston. That month a 10,000-man invasion force commanded by General Sir Henry Clinton landed on the coast below the city and began encircling it.

On April first 3,000 British troops and laborers moved down Charleston Neck to start digging siege trenches. Brothers John and William Wright were separated during the preparations to defend the city against the coming British assault. John was sent with Colonel Pinckney's First Regiment to Fort Moultrie on Sullivan's Island at the mouth of the Cooper River. Pinckney's riflemen supported Moultrie's artillery batteries guarding the entrance to Charleston harbor against the British fleet.

Thomson's Rangers were deployed on Charleston Neck several miles west of Fort Moultrie. William Wright was among the rangers holding the left flank of the main defense line between the Ashley River and the "Horn Work" fortification. Watson's and Bratton's New Acquisition militiamen were assigned to the South Bay waterfront batteries.[35] John Wilson's pay records show he was in Charleston during the siege and had been promoted by Watson to captain and wagon-master.[36] James Wright, Jr. may have been with him.

On April 8 the Royal Navy sailed past Fort Moultrie's blazing guns into the harbor suffering little damage to its warships. The British fleet now rained fire on the city at will. Meanwhile, on Charleston Neck's front lines deadly sniper fire from Hessian jaegers took a heavy toll on the defenders and kept them pinned down. On the night of April 23, Thomson picked 200 of his best men for a bayonet charge on the British trenches less than 800 feet away. It was a complete surprise and prompted the enemy's hasty retreat. The raid's success lingered into the next night when jittery British sentries fired on their own troops by mistake, but the relief was only temporary.[37]

By the first week of May the defenders were surrounded and pulverized by the British juggernaut. Pinckney surrendered Fort Moultrie on May 7. The next day American and British commanders began exchanging terms for the city's capitulation. By May 10 the British troops and sappers burrowing their way down the Neck had withstood constant fire from the American lines to get within 25 yards of them. On May 12 General Lincoln led his Continentals and militia through the Horn Work gate and stacked arms. One Hessian officer described the American soldiers as "extremely ragged, and on the whole the people looked greatly starved." But another German officer wrote it was "admirable that these people still fight for the chimerical freedom of America with such ardor."[38]

Fort Moultrie during the Revolutionary War

It is certain that John Wright became a British prisoner but his brother William's whereabouts at the time of the surrender is a mystery. There is no record of William being a prisoner and he seems to have eluded capture. Perhaps he was initially taken but later fell in with the hundreds of Americans who slipped away before the British could collect enough troops to guard them all. Given William's role as a trusted courier and guard at Stono Ferry he may have been handed a message to deliver out of the city during the siege. Being well known to Captain John Wilson, it is also possible that William was put on the detail that loaded the captain's wagon train with rebel government papers and escorted them out of Charleston several days before the surrender to keep them from falling into enemy hands.[39]

JOHN WRIGHT'S CAPTIVITY

The British bagged nearly 6,600 American and allied soldiers and sailors when Charleston fell, including about 3,500 Continental Army troops. The immediate impact on the American war effort and morale was calamitous. Most Continental officers were exchanged or paroled within a few months but the enlisted men's fates were quite different. Fewer than one in three would ever see their families again.

The surrender treaty included Sir Clinton's promise to General Lincoln that the militia "shall be permitted to return to their respective homes and be secured in their persons and property." Continental Line troops would "remain prisoners of war until exchanged" and "be supplied with good and wholesome provisions in such quantity as is served out to the troops of His Britannic Majesty."[40] Clinton's agreement to parole the militia was honored out of necessity because he had no means to hold them. His terms covering the Continental rank and file, however, were mostly ignored.

The 2,861 Continental enlisted men captured on May 12 were reduced to 2,322 by late July. The other 539 died or escaped. The rest of the prisoners were locked up below decks on six decrepit troop transport ships stripped of their masts and rigging with portholes and hatches nailed shut to prevent escape. The inert hulks and their human cargo, nearly 400 men per ship, were moored off Sullivan's Island.[41] From his dismal quarters John Wright could see Fort Moultrie where he last fought and surrendered.

In the summertime clouds of mosquitoes swarmed out of the swamps and rice fields into the harbor bringing malaria and yellow fever to the damned. Many American militiamen sent to Charleston after being captured in other engagements also caught small pox on the prison ships. The Continentals fared better because they were vaccinated against the dreaded pox when they enlisted. Nearly all suffered starvation, lack of clothing and beatings. One prisoner described a fellow inmate being flogged by guards "until his bowels were whipped out."[42]

Northern Patriots endured similar abuse aboard the British prison ship *JERSEY* in New York harbor where guards roused the inmates each morning shouting, "Rebels! Turn out your dead!" That was the order for prisoners to collect the fresh corpses from below and carry them up to the main deck where they were stripped and lowered over the side onto a "dead boat."[43] John Wright must have witnessed such atrocities in light of Dr. Ramsay's accurate estimate that 800 Americans perished on Charleston's prison ships.[44]

American Prisoners on Board a British Prison Ship,
by John Trumbull (1756-1843), Fordham University Libraries.

The British seized an opportunity in the prisoners' wretched conditions. Each man was offered the chance to join the Duke of Cumberland's Regiment raised by Lord Charles Grenville Montagu, the Governor of Jamaica. Montagu came to Charleston to inspect his reluctant recruits and found "the greater part of these Men were without a Blankett to sleep on & without a shirt or Rag to cover them."[45] Facing slow death and promised they would be sent to the Caribbean to fight only the French or Spanish and not their former comrades, 286 prisoners signed up with Montagu's regiment. Another 566 joined other British units and the Royal Navy.[46] After switching sides most turncoats could never go back home.

A year after Charleston's surrender a final prisoner exchange was negotiated. In early July, 1781 several British brigantines set out from Charleston bound for Jamestown, Virginia carrying the remaining 740 Americans who had not escaped, died or gone over to the enemy. John Wright was one of them.[47]

Fifteen months of captivity had reduced the survivors to a deplorable state. Some died soon after release, some were physically broken for the rest of their lives and most had to beg their way home. Facing a manpower shortage the Southern Department's new commander, Major General Nathanael Greene, ordered all freed Continental prisoners with unexpired enlistments to join their respective state forces.[48] While he was confined for over a year, John Wright's tour in the First and Sixth Continental Regiments had long since lapsed, but he complied with the spirit of Greene's order. After walking 350 miles from Jamestown back to his home on the Scape Whore Swamp, he joined Marion's Brigade the next year.

A decade after the war John Wright filed a compensation request with the South Carolina Senate stating he was among the Continental Army prisoners exchanged at Jamestown.[49] John's petition was supported by an affidavit from Captain Jesse Baker of the Sixth Regiment.[50] Baker attested, "John Wright was a soldier in the 6th Continental Regiment of South Carolina Commd. By Lt. Col. Wm. Henderson. That I was well acquainted with him at that time and that he was transferred into the 1st Regt. of the same."[51]

Captain Baker's corroboration of John Wright's service in the First and Sixth Regiments at Charleston gave proof that he had no chance of escape when Fort Moultrie surrendered. One can imagine why John may have been reluctant to tell his wife Alsey and their children about the horrors he survived for over a year in the dark holds of a floating hellhole. He was part of America's first "Greatest Generation."

TURNING THE TIDE

The King's new commander in South Carolina, Lieutenant General Lord Charles Cornwallis, was heartened by the outpouring of Tory support after Charleston fell. To secure his hold on the state Cornwallis built a chain of forts linking Augusta on the Savannah River with Ninety-Six, Camden and Georgetown on the coast 60 miles above Charleston. As Cornwallis's army marched through the upcountry, Loyalist recruits flocked to the Union Jack. The few

Continentals still in the field were in no shape to fight and many Patriot militiamen stayed home to protect their families from Tory and Cherokee raids. A North Carolina militiaman wrote of that period:

> The British were marching through this section of the country within such a distance as gave the disaffected a convenience of reaching out and joining them and to others becoming more bold and desperate in their acts of robbing and killing. In this situation in which the Tory War raged we had to go armed continually. Even while a person would take his rest by sleep it was common to sleep with his arms of defense.[52]

"In this situation in which the Tory War raged we had to go armed continually."

The fight for independence in the Carolinas degenerated into a vicious war of neighbors to settle political and personal scores.

At first the Americans were no match for Cornwallis's well-fed, equipped and disciplined forces, especially those led his aggressive cavalry commander Lieutenant Colonel Banastre Tarleton. On May 29, 1780 at Waxhaws, near the North Carolina border, Tarleton's Legion cut down Continental soldiers with sabers as they tried to surrender. "Tarleton's quarter," as the Patriots called it, was meted out again to defeated American troops at the Battle of Camden that summer.

The British were less apt to show mercy to lowly militiamen. Tarleton's adjutant, Major George Hanger, 4th Baron of Coleraine, scoffed that the Carolina backwoodsmen were more savage than the Indians with none of their virtues. The baron also disdained the way the locals fought:

> The crackers and militia in those parts of America are all mounted on horse-back, which renders it totally impossible to force them to fight, they dismount, and fasten their horses to the fences and rails; but if not very confident in the superiority of their numbers, they remain on horse-back, give their fire, and retreat, which renders it useless to attack them without cavalry for though you repulse them, and drive them from the field, you can never improve the advantage.[53]

The momentum in South Carolina began to shift on July 12 when over a hundred Tory dragoons from Tarleton's Legion led by Captain Christian Huck were surprised by New Acquisition militiamen led by Bratton, Hill and Lacey. Huck was a Philadelphia real estate lawyer before the war. His troops had murdered two civilians a few days after the Waxhaws massacre. As Huck rode through York County he stopped at Major Bratton's home where his men held a sickle to the throat of the major's wife, Martha, demanding to know his whereabouts. Martha kept silent and rushed a warning to her husband as soon as the Tories left.[54] Huck gathered some other women and, waving his sword, threatened to kill them too if their men refused to swear allegiance to the King.[55]

At daybreak the next morning, those husbands and sons suddenly emerged from the woods around the Tory camp and turned the tables on Huck. He was felled by two musket balls to the head as he leaped into his saddle. His men received "Tarleton's quarter" in a running battle from which only a few escaped. Major Bratton was severely wounded avenging Martha's mistreatment.[56] Although "Huck's Defeat" was relatively insignificant in military terms, Lieutenant Colonels Hill and Lacey later wrote in their memoirs about its enormous effect on Patriot morale. According to Colonel Hill:

> It was the first check the enemy had received after the fall of Charleston; and was of greater consequence to the American cause than can be well supposed from an affair of small magnitude as it had the tendency to inspire the Americans with courage & fortitude & to teach them that the enemy was not invincible.[57]

Colonel Lacey echoed Hill's sentiments:

> The entire overthrow of Huck's army was the first repulse the British arms had met with in South Carolina, after she was by many considered a subdued province, and proved that the British bayonet was not invincible.[58]

On October 7, 1780 some 1,100 Tories commanded by British Major Patrick Ferguson were annihilated by the "Overmountain Men" led by Colonels John Sevier and Isaac Shelby at King's Mountain, about 20 miles north of where the Wrights settled on Bullock's Creek. Three months later, Tarleton's Legion and the 71st Highlanders were lured into a trap set by General Daniel Morgan at Hannah's Cowpens 35 miles west of King's Mountain.

Morgan shrewdly gauged Tarleton's impulsiveness and baited the trap with a receding line of militia skirmishers designed to draw the British over a rise concealing a big phalanx of seasoned Continental veterans. Expecting another Waxhaws, Tarleton went after the militia. In an hour Morgan destroyed his Legionnaires and infantry as an effective force. Tarleton's adjutant Major Hanger recalled that his officers drew sabers and hacked down their own men to stop them from running away.[59] A few days later Morgan wrote to a friend, "I was desirous to have a stroke at Tarlton and I have given him a devil of a whipping."[60]

Lt. Col. Banastre Tarleton's clash with Col. William Washington depicted in "The Battle of Cowpens" by James Akin (1773-1846)

Many veterans of King's Mountain and Cowpens are still unknown. Some New Acquisition Regiment officers and enlisted men, including Colonel Hill's Light Dragoons, fought in both battles.[61] Lieutenant Colonels Bratton and Lacey were at King's Mountain. Colonel Samuel Watson and Captain John Lindsay were at Cowpens where Lindsay was killed leading a company of Brandon's Second Spartan Regiment.[62] Captain John Wilson is listed by a noted authority as a possible veteran of Cowpens.[63] If James Wright, Jr. served under any of those officers in late 1780 or early 1781, he would likely have been at Kings Mountain or Cowpens.

The timing of those victories galvanized Patriot will in the North and South to keep fighting when many believed the war was lost. After Cowpens the five Wright brothers served out their militia tours with Generals Marion, Sumter and Henderson who took over Sumter's Brigade in the last year of the war.

Breaking the Chain

Despite Cornwallis's initial prospects for victory, his control over the Carolina interior disintegrated within a year after Charleston's fall. In late 1780 General Greene took command of the southern Continentals at Charlotte and began a strategic retreat through North Carolina, leading Cornwallis in hot pursuit of the defeated American army. At Guilford Courthouse, Greene turned and fought the Redcoats to a draw on March 15, 1781. From there Cornwallis marched his badly depleted regiments to Wilmington and thence north to Yorktown, Virginia where he was surrounded by Washington's army in the autumn and surrendered in a decisive American victory.

After Guilford Courthouse, General Greene returned to South Carolina and made his headquarters in the High Hills of Santee a few miles west of the Wright farm. The Patriot strategy of isolating the British logistically and suppressing their Tory base was paying off. During 1781 James Wright, Jr. was in Captain John Wilson's company of Hill's Light Dragoons, Sumter's First Brigade of Militia. Wilson was still drawing extra pay for lending his wagon to the Revolution.[64] Sumter's Brigade participated in the sieges of Augusta and Ninety-Six which fell to the Patriots in June soon after the British abandoned their coastal fort at Georgetown. Sumter resigned at the end of August and Henderson was promoted to brigadier general to take over his command.

On September 8, Marion's and Henderson's Brigades linked up with General Greene's Continentals in a major battle at Eutaw Springs on the Santee River about 70 miles south of the Wright farm. Hill's Light Dragoons were among Henderson's forces. John Wilson was with Captain James Giles when Giles was wounded.[65] Richard and George Wright were then privates in Marion's Brigade. Thus, James, Richard and George were likely at the Battle of Eutaw Springs which saw heavy losses on both sides, including over 500 American casualties.

After Eutaw Springs, General Henderson sent some of Colonel Hill's troops, including Captain John Wilson and James Wright, Jr., to guard a river crossing at Colonel George Reed's mill eight miles from Abbeville in western South Carolina.[66] As the British fell back to Charleston they unleashed Loyalist bands on the civilian population, drawing Patriot forces away from the retreating Redcoats. The Tory raiders were led by the notoriously violent William ("Bloody Bill") Cunningham and Hezekiah Williams who attacked settlements along the east side of the Savannah River between Orangeburg and Abbeville. Although the conventional warfare in South Carolina was coming to an end, partisan fighting between the Patriots and Tories continued for another year.

THE SWAMP FOX CAMPAIGN

In the spring of 1780 Lieutenant Colonel Francis Marion was commanding South Carolina's Second Continental Regiment at Charleston as the British approached the city. Before the siege Marion was evacuated with a broken ankle he suffered jumping from a window as he tried to sneak out of a party. The fortuitous injury prevented his capture and he remained at large to lead the resistance from swampy hideouts east of the Santee River where Patriot sentiment flourished. Providence intervened more than once to spare Marion.

At age fifteen Francis was a deck hand on a schooner in the West Indies when a whale attacked and sank his ship in a real-life Moby Dick incident. He and the other survivors lived for days adrift with nothing to eat but a small dog. In the Cherokee War, Francis and his brother Gabriel were officers in the provincial militia. Francis distinguished himself as a platoon leader in Grant's expedition. After the fall of Charleston, Marion was made a brigadier general of South

Carolina militia. He proved so effective as a guerilla commander, the British made his death or capture a top priority.

General Francis Marion ("The Swamp Fox")

Marion's first action as a partisan leader occurred in the late summer of 1780 when he attacked a British column and freed 147 Continentals captured at Camden who were being herded down to the prison ships at Charleston. After the American victory at King's Mountain, Cornwallis's second-in-command, Lieutenant Colonel Francis, Lord Rawdon, reported to Sir Clinton, "the Majority of the Inhabitants of that Tract between the Pee Dee and the Santee are in Arms against us."[67] Even after the fall of Charleston and total expulsion of the Continental Army from South Carolina, the Camden and Cheraw Districts still remained hotbeds of rebellion. Marion drew from a deep well of support among the Santee people and he rewarded them with victories.

The Swamp Fox exercised strict discipline over his troops that would be unlawful under modern Western military codes, but not by eighteenth century standards. His courts-martial sat in permanent session. Those found guilty of insubordination, neglect of duty or drunkenness were routinely flogged or sentenced to doubling of their service periods. More serious crimes like murder, sedition and plundering were punished by hanging.

In early 1781, Marion's Brigade was operating in the region between the Santee River and Lynch's Creek where the Wrights lived. His men wore white cockades on their hats as a recognition sign to distinguish one another from Tories in the dense swamps. Their hit-and-run raids on the British and Loyalists between Camden and Georgetown crippled enemy communications and supply lines.

Marion made camp on March 1 near the Salem Church on the

Scape Whore Swamp a short distance west of Hannah Wright's home. That day Rawdon sent two detachments from Camden down the Santee and Pee Dee Rivers hoping to trap Marion in a pincer. Instead, the Swamp Fox ambushed Rawdon's column on the Santee between Murry's and Nelson's Ferries. Lieutenant Colonel Peter Horry's light horsemen attacked the British who replied with grapeshot and a bayonet charge. Both sides retreated. After a two-week siege of Rawdon's troops at Blakely's Plantation downriver they gave up any notion of capturing Marion and withdrew to Charleston.

In April, General Greene ordered Marion to join Lieutenant Colonel Henry Lee's Continental dragoons in an attack on the British-held Fort Watson on the Santee. At night the Patriots built a forty-foot high log tower that loomed over the fort's ramparts. From the top of the tower sharpshooters cleared the open ground inside the fort forcing the British to take cover. Fort Watson surrendered to Lee and Marion and they withdrew to Greene's camp in the High Hills to rest their men.

On July 17 Baxter's, Benton's and Hill's regiments clashed with British Colonel John Coates's 19th Regiment of Foot at Quinby Bridge and Shubrick's Plantation between Charleston and the Santee River. The Patriots sustained 27 killed and wounded, including Major Baxter who was struck down by three musket balls but lived. The British baggage seized by Hill's dragoons included a chest full of gold guineas that General Sumter divided up among his men. James Wright, Jr. may have used some of the captured British gold to buy confiscated Tory land after the war.[68]

In mid-1781, Marion's Brigade saw a rise in desertions caused by rumors that General Greene planned to take some of their horses for Continental use. Colonel Lee had told Greene about Marion's abundant supply of mounts without explaining that his men needed all of them to guarantee the mobility that made their operations so successful.[69] South Carolina pay indents record that after William Wright left Thomson's Rangers he was a link in the partisan network that maintained Marion's horse reserves and food supplies for Patriot forces. William received twenty-five pounds and fifteen shillings in 1781 for provisions and forage furnished to the Continental Army as well as pasturage for "25 publick horses."[70] On October 31 a North Carolina officer gave William Wright a receipt stating, "I received of William Rite forty bushels of corn for the use of Col. Shelby's ridgment on there march to General Marion for which the State of South Carolina is indebted to him for." Colonel Shelby's 600-man force passed the Wright farm on its way to reinforce the Swamp Fox after his heavy losses at Eutaw Springs.

William Wright received fourteen pounds, eight shillings and two pence from the United States for provisions to the Continental Army during July to December, 1781, including 165 bushels of corn and 1,350 bundles of fodder.[71] After the war South Carolina paid him eleven pounds, six shillings and four pence to settle "his Acct. of Provisions for North & South Carolina Militia in 1780 & 1781." The large quantities of materiel the Wrights supplied to the Patriot forces suggests their farm lands sustained high levels of productivity during the war when labor, including their own, was scarce.

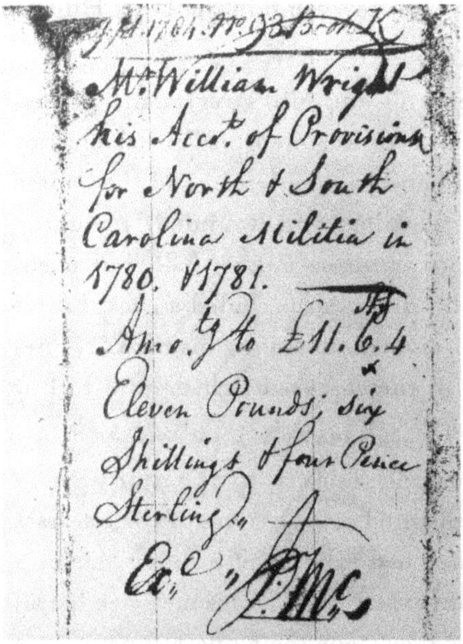
Mr. William Wright
his Acct. of Provisions
for North & South
Carolina Militia in
1780 & 1781.
Amo. £11.6.4
Eleven Pounds; six
Shillings & four Pence
Sterling

Receipt issued to William Wright in 1784 for provisions to the North and South Carolina militia

After the British evacuated Savannah on July 11, 1782 they remained garrisoned in Charleston until the end of the war. Greene's army was tasked with eliminating what was left of the Tory resistance and intercepting British foraging parties from Charleston. That year Benton's and Baxter's regiments of Marion's Brigade included William, John, Richard and George Wright in their ranks.[72] Captain John Wilson also served with Benton during the last year of the war.[73]

In the late summer of 1782, Marion's Brigade encamped on the Chehaw Neck peninsula between the Wadboo and Combahee Rivers above Beaufort. On August 31 a detachment of Marion's troops under Captain Galvin Witherspoon ambushed Tory dragoons led by Major Thomas Fraser. Fraser spotted Witherspoon hiding in the woods and bore down on him at full gallop with a saber. Witherspoon dropped the Tory officer with a load of buckshot at point blank range as his troops opened up on the Loyalist cavalry. Those were the Marion Brigade's final shots of the war.

The Swamp Fox knew the British would soon be leaving Charleston, but General Greene expected him to keep attacking their foragers. Instead, Marion gave them armed escorts and protested, "My Brigade is composed of citizens, enough of whose blood has been shed."[74] Marion's compassion for his vanquished enemies extended to the Tories whom he protected from reprisals after the war. Largely due to his efforts, more Loyalists stayed in South Carolina than in the other states.

On September 10, 1782, Marion discharged George Wright for illness after he had served over seven months. George and six other soldiers were found suffering from a "white swelling" that would be diagnosed today as tuberculous arthritis, a bacterial disease of the spine and weight bearing joints associated with anemia.[75] The disease may have been aggravated among Marion's troops by prolonged marching and poor diet.

"Francis Marion Crossing the Pee Dee" by William T. Ranney (1813-1857)

As General Marion's combat operations came to an end, it became harder for him to maintain discipline. His men were anxious to get back home for the fall harvest and more prone to insubordination and inattention to duty. Several days after George Wright was granted sick leave, his older brother John and nine other soldiers were court martialed for offenses that Marion's adjutant deemed too minor to describe in his orderly book. Each man's service period was doubled as punishment, but the war would soon be over for them in a few weeks.[76]

John Wright's five years of service to the cause included the Third Florida Expedition, defense of Savannah, Augusta and Charleston, over a year on a prison ship and finally as a Marion partisan. That he should face a petty disciplinary charge at the end of it all exemplifies war's capricious mix of heroism and injustice. In the closing month of 1782 the British sailed from Charleston and Marion's citizen soldiers finally went home.

ON TO GEORGIA

Soon after peace returned, Hannah Wright and her family left South Carolina to settle in northern Georgia. After the death of her first husband, James Wright, Sr., Hannah remarried to Daniel McCarty, Jr. from Lincoln County, North Carolina. Daniel was a matross in South Carolina's Fourth Continental Regiment (Artillery) from 1776 to 1781. He served under Colonel Barnard Beekman on Charleston Neck during the siege and was captured with his regiment. Daniel's discharge in August, 1781 indicates he was among the stalwart prison ship survivors released at Jamestown.[77]

The Wrights and McCartys certainly knew one another during the war as reflected by James Wright, Jr.'s appearance as a witness on a 1782 McCarty deed for land on the Catawba River in northeastern York County, South Carolina. Thus, Hannah and Daniel probably married before that year and it appears likely James and his wife Mary lived with Hannah and the McCartys in the border lands during the war.

Daniel and Hannah Wright McCarty later settled in Wilkes County, Georgia above Wrightsboro near her son James Wright, Jr. who established himself as a planter on the Little River. Hannah and Daniel had a son of their own named Cornelius. After Daniel died in 1794, Hannah retired to Clarke County, Georgia where she lived with her other children until her death in 1808. South Carolina was home to the Wrights for only three decades, but during those tumultuous years the founding generation created the unfinished experiment in liberty they gifted to us.

The Wright plantation on Harts Creek

4
In The Land of Cotton

In 1793 Massachusetts inventor Eli Whitney was visiting the widow of General Nathanael Greene in Savannah, Georgia when he saw one of her cats clawing the feathers from a captured bird. Inspired by this vision he devised an engine ("gin") to separate the seeds and fibers of short staple cotton. It used a nail-studded roller to pull the white filaments through a screen leaving the seeds behind. The gin could refine 50 pounds of cotton a day while processing by hand yielded only one pound. Whitney's machine revolutionized the production of cotton and the very foundation of the Southern economy. Like some other innovations it also carried a curse. The world's appetite for cotton addicted the South to slave labor as the most profitable mode of harvesting the valuable crop. In its origins American slavery was by no means a peculiarly Southern institution. When Whitney created his ingenious device New York had nearly as many slaves as Georgia.

At the end of the Revolutionary War many Americans yearned for an end to slavery and other forms of bondage. They recognized, at least tacitly, the patriotic services rendered by Black slaves and freedmen in the struggle for independence. In the North the growth of an economy based on industrial production and yeoman farming left no place for the helot. In the South, however, the rise of King Cotton gave a new lease of life to slavery which was highly adaptable to large-scale plantation agriculture. In 1800 cotton accounted for only 7% of United States exports. By 1860 that figure rose to 57%. Within a generation slavery became the distinctive and dominant feature of Southern culture. By this sad twist of fate the nation's two sections were set on a collision course.

Two generations of Georgian Wrights would become cotton planters and stakeholders in slavery. Not only slaveowners were enriched by the chattel system. In the North and South alike, manufacturers, lenders, shipowners and shopkeepers trafficked in the fruits of unpaid labor. Though the Wrights' slaveholdings were modest, possession of even a few bondsmen placed them among the privileged of their society.

James Wright Jr., the third son of James and Hannah, and his wife Mary Ray moved from South Carolina to northern Georgia in the early 1780s. This is deduced from several facts. Their eldest child, Mary Ann, was born in 1780 in North Carolina. James's militia service in South Carolina continued another year or more. By 1784 James and Mary were living in Columbia County, Georgia according to two land bounty certificates issued by Governor John Houstoun and Colonel Greenberry Lee of the Columbia-Richmond County militia district.

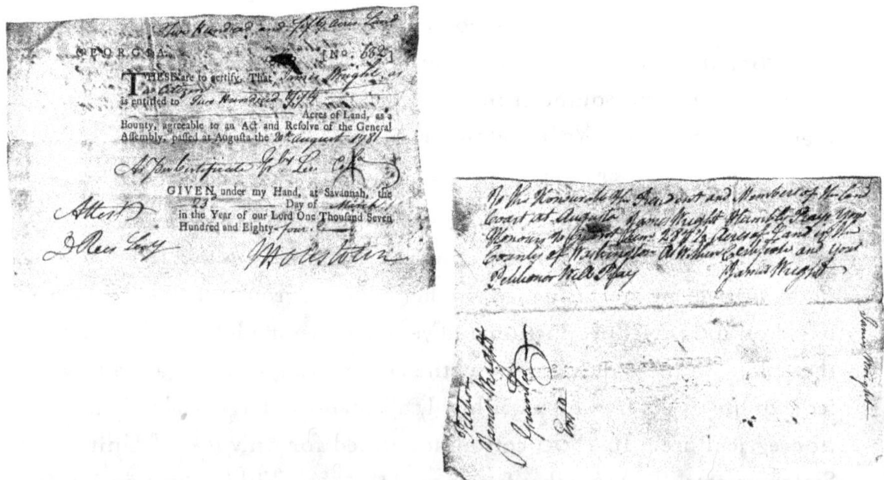
GEORGIA. [No. 682]

THESE are to certify, That James Wright

is entitled to Two Hundred

Acres of Land, as a Bounty, agreeable to an Act and Resolve of the General Assembly, passed at Augusta the 2nd August 1781

GIVEN under my Hand, at Savannah, the 23 Day of March in the Year of our Lord One Thousand Seven Hundred and Eighty-four.

Attest

Front and back of James Wright's 1784 Georgia land bounty certificate No. 682

STATE OF GEORGIA. At Col. Rich. County

THIS is to certify that James Wright hath steadfastly done his duty from the time of passing an Act at Augusta, to wit, the 20th of August, 1781 until the total Expulsion of the British from this state; and the said James Wright cannot, to my knowledge or belief, be convicted of plundering or distressing the country; and is therefore, under said Act entitled to a Bounty of Two Hundred and Fifty Acres of good land free from taxes for ten years.

Given under my hand, at Savannah the 23 day of February 1784.

Gb Lee Col.

* * * * * * *

No. 682

THESE are to certify, That James Wright as a Citizen is entitled to Two Hundred and Fifty Acres of Land, as a Bounty, agreeable to an Act and Resolve of the General Assembly passed at Augusta the 20th August 1781 as per certificate of Grby Lee Col. GIVEN under my hand at Savannah the 23 day of March in the year of our Lord One Thousand Seven Hundred and Eighty-four.

Attest

D. Rees, Secy J. Houstoun

The back of Governor Houstoun's Certificate No. 682 was endorsed and submitted by James to the Augusta Land Court with a notation in his own hand.

> To the Honorable President and Members of the Land Court at Augusta James Wright humbly prays Your Honours to grant him 284 1/2 acres of Land in the County of Washington as within Certificate and Your Petitioner will pray.
>
> James Wright

James's land certificates do not prove Revolutionary military service to Georgia but only his residence, loyalty and good character.[1] Similar certificates were issued to James's brothers William and John and father-in-law George Ray. In the original index of the certificates the abbreviation "Lt." (Lieutenant) precedes James's name indicating he was an officer in the Georgia militia after the war.[2]

In the 18th and 19th centuries settlers migrated south and west in large groups that provided safety and lessened hardship by spreading strenuous work among many hands. The Georgia land records suggest James and Mary made the trek from South Carolina to Georgia as an extended family that included their parents, siblings and in-laws. In northern Georgia they found fertile land along the Savannah River and its tributaries. Much of the land was still occupied by its first inhabitants, the Creek and Cherokee tribes.

The Wrights settled in Columbia County on the Little River about 10 miles northwest of the present town of Thomson in McDuffie County and 30 miles west of Augusta. A map of northern Georgia made by Henry Mouzon in 1775 designated the Little River as the boundary between Georgia and the Upper Creek nation. Northwest of the Creeks were the Cherokees. The area where the Wrights made their home was described by Mouzon as "High Rich Land." There Mary bore six more children. They were William (b. 1782); James, III (b. 1784); John (b. 1788); Elizabeth (b. 1790); Anne (b. 1795) and Moses (b. 1798).[3]

From James's personal effects we can surmise that he was a tobacco planter who turned to cotton farming by the end of the 1700s, acquiring significant wealth in Georgia. The key to his success lay in the nature of cotton. The growing demand for cotton offered enormous opportunities to ambitious farmers. It did not require a large investment in slaves and expensive tools. Compared with tobacco, cotton cultivation was uncomplicated and could be performed by slaves with minimum supervision. An industrious planter could accumulate capital to buy more land and slaves. Thus, cotton became the Southern road to riches and many planters made fortunes in it. James and his sons were among them.

During the 1790s James was a lieutenant of mounted militia in nearby Wilkes County.[4] The land records for Richmond and Columbia Counties reflect that James's holdings multiplied in the years after the Revolutionary War. On May 2, 1785 he purchased 250 acres on the Greenbrier Creek from Charles Crawford and on March 5, 1787 he acquired another 50 acres from Crawford. On October 24, 1792 James paid William Shields 45 pounds sterling for 280 acres in Columbia County. Thomas Willingham sold James 120 acres on September 22, 1797 for 60 pounds sterling. James bought the tract "together with all houses, orchards, gardens, woodways and waters appurtaining..." On February 10, 1801 James purchased 33 1/3 acres for $200.00 from Robert Allen. His last acquisition was on March 6, 1801 when he paid $583.00 to James Hall for 191 1/2 acres on the Fort Creek in Hancock County.

By then James's health was slowly deteriorating. This is evident from his will executed on June 21, 1800 two years before his death. He died in his early forties in the spring of 1802.

James Wright's Will Recorded April 10th 1802

In the name of God Amen

I, James Wright of the County of Columbia, State of Georgia, being weak in body but of sound mind and memory do make, constitute and ordain this my last Will and Testatment hoping that when my soul shall leave this tenement of clay that it will be received into the Mansion of eternal Joy and that my body be committed to its mother earth in the ordinary way.

I give and bequeath all of my estate both real and personal also all debts due or that may be due or owing to me also all rights and credits all increase and improvement of my said Estate or that I may die possessed of in the following manner that is today all lands which I hold by grant Deed or otherwise and all of the rest and residue of my Estate both real and personal with the increase of the whole to be equally divided between my wife Mary and all of my children to them and their heirs forever.

In the following manner the first that marries or attains the age of twenty one years old shall then and not till then draw from my Estate both real and personal one equal share of all of the Estate that there then is including increase to be laid off by my Executors in proportion to the value of the Estate in general and this my Executors are required to do with and for each child as they respectively marry or attain the age of twenty one years old.

It is also my will that all my Estate both real and personal be kept together for the support of the family and education of my children until each of their shares are respectively assigned them in manner before directed and it is my will and desire that all of my Estate both real and personal remain in possession of my wife for the benefit of herself and my children during her widowhood subject to the claim of my

> children on marriage or being at the age of twenty one years old in manner before directed and if my said wife should marry it is my will and desire that she shall have a child's part of all my Estate both real and personal at her own disposal forever to be assigned her in manner directed to be done in care of the children.
>
> If my Executors think it best to dispose of any part of my personal Estate they are hereby required to do it unless disapproved of by my said wife being then a widow, but no power to sell land. It is my will and desire that the annual profits of my lands be at the disposal of my wife for the use of the family whilst continue a widow. My Executors will proceed to collect all debts and dispose of the money for the benefit of my widow and children and I do hereby constitute and appoint John Stith, William Hogg, William Jones and Benjamin Lea Executors of this my Last Will and Testament.
>
> Jas. Wright

When James passed on he owned at least 1,400 acres that helped secure the prosperity of the next three generations of his descendants. His brother-in-law, attorney John Stith, prepared an inventory of his belongings several months after his death.[5] This list of the Wrights' worldly possessions gives us a window into their lives two centuries ago.

> Inventory of the personal Estate of James Wright deceased registered August 30th 1802 ---An Inventory and Appraisement of the goods & chattels of the Estate of James Wright late of the County of Columbia deceased.

one bay Mare Colt $100 one bay Mare $85	$185
one bay Gelding $120 one yellow bay Gelding $20	140
one bay year old Mare $40 one other ditto $35	75
one Wagon & Harness & Jack Screw	100
31 head of Cattle $145 44 head of hogs $73.25	228.25
plantation tools $16 Carpenter tools $7.12 1/2	23.12
one Loom Stays & Harness	5
Kitchen furniture (to wit) two pots, a pan, tea kettle	8
Pewter dishes, plates, basons & spoons	8
three bed steads, four beds and furniture	102
a cupboard & furniture $10.50 & sitting chairs $4	14.50
2 Tables & table cloth $3.25 two chests $2	5.25
a Small trunk $1.50 a Smoothing Iron 75 cents	2.25
2 Spinning Wheels & Cards $3 Books $6	9
Shot Gun $4 a Slate & Small looking Glass .50	4.50
Knives & forks $1 Steelyards $3	4
Shovel & Tongs $1.50 A Mans Saddle $9	10.50
2 Womans Saddles $10 Hogsheads & Barrell $4	14
a Coffee Mill $1 a Cutting Knife $2	3
Leather $4 59 wt bar Iron & 2 of Steel $5	9
Irons for a Cotton gin $42 17 Gin & Cotton $2.55	44.55
A Stone Jug & Jar $2 Plank at one dollar p. hundred	2
a Grind Stone $1.50 Six head of Sheep $11	12.50
5 Guns $2 Provisions 5 wt Sugar $46.50	48.50
	$1,057.92

Conspicuously absent from James's estate were slaves. If he possessed any when he died they would have been listed by John Stith. Either James owned no slaves or gave any he had to his children before his death.

Several months later Stith compiled a list of persons owing money to the estate. It suggests James was a generous soul who loaned large sums to his relatives and friends without demanding repayment. Two debtors, Robert Wiseman and John Baker, would figure prominently in the future of the Wright family.

> A list of the rights & credits belonging to the Estate of James Wright decd. by the Executor.
>
> A note given by Zach Ray to James Wright date 14th Jany 1801 no time of payment for 10 dollars 56 1/2 cents.
>
> A Rept. and obligation by John Baker to Jas. Wright & by the Credits on the note there appears to be only four dollars due.
>
> A note by Robert Wiseman to James Wright date 2 July 1801 payable in November after date for twelve dollars.
>
> A note given by Conrad Wall & Wm Ray to the Executor of Jas Wright date 27 August 1802 payable 12 months after date for 90 dollars (for a mare sold them by Exectr).

James's death left Mary with their youngest children, John, Elizabeth, Anne and Moses, still living at home. As propriety required, Mary remained in mourning for over a year before taking a new husband. On August 25, 1803 she wed Robert Wiseman, a close neighbor of the Wrights in the Little River area. That Wiseman had been a family friend before James's death is apparent from Stith's list.

Mary's marriage to Robert Wiseman was ill-starred. Generations later the descendants of her eldest son, William Wright, retold his stories about Wiseman being a severe disciplinarian with his step-children. He was especially harsh with 16-year-old John. William came to visit his mother one day and found Wiseman whipping John. Infuriated, William seized Wiseman and "wore him out."[6] William then gathered the younger children, lodged them with trusted relatives and left for South America on business.

Distraught, Mary sailed from Georgia with her husband to find William and make amends. En route to South America the ship called at St. Augustine, Florida where Mary disembarked to do some chores. She washed her kerchief and was spreading it on a rosebush to dry when she was bitten on the hand by a spider. After boarding the vessel Mary became so ill that she and Wiseman had to be put ashore on Cat Island in the Bahamas. Mary died on Cat Island and was buried there. When William learned of his mother's death he returned to Georgia, visiting her grave on the way home.[7] William found work managing Charles McCall's plantation in Screven County and married his daughter Mary in 1810. Wiseman also remarried that year.

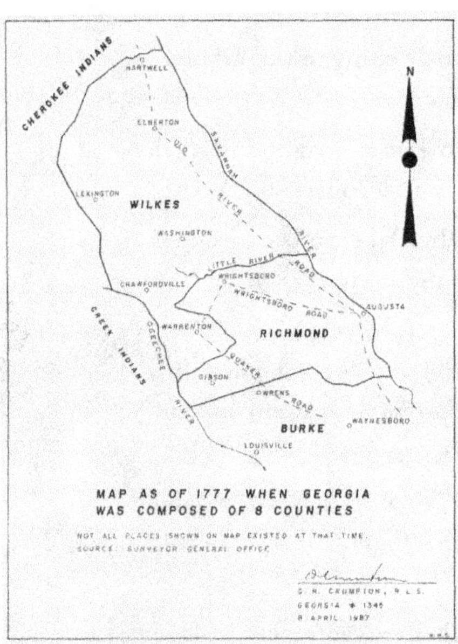

Early map of Little River area

When his mother died, James Wright, III was in his early 20s and living with his uncle John Wright in Jackson County about 50 miles northwest of the Little River plantation. James was a militia officer and commissioner of the joint academy of Clarke and Jackson Counties.[8] Over the next 20 years James, Jr. was a militia officer in Jackson, Putnam, Oconee and Columbia Counties which then formed the northwestern boundary between white-settled Georgia and the

Creek Indian territories in what is now western Georgia and eastern Alabama. Jame's military service and the constant danger of Creek attacks along the frontier may account for his transience in the early 1800s.

In 1805 James Wright, III turned 21 and bought two lots in the town of Clarke in Jackson County, Georgia. In 1807 the Georgia Legislature convened at its new capitol at Milledgeville. Among its first enactments was a lottery to distribute lands in Baldwin and Wilkinson Counties ceded under treaty by the Creeks to the United States. James, tried his luck and, drawing Lot No. 55, won 202 1/2 acres in Wilkinson County. By certificate, dated November 19, 1808, Governor Jared Irwin granted Lot No. 587 in Wilkinson County to "James Wright's orphans of the 7th district Columbia County..." The certificate suggests James gave his prize to his youngest sister and brother, Anne and Moses.

James Wright, III married Nancy Park of Jackson County and came back to Columbia County in 1809. It is not known whether any of his children were born to Nancy or whether all were by his second wife, Elvira Sarah Flynt. After James returned to his Little River home he accepted a lieutenancy in the 274th militia district company of Columbia County. The certificate granting his commission recites:

STATE OF GEORGIA

> By his Excellency David B. Mitchell Governor, and Commander In Chief of the Army and Navy of this State, and the Militia thereof.
>
> To James Wright Gentleman, GREETING
>
> We reposing especial trust and confidence in your patriotism, valour, conduct and fidelity, do, by these presents, constitute and appoint you Lieutenant of the 274th District Company of Militia formed for the defense of this State and for repelling every hostile invasion thereof. You are therefore carefully and

> diligently to discharge the duty of Lieutenant by doing and performing all manner of things thereunto belonging; and we do strictly charge and require all Officers and Privates under your command to be obedient to your orders as Lieutenant. And you are to observe and follow such orders and directions, from time to time as you shall receive from me, or a future Governor and Commander in Chief of this State, for the time being, or any other of your superior Officers, in pursuance of the trust reposed in you. This commission to continue in force during your usual residence within the district company to which you belong, unless removed by sentence of a court-martial, or by the Governor, or the address of two-thirds of each branch of the General Assembly.
>
> Dated at Milledgeville the 17th day of June one thousand eight hundred and ten and in the 35th year of American Independence.
>
> BY THE GOVERNOR, David B. Mitchell
> Hon. Marbury Scott

Columbia County probate records show that James Wright, III was still receiving distributions from his father's estate more than ten years after his death. In 1813 James received a total of $385.55 in legacy payments. On December 25, 1814 John Stith recorded in James Wright, Jr.'s estate ledger that he "caused to be admeasured and laid out to James Wright one of the legatees his full share and proportion of the Real Estate of the decd." Later records indicate that James acted on behalf of his brothers and sisters in paying taxes on 772 acres they inherited in Columbia, Early and Wilkinson Counties.

Columbia County's tax records for 1813 reflect that James Wright, III's eldest brother, William, operated a business in Wrightsboro.[9] The tax rolls describe it as "four improved lots in Wrightsboro val. $800" and "stock in trade ... $1500." Two slaves are also listed as part of William's taxable property.

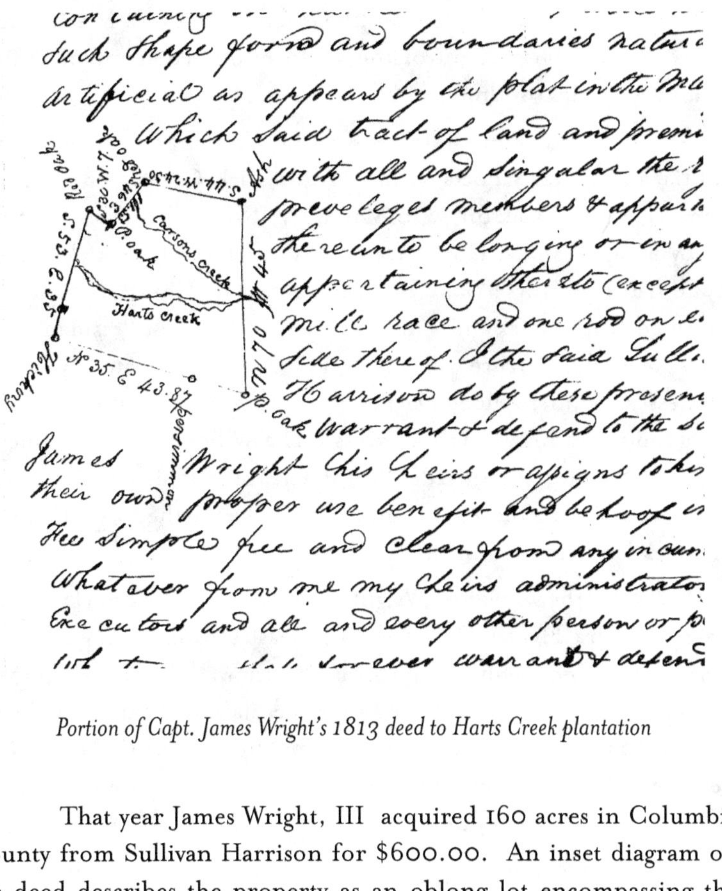

Portion of Capt. James Wright's 1813 deed to Harts Creek plantation

That year James Wright, III acquired 160 acres in Columbia County from Sullivan Harrison for $600.00. An inset diagram on the deed describes the property as an oblong lot encompassing the Harts and Carson (now Mill) Creeks which converged on its eastern boundary. This land now lies just east of Wrightsboro Road two miles northwest of Wrightsboro. James built a house on Harts Creek where his family lived for the next 23 years.

For three decades the settlers and Creeks were locked in a conflict known as the Oconee Creek Wars. These clashes culminated in the Red Stick War in eastern Alabama. The Red Stick War was ignited by settler land grabs and agitation among the Creeks by the British and the Shawnee chief Tecumseh during the War of 1812. At the outbreak of war with the Red Stick Creeks in the fall of 1813 James was called away from home. On September 28 Governor David B. Mitchell reassigned him as a lieutenant of the 312th militia company in Putnam County 50 miles southwest of Harts Creek.

The Red Sticks were crushed by United States troops, state militia and allied Choctaws and White Stick Creeks led by Major General Andrew Jackson. On March 27, 1814 a Tennessee company led by Ensign Samuel Houston broke through the Red Stick defenses at the Battle of Horse-Shoe Bend in Alabama. Houston was severely wounded in the attack and went on to become the first President of the Texas Republic. A truce with the Red Sticks was negotiated by another Tennessean soldier named David Crockett which made him a national hero and paved his way to Congress. The White Sticks' allegiance to the United States was rewarded by the seizure of their lands. General Jackson was among those who helped themselves to the 23 million acres of Creek land emptied by the Red Stick War.

After the war James Wright, III rose to the rank of captain and married Elvira Flynt. He fathered at least two daughters and three sons. The name of his eldest son is not known. His daughters were Amelia and Caroline Elizabeth and it is certain that the two youngest boys, William Cicero (b. January 6, 1818) and John Wesley (b. May 6, 1823) were sons of Elvira. James and Elvira named their youngest son for the English founder of Methodism.

Elvira was the eldest daughter of John Flynt born in 1758 in Culpepper County, Virginia and Sarah Porter Flynt born in 1768 in Orange County, Virginia. Elvira was a direct descendant of Richard Flynt who sailed on the ship *DIANA* from Ayton, Scotland to Jamestown, Virginia in 1618. John Flynt was a veteran of the Revolutionary War. After he married Sarah they settled in Wilkes County, Georgia.[10] Their children were Nicholas Porter, Elvira Sarah, George Washington, Augustus Wesley, Virginia Orange, Amelia Curtis and James Henry. John Flynt died on September 19, 1820 and Sarah on March 21, 1843. Their epitaphs read:

JOHN FLYNT

Pure as are thy Joys above the skies
And all thy Regions Peace,
No Wanton Lips or Envious Eyes
Can see or Taste thy Bliss.

SARAH FLYNT

Alas She is dead and Grief is Vain,
Nor would we wish her back again,
But still Affectionate Tribute
Would drop O'er her Memory.[11]

In 1820 James Wright, III had a cotton plantation on Harts Creek. He was also Captain of Columbia County's 274th militia district company and a justice of the peace.[12] The Wrights had four children under 10 years of age and their household included three male slaves and a female slave.[13]

James's youngest brother, Moses, was an Ensign in his militia company. In 1820 Moses purchased from his sister Elizabeth's husband, John Hannon, seven lots in Wrightsboro for $1,500.00 plus Hannon's interest in the firm of Hannon & Wright for $1,000.00. Moses' firm was ostensibly involved in cotton milling because the deed from Hannon recites that one of the seven lots contained a "store-house...with Ginhouse and gear of all kinds..." including "One stagewagon, slaves, gear, furniture, and farming tools." The cotton mill was mortgaged by Moses to Charles Stewart and George Hargrove for the sum of $4,878.87.[14]

Published references to the Wrights' slaves are a poignant reminder of that era. In 1808 an Augusta newspaper announced:

NEGRO INTELLIGENCE

In Granby Jail, an African boy named Congo says his master's name is James Wright, but he does not know where he lives...[15]

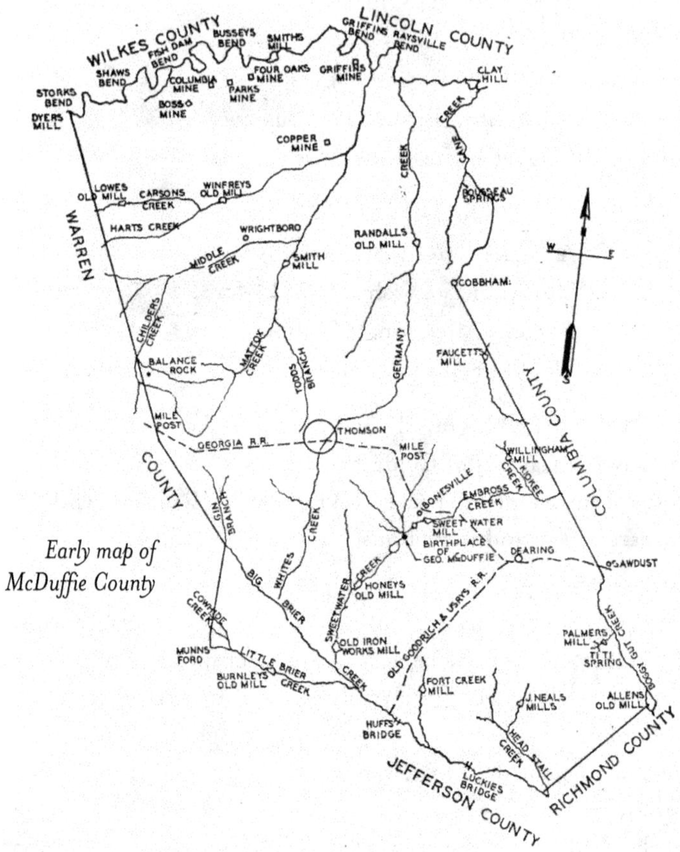

Early map of McDuffie County

Another notice for a fugitive slave appeared several years later:

TEN DOLLARS REWARD

Runaway from the subscriber on McBean's Creek, Burke county, on the 18th day of April last, a stout Negro Fellow named FED, about 25 years old, of dark complexion, has two or three scars on his breast that have grown above the skin larger than a goose quill and one on his back near where the short ribs and back bone join that is sunk deep enough to contain half a walnut. It is likely he has made for Columbia county, as I purchased him in Dec. last from Mr. James Wright of that county who informed me that he was raised by Mr. Alexander near Wrightsboro. Any person apprehending and lodging the said fellow in jail, so that I can get him, or deliver him to me, shall receive the above reward and all reasonable expenses paid. ELIJAH WALKER.[16]

Slaves were often traded privately among kinsmen rather than on the auction block. This is shown in two Wilkes County deeds, one between James Wright, III and his brother-in-law Augustus W. Flynt and another between James and his mother-in-law, Sarah. Captain Wright purchased a slave boy named Floyd for $300.00 and a girl named Burilla for $70.00. The deed for Floyd recites:

Augustus W. Flynt) Bill of Sale for
to) negro boy recorded
James Wright) 7th May 1822
Georgia) Know all men by the presents
Wilkes County) that Augustus W. Flynt

hath this day bargained and sold and by these presents do bargain sell and confirm unto James Wright of Columbia County and State aforesaid one certain negro boy known by the name of Floyd for and in consideration of the sum of three hundred dollars the receipt whereof I do hereby acknowledge and I warrant and defend the said negro boy for myself, my heirs and every other person whatsoever to the said James Wright, his heirs and assigns. Given under my hand & seal this 8th March, 1822.

What kind of treatment did Floyd and Burilla receive? What became of them? We can only wonder. Slave life was influenced by many factors, the master's temperament being the most decisive, but not all slaveowners were sadistic Simon Legrees. Most former slaves polled in a federal Works Project Administration survey in the 1930s testified that their owners were good men.[17] The relation between master and bondsman, however, was a contradictory affair. The master could be genteel or ruthless as it suited his purposes.

Article I, Section 2 of the United States Constitution defined the slave as three fifths of a person for purposes of taxation and representation in Congress. Southern legislatures enacted laws requiring that slaves be given adequate food, clothing, medical attention and care in their old age.[18] Sometimes the courts charged with enforcing the laws lectured masters on the rights of their slaves. In 1818 a Mississippi judge declared with remarkable candor, "Slavery is condemned by reason and the laws of nature. It exists and can only exist through municipal regulations."[19] Years later another jurist in Tennessee wrote:

"A slave is not in the condition of a horse. He is made after the image of the creator. He has mental capacities and an immortal principle in his nature that constitute him equal to his owner but for the accidental position in which fortune has placed him. The laws cannot extinguish his high born nature, nor deprive him of many rights which are inherent in man."[20]

The slave's rights were more honored in the breach than observance. He had no legal right to come and go as he pleased, earn money, own property, speak his mind or vote. A slave's marriage had no protected status and his family could be split up and sold at will. That the law recognized any slave rights was symptomatic of Southern society's intractable moral dilemma. Thomas Jefferson, a guilt-ridden slave owner, lamented that the master's son was "nursed, educated and daily exercised in tyranny" but even Jefferson was not above an occasional lashing. Perhaps he expected too much from lesser owners. Faced with the harsh demands of preserving a society built on extreme inequality they turned away from the democratic ideals of the American Revolution and took on the demeanor of an aristocracy. To Northern propagandists they were "The Slave Power."

William and Mary McCall Wright eventually moved from Columbia County to Augusta where he owned a merchant bank. Around 1837 William retired to his White Oak plantation near Augusta. He died in 1843 and is buried in Wrightsboro. William and Mary had four children; Augustus Romaldus, Anne, Moses Rochester and Edwin. Augustus attended the Litchfield Law School in Connecticut. In his first year at Litchfield he received a letter, dated June 14, 1833, from his father. William counseled his son, "You owe it to yourself to make a Herculean effort this year. I greatly desire that you may accomplish the law perfectly. The fag end of the bar is probably the last place this side of Hell that I should envy." Augustus returned to Georgia in 1835 as a lawyer and became a judge of the Cherokee Circuit. He served in both the United States Congress as a Democrat before the Civil War and in the Confederate Congress during the war.[21]

Augustus Romaldus Wright (1813-1891). Courtesy of Hargrett Rare Book and Manuscript Library, University of Georgia Libraries, Athens

James Wright, III's eldest sister, Mary Ann, married James Winfrey of North Carolina. They had a daughter, Ann, who wed Colonel James Patton Perkins of Rome, Georgia. John Wright married Elizabeth Walker in 1820 and they settled in Lincoln County. John was a Lincoln County Inferior Court Justice and a member of the Georgia Legislature during the 1830s. After

Elizabeth's death in 1846 John moved his family to Bulloch County, Alabama where he died in 1863. Elizabeth Wright's marriage to John Hannon yielded no less than 13 children. Moses Wright married and settled in Oglethorpe County where he owned a large plantation. Little is known about Anne Wright except that she married a man named James Neal.

James was not as reluctant as his father when it came to collecting a debt. In early 1823 he filed an assumpsit petition in the Columbia County Superior Court against Luke F. Clark. The petition complained that Clark, "although often requested," failed to pay a $142.00 promissory note. On March 20 a jury awarded James his money "with interest & cost of suit." Later that year James and Elvira lost their daughter Caroline who departed life on September 20, 1823.[22]

Captain James Wright, III came to his end a year later at age 40. His death may have been sudden because he had no will. His brothers came to the assistance of his widow Elvira and young children, shouldering the burden of managing his estate. On September 13 James's younger brother John was appointed administrator to marshal his assets and tend to the support of his family.

> I, John Wright do solemnly swear, that James Wright died without any will, as far as I know or believe, and that I will well and truly administer upon all and singular the goods and chattles, rights and credits of the said deceased, and pay all his just debts, as far as the same will extend and the law requires me, and that I will make a true and perfect Inventory of all and singular the goods and chattles, rights and credits and a just return thereof when thereunto required, so help me God.

Three weeks later John's appraisers completed their inventory.

> The List of the Appraisement of the Personal Property of James Wright Decd. October 8th 1824.

One Negro Woman named Critty and her child David	$450.00
Negro girl named Sylvia	175.00
Do [Ditto] Do Burilla	100.00
One Boy named Ned	150.00
One Chestnut Sorrel Horse	60.00
One Cow	12.00
18 Goats	36.00
2 Sows 7 pigs ea. $7	14.00
1 Spaid sow 2 years old	7.00
4 Pigs	1.00
1 Lot Corn say, 180 Bushels	62 1/2
1 Lot Cotton say, 4000 lbs. say	75.00
1 Ladder for	62 1/2
1 Yoke Steers & Old Cart	50.00
1 Lot plow Irons	1.50
2 plow stocks & Irons	1.50
1 Crop Cut Scow	4.00
1 Handsaw	1.00
2 Drawing Knives & cutting knife	.50
1 Coulter Iron	.87
2 Axes & 1 Mattock	2.25
1 Lot Gin	1.00
1 Scythe & Cradle	1.00
1 Grind Stone	1.50
1 Bell	.50
1 Side Board	40.00
1 Bed & Furniture	25.00
1 Do---Do	22.00
1 Trundle Do	10.00
1 Table	2.00
Do at Wrightsboro	3.00

1 Gun	15.00
1 Chest & 2 Trunks	4.00
7 Chairs	4.00
1 Looking Glass	1.00
2 Setts plates & Setts cups &	
Saucers & spoons	1.25
1 " Knives & forks	.50
4 Jars one a jug	2.00
2 Barrels & one Hogshead	.75
3 Cow Hides	2.50
1 Loom & Trimmings	5.00
1 Spinning wheel	2.00
1 Desk	1.00
1 Slab	2.00
1 Kitchen Cupboard	1.50
2 Water pails	.50
2 Pots & Oven	3.00
1 Coffee Mill	.12
1 Mans Saddle	8.00
1 Side Do	4.00
	$1,305.75

We do certify that we have appraised all the personal property of James Wright deceased that was shown to us by John Wright admr. of said deceased to the best of our understanding and knowledge.

Robert Wiseman

John Perry

David W. Low

John's inclusion of his old nemesis, Robert Wiseman, among the appraisers suggests Wiseman must have worked hard over the years to redeem himself with his stepson. On November 26, 1824 John held a sale of his brother's belongings. For Elvira to keep the things she needed for her home, she had to buy them back from the estate. The law of community property was still a distant notion.

In January, 1825 Burilla was sold by the Sheriff of Columbia County for $65.00 and on November 6, 1826 Ned was sold for $200.00. As time wore on, funds to support Elvira and her children had to be raised by selling Captain Wright's properties in other counties and most of the family farm on Harts Creek. In an 1827 petition to the Columbia County Inferior Court, John Wright attested:

> Your petitioner humbly showeth that the Estate of James Wright late of Columbia County stands indebted to the amt. of Four Hundred dollars and that your petitioner has no funds in his hands to discharge the same and prays for leave to sell the land whereon the said Decd. lived, the widow's dower excepted, also 4 adjoining lots in Wrightsboro in preference to the Negroes as there are but two Women & two children and four orphans which they contribute to support.

Under Georgia law a widow was entitled to a one third share, called dower, in her husband's real property. Accordingly, Elvira partitioned James's lands before they were sold. Pursuant to a writ of dower issued by Judge William Schley on March 16, 1827, Elvira was allotted 50 acres from the 160-acre Harts Creek plantation.

Georgia held another land lottery that year to distribute more territories yielded by the Creeks. As retribution for his agreement with Georgia to give up the region now encompassing Muscogee, Troup, Coweta, Lee and Carroll Counties the Creek chief, General William McIntosh, was put to death by his own people. The United States later paid the Creeks $28,000.00 for the land taken from them. When the 1827 lottery was over, the children of James and Elvira Wright were winners of three 202-acre tracts in Troup, Coweta and Lee Counties.[23]

Those fortuitously acquired properties were surely a great relief to Elvira in her dire financial straits. Just keeping up with the taxes on her Harts Creek home was becoming difficult. Her name appeared on Columbia County's list of tax defaulters in 1830. By then Elvira was in her mid-30s with a daughter between 15 and 20 years of age and three sons 8 to 15 years old. Her household also included the slaves Critty and Sylvia, both 36 to 55 years old, and Critty's son David who was under age 10.[24] Land lottery fever must have seized Elvira after her children's good fortune in 1827. She was among the winners in Georgia's 1833 drawing in which small tracts of less than 40 acres were awarded.[25]

Elvira's oldest son apparently died in the early 1830s because he did not inherit any part of his parents' estate. In the same period her elder daughter Amelia married a Virginian named Beader Proctor who settled in Taliaferro County. Amelia died a few years later and Proctor remarried.[26] In or about October, 1836 Elvira passed away leaving her two sons, William Cicero, age 18, and John Wesley, age 13, as orphans. The boys were placed in the care of their uncle James H. Flynt. The Wilkes County Inferior Court issued him a letter of guardianship.

> State of Georgia) By their Honors the Justices of the
> Wilkes County) Inferior Court of said County
> Sitting for Ordinary purposes.
>
> To James H. Flynt of said County; Greeting: Whereas William C. Wright & John W. Wright, orphans of James Wright deceased, and possessed in their own right of a considerable estate, by means whereof the power of granting the guardianship of the said orphans to us is manifestly known to belong, and for the letter securing

the estate and more ample maintenance and education of the said orphans and from the integrity and confidence reposed in you, we do hereby commit the tuition, education and guardianship of said orphans to you the said James H. Flynt, you assenting thereto by your acceptance of these letters: herein charging you, that you maintain and cause to be educated said orphans in such manner as shall be suitable to their interest and circumstances during their minority, and that you enquire into, and take charge of their estate, both real and personal, and all other things to do, which by law you ought to do for your said wards, of all which a true and perfect account you shall render to the first term of the Court of Ordinary for said county, in every year during your continuance in office. And lastly, we do hereby constitute and appoint you, the said James H. Flynt guardian of the aforesaid orphans during their minority.

Witnesseth the Honorable Lewis S. Brown one of the Justices of the said Court, this the 26th day of October one thousand eight hundred and thirty six.

John H. Dyson, C.C.O.

Elvira's only personal assets listed in James Flynt's appraisal were the slaves Sylvia and Critty.

Inventory and apraisement of the estate belonging to the minors of James Wright Decd.

No. 1 Sylvia a negro woman valued at	$400.00
No. 2 Critty Do Do " "	800.00
Total	$1,200.00
Deduct 1/3 for Beader Proctor as his distribution share in said negroes---	400.00
	$800.00

On April 27, 1837 William C. Wright wed Nancy E. Holladay in Taliaferro County. William established his farm on the eastern edge of the county near Williams Creek about five miles west of his parents' Harts Creek farm. John Wesley Wright left his uncle and lived with his brother's family for the next several years. On March 26, 1838 Flynt sold to Julius C. Alford for $910.00 the lot in Troup County won by the Wright children in the 1827 land lottery. He also tried to sell the Coweta County land but the bids were too low to suit him. In Flynt's next accounting to the Wilkes County Inferior Court on January 26, 1839, he wrote, "The lot of land in Coweta County was offered for sale on the First Tuesday in April last and as it did not bring near its value it was brought in for the minors and yet remaining unsold."

This is an opportune time to reflect on the state of the Union as it approached the 1840s. The nation was rapidly expanding westward while being pulled apart from within. From the moment of its birth the Republic contained the seeds of its own disunion. The Articles of Confederation ratified in 1781 established a loose bloc of semi-sovereign states. The Constitution that replaced the Articles in 1789 gave the federal government defined powers, leaving all others to the states. It was commonly believed in the north and south alike that the states retained the right to secede from the Union, although that right was neither reserved in any state's ratification nor in the Constitution's text. Secession was first threatened by New Englanders, however, not Southerners.

The War of 1812 was one of the most unpopular conflicts in American history. Nowhere was it more detested than in the north-eastern states where mercantile and shipping interests chafed under a government embargo on trade with England. They blamed the war and their financial ruin on the Virginians Thomas Jefferson and James Madison. In 1814 New England's leaders gathered in Hartford, Connecticut where, in the midst of war, they boldly debated a divorce from the United States. Some Hartford delegates declared, "If the Union be destined to dissolution...it should, if possible [!], be the work of peaceable times and deliberate consent." Had the would-be

Northern secessionists left the Union there is little reason to believe the other states would have forcibly restrained them. The example of the Hartford Conventioneers was not lost on Southerners when they later sought separation from a government inimical to them.

By 1820 slavery loomed ominously in sectional politics. When Missouri petitioned that year for admission to the Union as a slave state it provoked a chorus of protest in the North. The dispute was settled by the admission of Maine as a free state and a guarantee, later broken, that the territories now comprising Kansas and Nebraska would remain slaveless. During the Missouri Compromise debates the boundary separating Maryland and Pennsylvania, first surveyed in 1763 by Charles Mason and Jeremiah Dixon, was proposed to be extended down the Ohio River and westward to the Pacific. Some hoped the Mason-Dixon Line would be the permanent boundary between free and slave states. But an aging Thomas Jefferson wrote that the Missouri crisis, "...like a fire bell in the night, awakened me and filled me with terror. I considered it at once as the knell of the Union."

In 1825 and again in 1832 South Carolina threatened to declare federal import tariffs null and void within her borders. In the advocacy of states rights South Carolina was far ahead of her neighbors and stood alone on the nullification issue. It would take something much bigger than taxes to make the Southern states unite in common cause. For a long time Southerners openly aired their misgivings about slavery. Until the 1830s there were four times as many anti-slavery societies in the South as in the North.[27] In 1831 Nat Turner's bloody slave rebellion in Virginia sent shudders of terror through the South. After the Turner revolt audible criticism of slavery became very risky below the Mason-Dixon Line.

From then on, the debate between North and South over slavery intensified as did the Northern movement to abolish it. The abolitionists rested their arguments on religious precepts, hoping to cajole the South with moral suasion into freeing its bondsmen. Instead, the abolitionist message had the opposite effect. It debased the slaveowners' pride and they sought to convince the world, or at least themselves, that bondage was a positive good. Disputes between North and South continually flared and, for a time, they were settled within the framework of the Constitution. The North's growing economic might and the overarching shadow of slavery, however, created tensions of a lasting, irreconcilable nature.

In 1840 William C. Wright was a farmer in Taliaferro County at the head of a ten-member household. It included William, his wife Nancy, infant daughter Mary, brother John Wesley and six slaves including a male and female in their 20s and three boys and a girl under the age of ten.[28] William and Nancy produced another eight children; Ann, William Owen, Elvira, Vidalia, Felix, Wesley, George Norman and Josephine. On March 2 James Flynt distributed to each of his Wright nephews and Beader Proctor a one third share of the land in Troup County won by the Wright children in the 1827 land lottery. Proctor sold his wife's share back to her brothers for $327.60. On January 22, 1842 John received $233.13 from Flynt as a final distribution from his father's estate.

As William and John grew to manhood they maintained strong ties with those who had been intimate friends of their parents. It was natural that they would look for wives among the clans that were well known to them. On December 10, 1844 John married Frances Ann Baker of Warren County. Proof of a long amity between the Bakers and Wrights is found in John Stith's 1802 list of James Wright, III's debtors. Among the estate's credits was a partially paid note given to James by Frances Ann's grandfather John Baker.

John Baker and his two brothers served with distinction in the Revolutionary War before he came to Georgia.[29] John married Patty Harris in 1768 and they had two daughters and seven sons. John died in 1816 and Patty in 1824. Among their sons was Edwin Baker, born in 1780, who married Nancy Darden on May 13, 1810. Their children were Alfred, Henry, (Dr.) Lawrence, Lucinda, Frances Ann, Richmond and Emily. Edwin and his brother Jonathan were Georgia legislators in the 1830s.

248

Georgia, Warren County. To any Minister of the Gospel, Judge, Justice of the Inferior Court, or Justice of the Peace, to celebrate.

(CONSTITUTIONALIST OFFICE.)

These are to authorize and permit you to join in the Honorable state of MATRIMONY, John W. Wright of the one part, and Frances A. Baker of the other part, according to the rites of your Church, provided there be no lawful cause to obstruct the same; and this shall be your authority for so doing.

Given under my hand, as Clerk of the Court of Ordinary, of the County aforesaid, this Tenth day of December 1844

[illegible] Maddux C.C.O.

I DO HEREBY CERTIFY, That John W. Wright and Miss Frances A. Baker were joined in the HOLY BANDS OF MATRIMONY, by me, on the Twelfth day of December, 1844.

Recorded Jany 2nd 1845 by [illegible] Maddux clk.

Richard [illegible] Asbury, G.C.

Certificate of marriage of John Wesley Wright and Francis Ann Baker, December 10,1844

Frances's eldest brother, Alfred, joined the merchant bank of Bridges & Gibson in Augusta in 1829. Alfred was a financier and philanthropist who funded many scholarships for Augusta's young men and women. When the Civil War came he outfitted a company of infantrymen called "Baker's Volunteers" and always saw that his soldiers and their families were well cared for. After the war Alfred continued in banking and owned substantial shares in the Georgia Chemical Works and Bon Air Hotel Company. He was a deacon and trustee of the First Presbyterian Church of Augusta. Alfred was still working when he died on June 16, 1896 and was eulogized in these words. "Although he passed the eighty-fifth milestone on Life's highway he never seemed willing to shake off the burdens of responsibility. His bodily strength was impaired in the last years of his life, but his mind was clear and forceful to the last. Like ripened grain he was ready for the reaper and when the summons came to join the silent majority he sank to rest at his post of duty."[30]

Among Frances's first cousins was Colonel John H. Baker, a son of Jonathan. John fought in the Mexican War with the First Georgia Volunteers. At the start of the Civil War he raised Pike County's first unit, Company A of the 13th Georgia Regiment, and was elected its captain. John was wounded six times at Antietam, Gettysburg, The Wilderness, Richmond and Petersburg and was promoted to colonel in 1863. Colonel Baker was captured at Gettysburg in July, 1863 and interned at Johnson Island on Lake Erie and Fort Delaware below Philadelphia. He was exchanged in May, 1864 and returned to the fray. After one engagement John sent home a captured Union regimental banner. It was said to be "a beautiful thing with long gold fringe." To prevent the banner from being retaken by the Yankees during Sherman's march through Georgia, the Baker children buried it in a tin box in a swamp. The colours were later unearthed by their father and returned to the Union men who once held them aloft. Baker was elected without opposition to the Georgia legislature in 1870 and the senate in 1880. He died in 1905.[31]

John Wesley and Frances Ann Wright had nine children during their 28-year marriage. They were James Edwin (b. 1846); William H. (b. 1848); Linton Lafayette (b. 1849); Lawrence Baker (b. 1852); Mary (b. 1856); Henry (Harry) Lee (b. 1858); twins John Wesley, Jr. and Frances Ann (b. 1861) and Richmond (b. 1867).[32] The mid-1800s experienced a 50% infant mortality rate so the Wrights were relatively fortunate to lose only William in childhood.

In late 1845 the Wright brothers co-founded the Raytown Methodist Church three miles east of Sharon in Taliaferro County. On December 17 Mary S. Pearson sold to William C. Wright, John Wesley Wright, Beader Proctor, George W. Flynt, Nathaniel Parham, Aaron T. Kendrick, John C. Bird and John Phelts one acre of land on which they built their house of worship. The deed was witnessed by the Wrights' uncle

Augustus W. Flynt and John A. Durham, the husband of Flynt's daughter Mary Louisa. John and Mary Durham's son George would later join his cousins Linton and Lawrence Wright on their Texas odyssey.

Raytown Methodist Church (1845)

During the next several years John Wesley Wright acquired substantial holdings in Taliaferro County and eventually owned 1,038 acres on the Williams and Beaverdam Creeks. In 1847 the Wrights' uncle Samuel Jones died leaving them part of his immense estate in Wilkes County. Jones was the second husband of Elvira Wright's sister Amelia Flynt. When Jones died he owned a plantation on the Kettle Creek with 71 slaves valued at $29,975.00. William and John shared a $3,491.86 distribution and inherited the slaves "Little Daniel, Dolly and 2 children, Moses, Little Davy, Louisa, Chana, Aggy, Martina, Daniel a small boy, Mary, Amanda a small girl, Little Martin and Ellen."

In the late 1840s John Wesley Wright was elected as a justice of the peace in Taliaferro County. By 1850 John and Frances had three small sons, James Edwin, 4, William, 2 and Linton Lafayette, 1. John was a farmer with real property declared to be worth $1,000.00 and eight slaves. No names were given for the slaves who were listed only as four males ages 22, 21, 6 and 5 and four females ages 19, 14, 11 and 1.[33]

Around 1852 John moved his family and slaves to Marion County in southwestern Georgia. They settled 10 miles southwest of Buena Vista in the Church Hills community.[34] They were in Church Hills by the early part of that year because their fourth son, Lawrence ("Lonnie") Baker, named for Frances Ann's physician brother, was born on March 5 in nearby Americus. In September, John sold half his land in Taliaferro County to William F. Nance. During the 1850s John acquired 665 acres in Marion County on the Gill Creek and Pana Branch where he planted cotton and corn.

John's reasons for pulling up his stakes in Taliaferro County are not difficult to imagine. Land was cheaper and more plentiful further south and years of cotton production may have depleted his old plantation. In the 1850s fertilizers were not widely available in the slave states. Imported marl and guano were not affordable to most planters and the average plantation was too big for fertilization. Cattle manure was no solution because the cotton regions did not have large enough herds to produce it in useful quantities. The quality of livestock in Georgia was so deplorable that many families had to rely on imported pork and hunting to put meat on the table. The steady demand for cotton, dependence on unskilled slave labor and tight credit discouraged planters from rotating their crops to preserve the soil.

The Wrights spent the next 23 years in Buena Vista. Cotton was the mainstay there but wheat, oats, corn, sweet potatoes and wool were also produced in Marion County. Buena Vista was connected to the outside world by a hack service and would not see its first railroad until 1885. The Wright children may have been educated at Buena Vista's private academy or at one of Marion County's 18 common schools.[35]

It is fair to say the Wrights were content and prosperous in the decade before the Civil War. Elizabeth, the daughter of their fifth son Harry Lee, wrote of her father's youthful reminiscences, "My father often told me two things about his childhood. One was about his father's plantation and the rows of servants' quarters. He played very happily with the little Negro children. The other very vivid impression which he carried with him until the day of his death was of the beauty of his mother. He always wanted me to know how very beautiful she was."

The Chieftain's Museum, Rome, Georgia. Home of Judge Augustus R. Wright

In 1857 William C. Wright briefly owned 300 acres near Buena Vista but soon sold the land to John. William lived out his days in Taliaferro County. After the Civil War he and his sons William Owen and George Norman owned a tavern in Crawfordville. William died in 1883 and is buried at the Raytown Methodist Church.

The 1850s witnessed an alarming polarization of the nation. The obsession with slavery erupted again over how to absorb the immense new territories acquired by the United States in the Mexican War. After long and bitter debate Congress reached another compromise in 1850. California was admitted as a free state and the slave trade was banned in the District of Columbia. In return Congress passed the Fugitive Slave Act to facilitate the capture and return of escaped bondsmen to their owners. The people in the North were outraged over being forced by federal law to aid the slavehunters.

In 1852 Harriet Beecher Stowe's novel "Uncle Tom's Cabin" sold over 300,000 copies in the North swelling the ranks of the anti-slavery cause. Two years later Congress voted to undo the Missouri Compromise of 1820 and open Kansas and Nebraska to slavery if a majority of their citizens wanted it. The Kansas-Nebraska Bill was a clarion call to wholesale violence as pro and antislavery settlers poured into "Bleeding Kansas." The bloodshed was but a dim shadow of the coming holocaust.

In 1857 the United States Supreme Court declared the Missouri Compromise unconstitutional in its famous Dred Scott decision. The Supreme Court reasoned that Congress could not give less protection to slave ownership than to other property rights and held that slavery could not be banned by the states. Chief Justice Roger B. Taney, who freed his own slaves, wrote that the slave and his descendants, whether free or not, "...had no rights which the white man was bound to respect..." Dred Scott vindicated the slaveowners' belief that the right to possess others was guaranteed by the Constitution. It also stiffened their resolve never to live under any regime that would not safeguard that right.

Two years later the militant abolitionist John Brown seized the federal arsenal at Harpers Ferry, Virginia and bid slaves to rise up against their masters. Ironically, the first man killed by Brown's raiders was a free Black. Brown's summons to insurrection went unheeded and he was captured and condemned. The Harpers Ferry raid, however, deeply impressed upon the South that it could expect more such forays and that a national government controlled by the new northern Republican Party would encourage them. The poet Ralph Waldo Emerson echoed the sentiments of many in the North when he likened John Brown on the gallows to Jesus Christ at Calvary. By the end of the 1850s it was nearly impossible to be neutral about slavery. The nation had truly become a "house divided."

In early 1860 the Wright brothers' aunt Amelia Flynt Jones died leaving them and their Flynt cousins as beneficiaries of her estate.

Amelia left, among other things, 16 slaves to be divided among her nephews. By then John and Frances had five children; James Edwin, 14; Linton Lafayette, 10; Lawrence Baker, 8; Mary, 4 and Harry Lee, 1. Linton and Lawrence were in school. John was a farmer with personal property worth $9,900.00 and land worth $2,000.00. Most of his personal property value was in eight slaves; four men ages 30, 25, 17 and 15 and four females ages 26, 13, 11 and 2. Except for the 25-year-old man who was listed as a "mulatto," all the slaves were Black and shared two houses.[36] Perhaps Harry's remembrance of "rows" of servant quarters was a bit fanciful.

The following March, Frances gave birth to fraternal twins who were named for their parents. Even with slave help Frances had little time to worry about the larger events going on around her. Yet each day while she rocked her newborns to sleep the nation was edging toward a cataclysm of unimaginable dimensions. When it was over her world would never be the same again.

"Mother, I will say to you not to be uneasy about us for we are in the hands of the Lord."

5

Secession and Reconstruction

There can be little debate that the Civil War was the most tragic event in American history. Its profound effect on our destiny demands some consideration of its origins. In a sense the war is unfinished. The issues over which it was fought, majority rule, the status of Blacks and states rights versus federal authority, still persist. The American Revolution embodies our highest ideals but the Civil War shows us as we really are, a nation of diverse peoples and interests united by circumstance.

The cost of preserving the Union and purging its original sin of slavery was appalling. Nearly 620,000 perished, many more than the 405,000 Americans lost in the Second World War. Northern casualties were triple those of the South yet one of every four Southerners in uniform were dead by the end of the war. At the Battle of Shiloh in 1862 more Americans were killed and wounded in just two days than in the Revolutionary War, the War of 1812 and the Mexican War combined.

The War Between the States was a resounding echo of England's Civil War of 1642. The Southern gentry saw themselves as scions of the English Cavaliers and their neighbors to the North as lowly offspring of Puritan commoners. To Northerners, Southerners were decadent aristocrats who amassed ill-gotten wealth on the backs of slaves. Southerners viewed Northerners as vulgar merchants who exploited poor whites and immigrants.

Economically, the North and South were at cross purposes. The South had little manufacturing industry and its agrarian economy was geared to production of cotton, tobacco, rice and other crops for export. Consequently, the South had to import many of its needs and wanted access to cheap foreign goods. It resented the tariffs sponsored by Northern legislators to protect their wares from foreign competition at the expense of the South. The economic disparities between the two sections naturally spilled into the political arena.

With the entry of each new free state into the Union, Southern leaders demanded a matching slave state. The election of Abraham Lincoln upset that balance. Lincoln and his Republican Party vowed to stop the admission of slave states and bar slavery from the territories. Lincoln's agenda meant the slaveowners were doomed to become a minority in the national government. They perceived their way of life as threatened with slow strangulation by the North. Their choices were to accept that fate or secede from the Union and found their own republic.

Strictly speaking, the Civil War began over the extension of slavery, not its existence. When first elected Lincoln did not favor outright abolition of the "peculiar institution." In his debates with Senator Stephen A. Douglas in 1858 only three years before the war, Lincoln predicted that slavery in the United States might last for another century. Lincoln's early belief that slavery should die a natural rather than a sudden death was shared by a majority of Northerners. Few approved of slavery but still fewer advocated its violent overthrow. The idea of a war over slavery was unthinkable to most Americans on both sides of the Mason-Dixon Line.

As a Northern objective, the abolition of slavery was an afterthought. For the first year and a half of the war Lincoln avoided making slavery an issue. In the Emancipation Proclamation he declared on September 22, 1862 that effective January 1, 1863 slavery would be abolished only in those Southern states that were "then in rebellion against the United States." Lincoln's decree left open the possibility that slavery might survive in the border states and even in Confederate states that would give up the fight for secession. In response to Lincoln's election on November 6, 1860 delegations in the slave states convened to vote on articles of secession. They fervently argued that the Constitution sanctioned the right of the states to secede. The secessionists insisted their grandfathers would never have joined a Union they could not leave. Had not the thirteen colonies seceded from England? Were not many of the Founders slaveowners?

In Georgia 1,403 delegates assembled in the old capitol at Milledgeville on January 16, 1861 to hold a secession convention. On January 19 the Georgians approved articles of secession by a vote of 944 to 459. The citizens of Buena Vista held a tumultuous torchlight parade and bonfire that night to celebrate Georgia's departure from the Union.[1] The Wrights were undoubtedly there with their neighbors to cheer the cause of Southern independence. On March 7 a second convention in Savannah adopted the Constitution of the Confederate States of America. One of the signers of the new Constitution was John Wesley Wright's first cousin, Judge Augustus R. Wright, who had voted against secession at Milledgeville.

An ardent Unionist before the war, Judge Wright remained loyal to the Southland when secession came and was made colonel of the 38th Georgia Regiment at Savannah. He was soon drafted into civil service as a member of the Rebel congress which made its first capital at Montgomery, Alabama. Augustus was unwavering in his allegiance to Georgia but did not conceal his disdain for the "fire-eaters," the fanatical secessionists he blamed for the crisis. The distinguished political maverick set down his views in a prophetic letter he sent from Montgomery to a friend in early 1861 before the outbreak of the war.

"In my opinion I am looked upon with suspicion here, as other Union men. I have been invited to but two parties, or dinings, since I have been here, both with Union men--am wholly ignored by the seceders, and this is a powerful seceding place. My opinion is the ultras will take charge of the government, and as soon as they feel settled in power, will 'put the screws' to all outsiders. The more I see of the disposition of some of the controlling spirits here, the more fears I have of our future peace and prosperity. We have more to fear in my opinion from bad men at home--fierce, ferocious, plunder-seeking men, than from the republicans. If they fight us, as they probably will, we shall whip them after a while. These other fellows will then fasten on us like vampires, and by their exclusive patriotism, and self devotion, and constant appeals to the lowest passions, finally control the country. Montgomery is now equal to Washington in fast men and women--so I judge from what I see and hear. When it has a chance to improve by having the Capitol awhile, Paris and the Tuileries will have a competitor in the cunning deceptions and amours of a court. I greatly fear sometimes, from my inside peep into the scenes that we, like other nations, shall be 'dashed in pieces as a potter's vessel' for our transgressions."[2]

Lincoln watched Montgomery with consternation but made no overt move against the Confederacy. At his inaugural address on March 4, Lincoln implored the South to return to the fold. "We are not enemies, but friends. We must not be enemies. Though passion may have strained, it must not break our bonds of affection. The mystic chords of memory, stretching from every battlefield and patriot grave to every living heart and hearthstone all over this broad land, will yet swell the chorus of the Union, when again touched, as surely they will be, by the better angels of our nature." The secessionists were not appeased.

The stand-off ended at 4:30 in the morning of April 12 when shore batteries in Charleston, South Carolina fired on the Federal garrison at Fort Sumter. The Rebel gunners were commanded by General Pierre Gustave Toutant Beauregard. The next day Fort Sumter was surrendered by U.S. Army Major Robert Anderson, Beauregard's former West Point artillery instructor. Coincidences of this sort were common as former comrades, friends and even relatives met as enemies on the battlefield.

As in most wars each side underestimated the other. Northerners believed they would subdue the "seceshes" in a few weeks. The South had less than a fourth the manpower of the North and its navy was vastly inferior to the Union's. Still, many Southerners were deluded by the notion that their opponents were cowards and unfit to fight. Hence the popular adage that one Rebel was worth ten Yankees. The South did have several advantages at the outset. Its officer corps and cavalry were superior to the North's. The Union soldier was about as likely to be a farmer as the Confederate, but the latter was often more skilled in the use of arms.

Southerners enjoyed far greater morale and unity when the war began. They were fighting for independence from a government hostile to them and to defend their lands from invasion and plunder. The North's objectives, military conquest and economic domination of the South, were more difficult to justify. Many wanted to save the Union but there were also numerous dissenters in the North who preferred to let the South go its own way. Only after the Federal government paid dearly in blood and Lincoln offered a moral purpose for the war, the destruction of slavery, did the Union gain the will and cohesion to win it.

It would be simplistic, however, to think that so many sacrificed themselves out of love or hatred of slavery. Appeals to sectional patriotism, family honor, religion and comradery all played a part in motivating the soldier. Supreme Court Justice Oliver Wendell Holmes, Jr., a Union veteran wounded three times, wrote, "Through our great good fortune, in our youth our hearts were touched with fire. It was given to us to learn at the outset that life is a profound and passionate thing."[3] With this fire in their hearts the flower of the North and South marched off to do their duty as they saw it.

In the spring of 1861 Marion County, Georgia generously

answered the call to arms. A year later three fourths of Marion County's white males were in the Confederate States Army. On April 20 "The Buena Vista Guards," 106 strong, set out to join what would become General Robert E. Lee's Army of Northern Virginia. Two months later another 138 men were organized as "The Marion Guards" and they too joined Lee. Both companies were in most of the major battles of the northern campaign including Bull Run, Fredericksburg, Gettysburg, The Wilderness, Spotsylvania and Cold Harbor.[4] The largest unit organized in Marion County was Company H of the 46th Georgia Infantry Regiment, "The Marion Volunteers." Company H was raised by Captain Eleazar Taylor with 191 recruits on March 4, 1862.

That day the eldest son of John Wesley and Frances Ann Wright, sixteen-year-old James Edwin, enlisted in Company H as a private. In joining The Marion Volunteers, James was continuing a long family tradition of military service to Georgia. According to regimental muster rolls he received $11.00 a month in his first paying job as a Confederate foot soldier.

Gen. States Rights Gist
The Library of Congress

The 46th Georgia was commanded by Colonel Peyton H. Colquitt whose credentials were presented by the Atlanta press. "Peyton H. Colquitt is a son of Hon. Walter T. Colquitt--well known to every Georgian, and every prominent man in America, as a statesman and orator. Col. Colquitt is a lawyer and has been for years editor of the Columbus 'Times.' He served through the Mexican war and has been captain of a company on the Peninsula during the last year. He is a handsome man of pleasing manners, superior talents, good morals and every way suited to the command for which he is chosen."[5]

Colonel Colquitt's regiment was brigaded under General States Rights Gist, a Rebel in both name and deed. The 31-year-old Gist was a graduate of Harvard Law School and son of South Carolina Governor William Gist. He was Beauregard's second-in-command at the siege of Fort Sumter and a hero of the First Bull Run. For the next three years General Gist would lead the 46th Georgia in some of the fiercest fighting in the southern theater. What follows are the major events of the War Between the States in which James Wright and his regiment participated.

SOUTH CAROLINA

The 46th Georgia's first order was to report to Camp Stephens near Griffin 50 miles south of Atlanta. Its training completed within the month, the regiment marched to Savannah to draw weapons and was transferred to the Second Military District of South Carolina. The 46th Georgia arrived in South Carolina in April, 1862 and bivouacked at Pocotaligo, Coosawhatchie, Grahamsville, Charleston and James Island. In its first year of service the regiment was held in reserve and assigned coastal defense duties.

On April 6 William R. King of Company F wrote to his girlfriend, Miss Georgia Wilkinson. "We are encamped in the piney woods on open, level wiregrass country fifty three miles from Savannah...I have nothing to plead for not having written before but beg you will not censure me too greatly...I could not come to see you before I left home it was almost an impossibility...We left Camp Stephens on the 21st, lost 3 nights sleep on the road which made us all sick with colds. We have fared tolerably well since...The Yankees played a trick on us the first of April, intended I suppose for an April fool, and if it was, their object was accomplished to a certainty."

As a reserve unit the 46th Georgia remained on the fringes of combat during its tour in South Carolina. James got his first taste of action on June 16, 1862 when Union forces assaulted the Rebel stronghold of Fort Johnson at Secessionville on James Island. The attack was beaten back by intense artillery fire leaving over 400 Northern casualties. There were 204 Confederate dead and wounded.[6] The green levies of the 46th Georgia had to watch the battle from the sidelines but later saw some of the results. On July 2 Bill King wrote to his cousin, "I have been running from place to place trying to get in a fight all over the Island but have not yet succeeded. I was on picket advance post when that battle occurred and not more than 1 1/2 miles distant at the time. I was taken off and carried there forthwith the battle was over but the dead, the dying and wounded were there the sight of which and the groans of which were enough to appall the stoutest hearts. I could not describe the scene were I to wish all day, so I will let it pass."

By the end of the summer of 1862 both sides had given up hope that the war would soon end. Gloom and demoralization were the constant companions of every soldier. On August 21 Captain Malcolm Gillis of Company G wrote to his sister Mary about the homesickness of his men and his own despair. "I have a great many men who are home sick, in fact it is the most prevalent disease of the camp, it actually kills some men. I'm trying to kill off time as best I can. I'm told the people at home think this war will close shortly. I've long since discarded any such hopes. The next generation of people will only come along to build the breast works and walls around the cities higher. I'm pretty well satisfied that without the interference of foreign powers, the war will not close at least in my day. You may think the future looks dark to me and so it does."

Two months later several Union regiments stormed ashore near Pocotaligo and were repelled. Captain Gillis's younger brother Walter, plainly exasperated at missing another chance to get into the show, sent a letter to sister Mary complaining, "The Yankees came out from MacKees Point to Pocotaligo to take the railroad. Our Regt. was telligraphed for they got there the day after the fight, just as they always do. The fight came off Wednesday and they got there Thursday. There was a great many Yankees killed, some say

300...We lost very few men. The Yankees retreated back to their gun boats and seam like they are satisfied to let Pocotaligo alone at least for a while...George Terry came back yesterday very sick. He says he saw a great many ded Yankees and that our boys got a great deal of Yankee plunder such as belts, blankets, etc. What a pity it was that I was not along to get my shair of the plunder."

Private Jonathan H. Purvis of Company B wrote to his parents in Marion County about the fight at Pocotaligo. "A battlefield is a sight I never want to see again. I tell you it is no pleasant sight to see dead men lying on every side of the road and that was the case last Thursday morning. They were mostly Yankees. I saw three or four of our own men dead. Our regiment was like they was at Secessionville. We came in a day after the fight. The Yankees got the worst of the fight from the signs along the road...They may make the effort to come out again and attack us, but I hope we will drive them back again and make them skidaddle faster than they did before...We are under the command of Major A.M. Speer, as fine a man as is living I think. Mother, I will say to you not to be uneasy about us for we are in the hands of the Lord. He is just as able to save us here as he is at home. In him I put my trust that it will be his will for us all to meet again on this earth and if we don't meet any more in this world of trouble and sorrow, I hope we will meet in heaven where there is no more parting and no more sorrow--where pleasure never ends."

Gist's brigade remained in South Carolina and Wilmington, North Carolina until the spring of 1863. Regimental records reflect that James Wright was sent home on sick leave from March until June with an unidentified illness. Dysentery and consumption, not bullets, were the major causes of absence from duty. While James was home his regiment participated in the defense of Fort Sumter against a Union naval bombardment that lasted for four days.[7]

MISSISSIPPI

In early May the 46th Georgia was transferred by rail to Jackson, Mississippi to confront General Ulysses S. Grant's forces. By then Gist's brigade had earned a solid reputation as a crack unit. When Confederate General Beauregard dispatched it to Mississippi on May 5 he wired General John C. Pemberton, at Vicksburg, "I send Gist's and Walker's brigades (best troops) and two batteries. Keep them together, if practicable, under Gist."[8]

The 46th Georgia clashed with General William Tecumseh Sherman's Fifteenth Army Corps on May 14 at Jackson. Outnumbered two to one, the Rebels withdrew from Jackson but not until Colonel Colquitt's boys gave a good account of themselves. The Confederate commander reported, "Owing to the well-directed fire from Captain J.A. Hoskin's battery and the fire of Colonel Colquitt's skirmishers as well...the advance of the enemy was very slow and cautious...The utmost good order prevailed and during the fight the troops engaged behaved with the most determined coolness and courage."[9] Gist's brigade lost 198 killed and wounded at Jackson.[10]

After the Confederates abandoned Jackson western Mississippi was firmly in the hands of the Federals who surrounded Vicksburg on the Mississippi River. On May 30 the 46th Georgia marched to Yazoo City and awaited orders to break the Union stranglehold on Vicksburg. When the orders finally came they were too late to save the city. In the first week of July the South suffered two catastrophic defeats from which it never recovered. After a one-month siege Pemberton surrendered Vicksburg to Grant on the Fourth of July. At the same moment Lee's army was decimated in a desperate three-day battle at Gettysburg, Pennsylvania. The fall of Vicksburg gave the Union complete control of the Mississippi River cutting the Confederacy in half. After Gettysburg, Lee's army retreated back to Virginia and never left it again.

CHICKAMAUGA

The tide of the war had turned and the North's superiority in numbers and materiel began to tell. No longer could the South boast that one Rebel was worth ten Yankees. With both the eastern and western wings of its front secured, the Union devised a plan to split the Confederacy again. The strategy called for a thrust by Sherman's armies from Tennessee into Georgia to capture Atlanta with its vital war industry and rail center. In the late summer of 1863 Confederate forces in the southern theater regrouped. The 46th Georgia remained with Gist's brigade which was reassigned to Major General William Walker's division, Lieutenant General Daniel H. Hill's corps, General Braxton Bragg's Army of Tennessee. By July, James Wright was well again and back with his regiment in Rome, Georgia.

In early September the Union Army of the Cumberland under General William S. Rosecrans moved south from Tennessee into northern Georgia. Rosecrans believed Bragg's army had fled toward Atlanta. Bragg was preparing a surprise for him. Rosecrans ventured 12 miles into Georgia and established a lodgement on the Chickamauga Creek. Appropriately, Chickamauga was a Creek Indian word meaning "river of death." On September 19 Bragg attacked Rosecrans with 65,000 troops. At nine o'clock in the morning on Sunday, September 20 Confederate corps commander D.H. Hill summoned General Walker's division into the fight. In his battle report Walker recounted, "General Hill informed me on my arrival that he wanted a brigade. I told him there was one immediately behind him. He remarked he wanted Gist's brigade. I informed him that it was to the left and had just come up...He ordered Gist's brigade immediately into the fight in the rear of Breckinridge, a part of whose division had fallen back and the whole of which was hard pressed. General Gist was then ordered by me to move his division in the direction of the enemy."[11]

General Gist issued his own report on the Battle of Chickamauga. After an all-night march from Ringgold, Georgia his men arrived at Alexander's Bridge on the Chickamauga Creek, crossed the Creek at sunrise and waited a mile from the bridge for orders. Gist's report graphically describes the situation that Sunday morning.

"Upon reporting my command I was ordered by Major-General Walker to at once assume command of the division. [My] brigade being now under the command of Col. Peyton H. Colquitt of the Forty-Sixth Georgia Volunteers, he advanced his command in the direction indicated, being cautioned that he was to support General Breckinridge. Colonel Colquitt, upon advancing a few hundred yards in the woods before him, found himself in the presence of the enemy, strongly posted and massed behind a breast-work of logs, the troops reported in his front having retired before the galling fire of the enemy. The direction taken by Colonel Colquitt was too far to the right, and the left regiment only came directly upon the enemy's lines, which were so disposed by a salient as to rake the entire front of the brigade as it came forward with a severe and destructive enfilading fire.

"The brigade could not have changed direction, as the position of the enemy was not discovered by Colonel Colquitt until the left was within a short distance of the breastworks. The right, however, changed front sufficiently to become directly engaged. Colonel Colquitt did not reconnoiter the position, as he was instructed that our troops were in his front. The enemy now poured forth a most destructive and well-aimed fire upon the entire line, and though it wavered and recoiled under the shock, yet, by the exertions of the gallant Colquitt, nobly seconded by Colonels Stevens, Capers, and other brave and true officers, order was promptly restored, and for some twenty-five minutes the terrific fire was withstood and returned with marked effect by the gallant little band."

"It was here that the lamented Colquitt fell mortally wounded while cheering on his command, and in quick succession the iron-nerved Stevens and the intrepid Capers were seriously wounded, and many others who deserve to live in their country's memory yielded up their life's blood. One-third of the gallant command was either killed or wounded. Reeling under the storm of bullets, having lost all but 2 of their field officers, the brigade fell back fighting to the position from which they advanced...Our lines being re-established, we remained in position until about 4 p.m., when a general advance was ordered. Maj. A.M. Speer with seven companies of the Forty-Sixth Georgia Volunteers having come up, my own brigade, now under command of Lieutenant-Colonel Napier, was increased to some 1,400 men and officers. I was directed by Major-General Walker to support the advance of General Liddell's division. Upon reaching the Chattanooga Road, General Liddell found his command exposed to a heavy fire upon both flanks and fell back to my rear.

"The gallant Forty-Sixth Georgia Volunteers, occupying the right of the brigade, eager to avenge their beloved colonel, the brave Captain Cooper, and other true officers of the regiment, with a loud cheer, led by their brave major [Speer], charged through the wood before them, driving the enemy and capturing some 40 prisoners... The firing ceased, loud cheers went up to heaven, and the grandest, most important battle of the war was fought and won...I cannot close my report without expressing my satisfaction at the conduct and efficiency of the officers, and my admiration for the brave and soldierly bearing of the men of the division which I had the honor to command in the battle of Chickamauga. Their rolls of killed and wounded testify to the place which they occupied in the picture."[12]

Rebel battle line at Chickamauga

Gist's brigade went into Chickamauga with 980 troops which were reinforced by another 400 from the 46th Georgia as the battle progressed. Of that combined number 57 were killed and 254 were wounded in the attack on the breastworks held by General Absalom Baird's Union division. James Wright was among those wounded in the final charge led by Major Speer that Sunday afternoon in front of the Kelly House.[13] Although the 46th Georgia's records do not mention the nature of James's injury, it was not serious enough to warrant a discharge and he remained with his regiment after the battle.

In the sullen aftermath of Gettysburg and Vicksburg, Chickamauga was a rousing Southern victory. It might have ended in the annihilation of the Union Army of the Cumberland but for the conduct of two opposing generals. General George H. Thomas held the Yankee left flank together long enough to enable the rest of Rosecrans's army to escape back to Chattanooga. Thomas was christened the "Rock of Chickamauga" for his tenacity. Grant fired Rosecrans and placed Thomas at the head of the Army of the Cumberland.

Confederate General Bragg failed to capitalize on his victory by chasing the fleeing Yankees back to Chattanooga. By his inaction Bragg incurred the everlasting wrath of his subordinates. General Leonidas Polk complained to Confederate President Jefferson Davis, "General Bragg did not know what had happened. He let down as usual, and let the fruits of the great but sanguinary victory to pass from him by the most criminal negligence."[14] After the battle General Nathan Bedford Forrest thundered at Bragg, "You have played the part of a damned scoundrel, and are a coward, and if you were any part of a man I would slap your jaws and force you to resent it. You may as well not issue me any more orders for I will not obey them."[15] Bragg was later relieved by President Davis and replaced by General Joseph E. Johnston, a grand nephew of the patriot Patrick Henry. Besides Robert E. Lee no Confederate general was more beloved by his troops than Johnston.

The Confederate Army of Tennessee approached Chattanooga but, instead of attacking, took up fixed positions on Missionary Ridge and Lookout Mountain overlooking the city. Grant took full advantage of the lull by bringing in four corps of reinforcements from Memphis and Virginia. With a six to one advantage the Yankees charged up Lookout Mountain on November 24 and pushed the Rebels off. The next day the Confederates were driven from Missionary Ridge back into Georgia. The 46th Georgia defended the Confederate right flank on Missionary Ridge and was one of the last Rebel units to withdraw from the battle. Several of its troops were captured in the retreat. By the end of 1863 the 46th Georgia numbered 628 men and 513 arms.[16] The Army of Tennessee encamped that winter 20 miles below Chattanooga at Dalton, Georgia.

THE ATLANTA CAMPAIGN

On May 6, 1864 Sherman resumed the Georgia campaign with a march on Dalton. At the head of over 100,000 Federals, Sherman was determined to take Atlanta and destroy the Army of Tennessee which totaled about 60,000 troops. His standing order from Grant was to "go for Joe Johnston." Sherman tried to avoid head-on collisions with Johnston, preferring wide flanking maneuvers to force the Rebels to give ground and fall back to Atlanta. The 46th Georgia nevertheless saw continuous fighting at Dalton, Calhoun, Resaca, New Hope Church, Cass Station, Pine Mountain and Kennesaw Mountain. At Kennesaw, Sherman chose to make a frontal attack on Johnston with disastrous consequences for the Yankees. On June 19 Walker's division dug in on the southwest base of Kennesaw near Marietta. The next day began one of the bloodiest battles of the Atlanta Campaign. Colonel Ellison Capers of the 24th South Carolina Regiment, part of Gist's brigade, reported the action.

"The line was strongly intrenched with head logs on the work and obstructions in front. The enemy appeared in force on the 20th and pressed up against our pickets. The fighting on the picket-line was severe all day...The enemy established his line of battle about 300 yards in our front, and his fire, both of small-arms and artillery, was so constant and severe that the men had to keep close behind the work and constantly on the watch. The weather was very bad and the position of the troops behind the works most uncomfortable. The fighting was incessant and the men got but little rest. On the 27th of June, early in the morning, the enemy began a general shelling of our line. About 9.30 o'clock he moved gallantly forward to a general assault."

"Our pickets were driven in and the enemy came on to the assault of our position. The steady fire of our line, and the raking artillery fire which General French sent down our front from his batteries upon our right, repelled every charge and finally drove the enemy back to his fortifications. But he succeeded by dark in fixing his line of battle within 100 yards of our position and poured in a galling fire of musketry. We could have no pickets and the men were constantly firing and watching. For one week we held our position under this fire and on the night of the 2d of July, after thirteen days of unceasing exertion, fighting and watching we retired from the position."[17]

During the battle the 46th Georgia squared off with the 40th Ohio Regiment which had built a line of breastworks from which to shoot at the Georgians. Captain Eleazar Taylor of Company H, now the 46th's commanding officer, was ordered to drive the Ohioans back. Taylor rallied his troops and led them in a sudden rush on the breastworks. The Georgian thrust was a complete surprise and resulted in the capture of the entire Union regiment. The charge was so swift and overwhelming that Colonel Watt of Ohio had to surrender his sword to Private Campbell of Georgia.[18]

Captain Taylor and his troops were lauded by Generals Walker and Gist who sent them letters of commendation. Gist wrote Taylor, "It affords me pleasure to transmit through you to your splendid regiment the accompanying complimentary letter from Maj. Gen. Walker and to add my testimony to the gallant conduct of the officers and men of the 46th Georgia Volunteers. From the reputation of this regiment much was expected; it has more than fulfilled anticipation and I feel assured before the campaign is over will add fresh laurels to those already won and modestly worn. I sorrow with you for the loss of gallant officers and brave men. Let us emulate their examples and revenge their deaths. The occasion will soon be presented, let each man again do his whole duty. Your charge upon the enemy was dashing and effective, accomplishing all that was desired. Success, freedom awaits us--to each man buckle on his armor and all will yet be well with our suffering country."[19]

Dragging guns up Kennesaw Mountain

The Battle of Kennesaw Mountain was Sherman's cardinal error of the Atlanta Campaign. It cost the North nearly 9,000 killed and wounded with half as many Confederate casualties. The 46th Georgia sustained 147 killed and wounded. Company H lost four killed and eleven wounded. The stench of death became so unbearable under the searing 110-degree sun a truce was declared so that the hundreds of corpses covering the field could be buried. On July 9 the Army of Tennessee withdrew to a position between the Chattahoochee River and Atlanta. Later that month Gist's brigade was reassigned to General Benjamin F. Cheatham's division, General William J. Hardee's corps.

General Johnston had been warned by Confederate President Davis that Sherman was not to be allowed to cross the Chattahoochee River. Sherman crossed it anyway on July 15 and Johnston was sacked three days later. In his place Davis appointed General John Bell Hood, a bulldog fighter from Texas. Hood's left arm was crippled at Gettysburg and he lost his right leg two months later at Chickamauga. He had to be strapped to his horse each morning. Hood was only 33 years old when he was given command of the Army of Tennessee. His promotion was a signal to Sherman that he faced an all-out fight for Atlanta.

Sherman began encircling Atlanta but Hood was not one to sit still while Sherman tightened the noose. As Sherman approached the city he divided his forces directing General George H. Thomas to cross the Army of the Cumberland over the Peachtree Creek five miles north of Atlanta. Hood thought he saw a chance to crush Thomas and attacked him with Hardee's corps on July 20 as the Yankees forded the Creek. Ever resilient, Thomas got his artillery across in time to fend off the Rebels.

The 46th Georgia suffered many casualties before retreating to Atlanta. There were three killed and three wounded from Company H. Two days later Hood attacked the rest of Sherman's army east of

Atlanta along the Georgia Railroad line. Cheatham's division performed splendidly, splitting the Yankees and forcing them to fight on two fronts. The Rebels even killed Sherman's favorite general, James B. McPherson, a West Point classmate of Hood. At the end of the day, however, the Confederates were sent reeling back to Atlanta again. In two days Hood took 13,000 casualties he could ill afford. Throughout August, Sherman subjected Atlanta to a relentless artillery siege.

On September 1, 1864 Gist's brigade engaged Federal cavalry at Jonesboro 20 miles south of Atlanta. Assigned the defense of Hood's supply and ordnance wagons, the brigade's role in the battle was critical. The 46th Georgia was posted on the right flank behind a log fortification. Colonel Ellison Capers described the engagement. "Rapid firing began in my front about 4 o'clock and in half an hour my skirmishers came in, closely followed by the assaulting line of the enemy...The firing of the enemy for the most part was wild and entirely over us. I attribute this to the confusion in his advance and attack caused by our abatis[20] for there was no lack of spirit in his attacks. Our small loss in killed and wounded is attributed to this wild firing on the enemy's part...I have counted over 200 graves in our front, most of them marked. The battle began about 4.30 p.m. and lasted until dark."[21] At twilight the 46th Georgia foiled an attempt by a Yankee brigade to slip around its right flank.[22] With nightfall the fighting ceased. After Jonesboro, Hood gave up trying to hold Atlanta and evacuated the city.

Gen. Ellison Capers
Valentine Richmond History Center

Two months later the conqueror of Atlanta began his "March to the Sea" ending in the capture of Savannah. Along the way Sherman let loose 75,000 of his soldiers and urged them to "make Georgia howl." Sherman's troops fanned out along a sixty mile wide front. Meeting little resistance they cut a swath of pillage and destruction across northern Georgia. Fortunately for the Wrights, Marion County was out of harm's way. Their relatives and former neighbors in Warren and Taliaferro Counties, however, bore the brunt of Sherman's juggernaut.

James Wright's brother Harry was only six years old at the time of Sherman's march but recalled it seventy-six years later in a seething passage. "Sherman's raid passed our farm and destroyed houses, barns, cotton, hogs, all livestock, food and fuel, leaving in his wake helpless women and children without food, raiment or shelter on the bleak and barren earth, so recently made so by fire and sword by the U.S. soldiers who ravished women and girls and left their bodies for food for the vultures of the air and beasts of the jungle; and innocent babies slowly starved to death under the orders of that 'Child of Hell', General Sherman."

Sherman's devastation seems a foregone conclusion to his Atlanta campaign but President Lincoln delayed it to pursue a separate peace with Georgia. As Sherman's armies approached Atlanta, Judge Augustus R. Wright and his family abandoned their home in Rome and fled twenty miles west to a sanctuary on the Coosa River in Alabama.[23] Several days after the capture of Atlanta, Augustus was awakened at midnight by a Yankee squad and taken away in the darkness. The remarkable events that followed were narrated in an 1879 letter from Judge Wright to Colonel Isaac W. Avery.

"I was immediately sent to Atlanta where I spent a day with Gen. Sherman, dined with him alone and had much conversation with him.[24] He was exceedingly anxious to make peace. I must do him the justice to say, not so much, it appeared to me, from any fear of ultimate and complete victory, as the terrible devastation of the country which must ensue from further prosecution of the war. He desired to send me personally to Washington to see and converse with President Lincoln and to convey to Mr. Davis the liberal sentiments of the

President which he seemed to think, if known by President Davis, would incline him to peace. He also desired me to say to Governor Brown that if Georgia would treat separately for peace...he would countermarch his army from Georgia soil and permit no further ravages of war.

"I spent some two weeks at Washington with Mr. Lincoln and talked with him more or less almost every day. I was received by President Lincoln with great cordiality. The President then said to me that he had his proclamation of amnesty written for the whole South, from Mr. Davis down to the humblest citizen, and though a part of his cabinet was opposed to it, the day we laid down our arms it would be published, and the South restored to her rights in the Union, as far as was in his power. He desired me to see Mr. Davis personally and to say to him that slaves already freed would not be remanded to slavery, but the general manumissions of slaves in twenty one years would be satisfactory. He certainly intimated longer time would be granted if made a point. He asked me if I did not think I could be of service to the Federal Government as Military Governor of Georgia. I replied that upon the restoration of peace, whenever it did come, I thought I might be of service to the people of Georgia, and also to the Federal Government; but that as long as my people stood in an attitude of hostility to the Government he must regard me as identified with them."[25]

President Lincoln knew of Judge Wright's record as a Unionist in Congress before the war and an anti-secessionist at the Milledgeville convention. This was undoubtedly why the President sought to enlist the Judge as an emissary to Jefferson Davis. Augustus well knew, however, that the Confederate leader would never accept Lincoln's olive branch and so he did not see Davis. Considering Lincoln's certainty of victory when he met with Judge Wright, his proposal that the North would sanction slavery for at least another 21 years if the South would sue for peace was astonishing. Had Davis accepted Lincoln's terms it would have meant nullification of the Emancipation Proclamation which decreed freedom for all slaves in the Confederate states only two years earlier.

Gen. John Bell Hood

While discussing the nation's destiny with President Lincoln, Judge Wright interceded on behalf of a former Rome business partner, Colonel Alfred Shorter. Shorter owned a large cache of cotton that was about to be expropriated by the Yankees. In response to the former Georgia Congressman's plea for help Lincoln replied, "I am sorry I can't furnish you men to transport it, but if you can arrange that detail I will probably be looking the other way."[26]

As all hope of stemming the Yankee flood into Georgia faded General Hood faced some difficult decisions. He could retreat into winter camp and let the Army of Tennessee disintegrate or he could strike his enemy at a place and time of his choosing. Hood had no good options left. He resolved to move his forces into central Tennessee to attack Sherman's rear. If Hood could smite the Union on its western front he might draw Sherman out of Georgia and then cross the Appalachians into Virginia to rescue Lee. The prospect of Hood actually reaching Lee did not worry Sherman. When he learned of Hood's ambitions, he declared, "Damn him, if he will go to the Ohio River, I'll give him rations...Let him go North. My business is down South."

From Jonesboro, Hood turned northwest back toward Dalton where the Atlanta Campaign had begun only four months before. On October 13 Hood arrived at Dalton where Sherman had left 800 colored troops and 100 white cavalrymen. As soon as Rebel artillery was placed on a hill above them the Yankees surrendered without a shot. Hood's bloodless victory at Dalton provided him with badly needed food and arms. A few days later the Army of Tennessee crossed into Alabama. As the cold autumn fell, the Rebels lacked basic necessities. Many were barefoot. Despite the shortages, foraging and straggling were strictly forbidden.

FRANKLIN

On November 18 Hood was joined by Forrest's cavalry at Tuscumbia. Together they turned north into Tennessee with 38,000 ragged fighters.

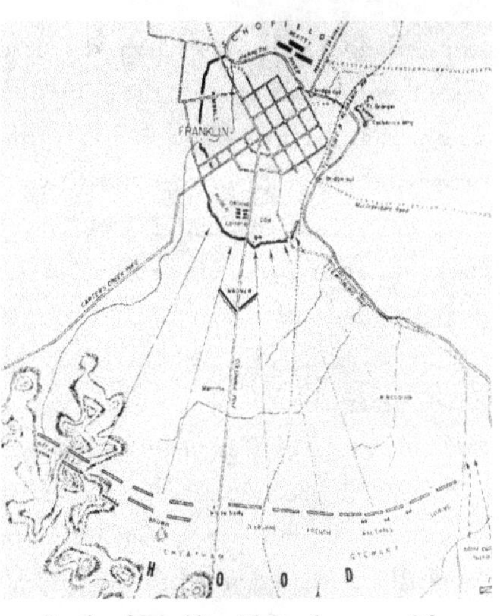

Battle of Franklin, November 30,1864

At Columbia the Confederates bivouacked a few days to ride out rain and snow storms. In late November Hood learned that 32,000 blues under General John M. Schofield, one of his West Point roommates, were moving east of his position toward Nashville which was in the hands of Union General George H. Thomas, the "Rock of Chickamauga." To thwart Schofield's rendezvous with Thomas, Hood raced north to intercept him at Franklin 18 miles south of Nashville. Hardee's corps was now commanded by Cheatham. An element of Cheatham's corps, Gist's valiant brigade was one of those chosen to lead the assault on the Federals who were strongly fortified and waiting. Hood's junior officers quickly realized the long odds against them. To get at the Yankees they would have to lead their men across two miles of wide open terrain. Worse still, Schofield would have cannons aplenty trained on them as they came forward. Hood was too impetuous to wait for his own artillery to come up from the rear. Consequently, his infantry faced an enemy line unfazed by shelling. Captain Robert W. Banks of the 37th Mississippi remembered the mood at breakfast on the last day of November.

"The meal was eaten in haste, each officer with his belt buckled on and side-arms in place, for momentarily they were expecting orders to move upon the enemy in the fortified town. While eating, the impending battle was freely discussed by those eight officers, all of whom were in a serious, thoughtful mood. Two only were optimistic. The other six took a gloomy view of the situation. The latter frankly expressed their opinion that the approaching battle would end the chapter of their respective lives. They anticipated it was to be the finale to their individual endeavors as Confederate soldiers. They had presentiments that when it was over their records for time and eternity would be made up; that for them the curtain would not only be rung down upon the last scene of the last drama of the war, but that with its fall the end to their earthly careers would be at hand. And they substantially so expressed themselves. Sadder prognostications it would be difficult to imagine. Prognostications more swiftly, and direfully, fulfilled it would be impossible to discover. Before the sun went down six of the eight received mortal wounds."[27]

Colonel Ellison Capers recounts the ferocious battle at Franklin. "The enemy was intrenched in a semicircle in front of Franklin with his flanks refused and resting on the Harpeth River in his rear...The distance from our position to this advanced force seemed to be about a mile and a quarter. At about 4 o'clock the two corps moved down the hills, our division marching by the right flank of regiments until we descended the slopes, then forming forward into line. As we advanced the force in front opened fire on us and our line moved steadily on, the enemy retreating as we pressed forward. Just before the charge was ordered the brigade passed over an elevation, from which we beheld the magnificent spectacle the battlefield presented--bands were playing, general and staff officers and gallant couriers were riding in front of and between the line, 100 battle flags were waving in the smoke of battle, and bursting shells were wreathing the air with great circles of smoke, while 20,000 brave men were marching in perfect order against the foe."[28]

This was the last great Confederate infantry charge of the Civil War. In sheer numbers it was much bigger than the more famous, ill-fated "Pickett's Charge" at Gettysburg. The awesome sight of the tattered gray and brown legions descending on Franklin was eloquently described by a Union officer who was on the receiving end of their attack and lived to tell about it. "It was a grand sight such as would make a lifelong impression on the mind of any man who could see such a resistless, well-conducted charge. For the moment we were spellbound with admiration, although they were our hated foes and we knew that in a few brief moments as soon as they were within firing distance, all that orderly grandeur would be changed to bleeding, writhing confusion, and that thousands of those valorous men of the South, with their chivalric officers, would pour out their life's blood on the fair fields in front of us."[29]

Colonel Capers continues his narrative. "General Gist...rode down our front, and returning, ordered the charge in concert with General Gordon. In passing from the left to the right of the regiment, the general waved his hat to us, expressed his pride and confidence in the Twenty-fourth, and rode away in the smoke of battle, never more to be seen by the men he had commanded on so many fields. His horse was shot, and dismounting, he was leading the right of the brigade when he fell, pierced through the heart. On pressed the charging lines of the brigade, driving the advance force of the enemy pellmell into a locust abatis where many were captured and sent to the rear; others were wounded by the fire of their own men. This abatis was a formidable and fearful obstruction. The entire brigade was arrested by it.

"Gist's and Gordon's brigades charged on and reached the ditch of the work, mounted the work, and met the enemy in close combat. He never succeeded in retaking the line we held. About dusk there was a lull in the firing west of the pike. Torn and exhausted, deprived of every general officer and nearly every field officer, the division had only strength enough left to hold its position. Strahl's and Carter's brigades came gallantly to the assistance of Gist's and Gordon's, but the enemy's fire from the houses in the rear of the line and from his reserves, thrown rapidly forward, and from guns posted on the far side of the river so as to enfilade the field, tore their line to pieces before it reached the abatis. But there was no backward movement of this line."[30]

General Gist fell in front of the 46th Georgia just as it reached the Union entrenchment. Private Samuel R. Watkins of the First Tennessee Regiment wrote, "General Gist, a noble and brave cavalier from South Carolina, was lying with his sword reaching across the breastworks still grasped in his hand. He was lying there dead. All dead! I loved General Gist and when I mention his name tears gather in my eyes. I think he was the handsomest man I ever knew."[31]

When Gist's men broke through the line held by the 72nd Illinois a few yards from the Carter House, the 183rd Ohio rushed in to stop them. For a while the 46th Georgia and Yankees stood toe-to-toe trading volleys only 15 yards apart.[32] The dead were so densely arrayed some remained standing. One Confederate survivor described it as the "grand coronation of death." Captain Banks recalled, "So thick were the dead and wounded in the ditch there, it became a sort of out-door chamber of horrors. When night came, the groans and frenzied cries of the wounded on both sides of the earthworks were awe-inspiring. The ravings of the maimed and mangled victims were heartrending. Crazed by pain, many knew not what they did or said. Some pleadingly cried out, 'Cease firing! Cease firing!' while others agonizingly were shouting, 'We surrender! We surrender!'"[33]

Captain Malcolm Gillis of Company G found himself the ranking officer in Gist's brigade when the shooting stopped that night. The rolls of the 46th Georgia testify that it lost 23 killed, 25 wounded and 17 captured including two killed and six wounded from Company H. Somehow James Wright survived the carnage after charging into the Yankee fire with the first Rebel assault wave. We can but imagine the horror he witnessed that day. The intensity of the killing must have stunned even him, a hardened veteran of three years at age nineteen. By then James was a Second Sergeant in Company H.

The Carter House today still showing bullet holes from the Battle of Franklin

The day after the battle Augustus G. McGehee of Company I wrote to his mother about it. "They could see us coming in plain view in an open field and volley after volley the deadly missiles would come killing my comrades on every side, many of my friends fell to whom I had become endeared. I loved them but onward I went double quicking over rocks, through cornfields until I reached the enemy's works. I was with the first who reached the works and I say it to the honor and bravery of the 46th. Her colors were the first to be planted upon the works. As soon as they were planted we rallied to them and then poured volley after volley into them for several long hours. I thought of your prayers all the while I was in the fight. I feel they alone saved me for the bullets fell around thick as hail. We will now move on towards Nashville. Pray for me. Love to all. Your son, Gus."

NASHVILLE

In five hours the North sustained 2,200 casualties and the South 6,300 losses at Franklin, a Pyrrhic victory for Hood at best. Despite Hood's desperate attack, Schofield withdrew from Franklin and linked up with Thomas in Nashville. Hood moved his remaining forces into the Harpeth Hills three miles southeast of Nashville and dared Thomas to come out and fight. Grant

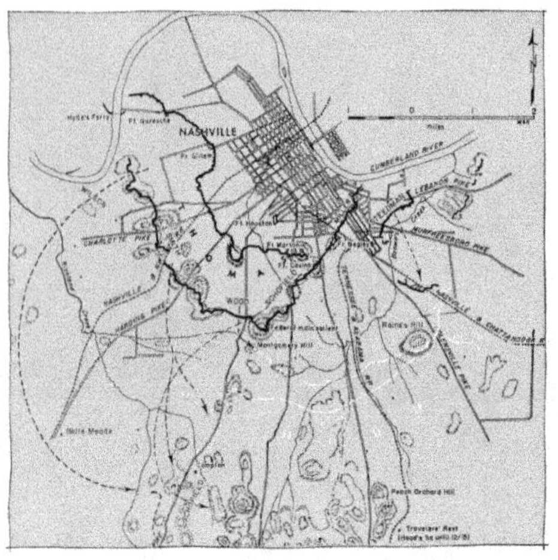

Battle of Nashville, December 16, 1864

began telegraphing Thomas ordering him to launch an immediate attack on Hood and drive him out of Tennessee. With more than twice Hood's strength, Thomas ignored Grant's orders and waited until he was sure the time was right. Outside Nashville, Cheatham's corps formed Hood's right flank which stretched across the Nolensville Pike. On December 8 freezing rain coated Nashville with a sheet of ice. Thomas stalled another week and Grant prepared to relieve him of his command. On the 15th the ice began to melt and Thomas decided to strike. Sergeant Wright awoke that morning in a dense fog through which 55,000 bluecoats were streaming toward him. Just before dawn Thomas sent General James Steedman's colored troops charging into Cheatham's corps where James was at his post. It was only a feint. Shortly, the real assault began on Hood's left and center. As the Union attack progressed, Hood's left flank began to falter and he ordered Cheatham to move over and shore it up. That night Hood fell back two miles and tightened his perimeter. Cheatham's corps was now positioned on Shy's Hill anchoring the Rebels' left flank.

The next day "The Rock" waited until three o'clock in the afternoon before launching another crushing attack on the Confederates. An hour later Thomas concentrated his fury on Hood's left. With artillery fire, infantry charges and dismounted cavalry wreaking havoc in Hood's rear with new Spencer repeating rifles, Thomas brought the Army of Tennessee to heel. James was among those who absorbed the onslaught against Shy's Hill. During the fighting he was grazed in the right leg by a ball that was probably fired by a lad from Minnesota. Soon the Confederates were in headlong flight.

The melee was described by Sam Watkins who was not far from

James Wright. "Such a scene I never saw. The army was panic-stricken. The woods everywhere were full of running soldiers. Our officers were crying 'Halt! Halt!' and trying to rally and reform their broken ranks. My boot was full of blood and my clothing saturated with it. I was at General Hood's headquarters. He was much agitated and affected, pulling his hair with his one hand (he had but one) and crying like his heart would break. I pitied him, poor fellow."[34]

Hood's hasty retreat from Nashville was covered by Forrest's cavalry but Forrest could do little more than annoy his pursuers. The Battle of Nashville was a defeat such as the South had never seen. It was the only engagement in the war in which a large Rebel force left the field in utter chaos. During the night of December 16 James limped south along the Franklin Pike in a driving rain. The road was clogged with retreating Rebels and some were ad-libbing a new song about their commander. It was sung to the tune of "The Yellow Rose of Texas."

So now I'm marching southward;
My heart is full of woe.
I'm going back to Georgia
To see my uncle Joe.
You may talk about your Beauregard
And sing of General Lee,
But the gallant Hood of Texas
Played hell in Tennessee.

BATTLE OF NASHVILLE
Shy's Hill
On this hill was fought the decisive encounter of the Battle of Nashville December 16. 1864. At 4:15 P. M. a Federal assault at the angle on top of the hill broke the Confederate line. Col. W. M. Shy. 20th Tenn. Inf. was killed and Gen. T. B. Smith was captured. The Confederates retreated over the Overton Hills to the Franklin Pike.

Historical marker at Shy's Hill, Nashville

By morning James covered 13 miles on his wounded leg and was back in Franklin. The Yankees were close behind and the healthy Rebels had to keep moving. Only hours after James arrived in Franklin he was captured by General James H. Wilson's cavalry along with 1,800 other Confederate wounded. James was transported to the Federal hospital in Nashville where he was admitted on December 26. He was assigned hospital number 12946 and placed in the care of U.S. Army surgeon Major Bowman Bigelow Breed. Dr. Breed noted that James had a "simple flesh wound" to his right leg. Given the primitive state of medicine and the conditions in which the wounded were kept, even slight wounds quickly festered.

In an attempt to relieve the growing infection in James's leg Dr. Breed performed a venisection. The procedure involved opening a vein with a scalpel to let "bad" blood from the wound. Dr. Breed's best efforts failed. The Union army hospital records reflect that James's leg turned gangrenous and had to be amputated above the knee as shown by the grim notation "upper 3d sev." Any anesthesia would have been rudimentary while the surgeon's saw did its ghastly work in a few seconds. James lingered for over a month and was given "stimulants & tonics, warm formulations locally" to ease his pain. He succumbed to his wound on February 1, 1865. The hospital records further reflect that James was 19 years old, single and had no personal effects when he died. He was buried under grave marker 11792 at the Nashville City Cemetery.

W | Confed 46 | Ga.

James E. Wright

Rank Sergt.; Co. H, 46 Reg't Ga. Reb.

Admitted Dec 26, 1864,

To No. 1, U. S. A., Gen'l Hosp. Nashville, Tenn.

From Franklin Tenn.

Diagnosis, Simple fl. wd. of Rt leg upper 3d sev

Missile, Con. Ball

W'd at Nashville, Dec 16, 1864.

Treatm't, Stimulants & Tonics warm formulations locally

Ret'd to duty ...., 18 .

Transf'd to I. C. ...., 18 .

Transf'd to ...., 18 .

Furloughed ...., 18 .

Deserted ...., 18 .

Disch'd from service ...., 18 .

Died Feb 1, 1865.

Re-adm'd from furlo' or des'n ...., 18 .

Remarks: Exhaustion from U.S.G. Rt leg

Age 19

H # 12946

Tenn. Reg. No. 37; Hos. No. ; Page 66

Lindsey, Copyist.

Sgt. James E. Wright's last muster roll

JAMES EDWIN WRIGHT
2ND SERG CO H 46 GA INF
CONFEDERATE STATES ARMY
1846 1865
MOTHER COULD NEVER BECOME
RECONCILED AT JAMES' DEATH

Grave marker at Confederate Circle Mt. Olivet Cemetery, Nashville

U.S Hospital No. 1 where Sgt. James E. Wright died as a prisoner of war.
National Archives

Four years later James's remains were disinterred and reburied in the Confederate Circle at the Mount Olivet Cemetery in Nashville with those of 1,500 other fallen of the Army of Tennessee. A Nashville newspaper commemorated the occasion. "Once entombed in a final resting place so sweet and acceptable, no other duty will have to be performed toward the gallant dead save the enshrinement in our memories of their noble deeds, for danger and death have ridden unbridled over their breasts and the smoldering holocaust claims, aye, demands the sweetest remembrance. Here youth had chivalry, undying faith and lofty valor meet and mingle dust with dust..."[35]

The South suffered 4,500 and the North 3,000 killed and wounded at Nashville. Four fatalities were from Company H of the 46th Georgia. In the larger scheme James's death was merely an infinitesimal part of our great national tragedy. It was, however, nonetheless devastating to his parents. Their grief over the loss of their first-born son left a permanent imprint on the younger children. Harry wrote, "Mother could never become reconciled at brother James's death." Even now it is difficult to accept that James survived three years of brutal warfare only to die from a superficial wound received at the end of the last day of the last major battle fought by his regiment.

After Nashville, Hood brought what was left of the Army of Tennessee to Tupelo, Mississippi and resigned his commission on January 23, 1865. En route to Mississippi, Hood sent Beauregard a telegram concealing the disaster at Nashville. "The army has recrossed the Tennessee River without material loss since the battle of Franklin."[36] After Hood's resignation his troops were returned to General Johnston from whom they had been taken before the fall of Atlanta.

The 46th and 47th Georgia regiments were consolidated in early 1865. Gist's old brigade was sent to the Carolinas under Brigadier General Ellison Capers to resist Sherman's march north. On March 19 Johnston rallied his soldiers for a final victory over part of Sherman's army at Bentonville, North Carolina. Bowing to the inevitable Johnston surrendered the Army of Tennessee to Sherman at Greensboro, North Carolina on April 28 three weeks after Lee surrendered to Grant at Appomattox, Virginia. No command ever fought more bravely for its homeland than the Army of Tennessee. None was more doomed by the inexorable tide of history.

THE AFTERMATH

Federal troops arrived in Buena Vista in May and imposed martial law. Thus, John Wesley Wright was the last of his family to hold slaves. Twenty miles east of the Wright farm the military prison camp at Andersonville was liberated. The stockade was designed to hold 10,000 prisoners, but when exchanges were ended by Grant in 1864 the population at the 16-acre camp swelled to 35,000. Conditions at Andersonville became horrific and more than 13,000 Northern soldiers died there. After receiving an amnesty from Sherman, Andersonville's commandant Major Henry Wirz was tried for war crimes and hanged by a Union military tribunal. Andersonville is imbedded in our national memory and rightly so. It is more easily forgotten that Southern prisoners died in greater numbers under similar conditions in Northern camps like those at Elmira, New York, Point

Lookout, Maryland and Camp Douglas, Illinois.

Early in the war Judge Augustus R. Wright was chairman of a Confederate congressional committee that investigated conditions in military prisons in Richmond, Virginia. In a September, 1862 report to Confederate Secretary of War George W. Randolph, a grandson of Thomas Jefferson, Chairman Wright advised that conditions in one of the facilities he saw were "terrible beyond belief... the committee could not stay in the room over a few seconds." He added, "[T]he committee makes the report to the Secretary of War and not to the House because in the latter case it would be printed and for the honor of the nation such things must be kept secret."[37]

Before the Civil War southwest Georgia was called "Little Egypt," a biblical reference to its fertile lands and rich harvests. At the war's end 80% percent of Marion County's wealth was gone and the value of its land was halved.[38] The future must have seemed dismal to those who had lost so much. Yet in 1867 John and Frances Wright celebrated the birth of their ninth child, Richmond. A year later Georgia was readmitted to the Union.

The decade after the Civil War is known as the Reconstruction period. For the vanquished, Reconstruction meant Federal military occupation and Republican state governments controlled by the Yankees, their white collaborators ("scalawags") and Black freedmen. Those who had supported the Confederacy, particularly veterans, were disenfranchised and barred from national office. For the enslaved, Reconstruction was their first taste of freedom after 250 years of bondage.

On August 12, 1870 Buena Vista's census taker, Deputy L.M. Wall, found the Wrights living in Tazewell several miles north of Buena Vista. John was listed as a farmer and Justice of the Peace with real property valued at $4,000 and personal property worth $1,000, less than half his wealth before the war. Frances was keeping house and listed as unable to read and write. The younger children were Mary,

14; Harry, 12; John, Jr. and Frances, both 9; and Richmond, 3. Eighteen-year-old Lawrence was working in his father's fields and 21-year-old Linton was employed away from the family farm. Some of the Wrights' neighbors in Tazewell, like Charles Bridge and Lazarus Dimmack, were Black sharecroppers with large families.[39] Without doubt they had tilled the lands of others just a few years before as slaves.

According to Harry Wright his mother Frances Ann died exactly two years later on August 12, 1872 at age 45. A widower, John was left with five young children to care for with the help of Linton and Lawrence. To shield the children and his few remaining possessions from creditors, John sought protection under Georgia's Homestead Act. The Act permitted families to declare some land and personal property exempt from attachment. In late 1872 John filed a petition in the Marion County Ordinary Court.

"The petition of John W. Wright of said County respectfully showeth that he is the head of a family consisting of six minor children and that he desires to have laid off and set apart to be exempt from levy and sale as a Homestead for the use of his said family an amount of or fraction of the value of said real estate not to exceed the value of two thousand dollars in specie...The petitioner further desires to have set apart to be exempt from levy and sale, and for the use and benefit of said family, certain personal property, not to exceed one thousand dollars in specie, a schedule of which said personal property is attached and marked exhibit "A" to which reference is hereby made. Your petitioner therefore asks that the usual notice in such cases may issue and be published, as is by law required and as in duty bound petitioner will ever pray."

Exhibit "A"

1 Dark bay Horse Mule$130.	
1 Dark bay Mare Mule $130	$260.00
1 Black Horse	100.00

21 Head of Hogs $125. 4 Head of Cows $40	165.00
130 Bu Corn $112.50. Fodder 1500 lbs. $11.25	123.75
300 Bu Cot Seed $45.00.	
Household & Kitchen Furniture $150	195.00
2 Wagons $60.00. 1 Buggy $10.00.	
Plantation Tools $8.00	78.00

Approved this Decr. 19, 1872	Recorded Oct. 13, 1874
Jas. M. Lowe, Ordy	Thos. B. Lumpkin, Clerk

By the end of 1873 the United States was in the throes of the worst financial panic in its history. The depression weighed most heavily on the South. John Wesley Wright and his elder sons began to look westward for a more promising future. Like many of their fellow Georgians they saw Texas as the place where a new life could be made.

"I would not have a man in my company that I didn't think was as good as I am."

6
Joining Captain McNelly

Its sprawling territory set back from the Civil War's main arena, Texas was spared the devastation that befell other Confederate states. Texas did not, however, escape Reconstruction and Union rule. A month after Abraham Lincoln's assassination President Andrew Johnson ordered General Philip Sheridan with 50,000 troops to the Rio Grande Valley. Their presence discouraged diehard Rebels from fomenting border trouble in league with Emperor Maximilian, the French-supported puppet ruler of Mexico. Washington installed another Union general, Edmund J. Davis, as Governor of Texas.

During the war the famed scouts, the Texas Rangers, were mostly absorbed into the Confederate cavalry. After the war Governor Davis abolished the Rangers. In their place a new State Police force was formed by the Republican government. Davis needed Texans with military experience to head his State Police but by and large such men were only to be found among his recent foes.

One former Confederate who caught Davis's attention was Leander H. McNelly. The son of a Methodist minister, McNelly moved from Virginia to central Texas as a child. At age 16 he joined General Henry H. Sibley's Texas cavalry brigade. Despite his youth McNelly was quickly recognized for his natural ability as a leader. He also gained a reputation for conducting himself in battle as if he cared not whether he lived or died. At seventeen McNelly was given command of a company of mounted troops in Colonel Thomas Green's regiment.

McNelly's partisans mainly operated behind Union lines in Louisiana. In 1863 McNelly was sent to reconnoiter near Brashear City where the Federals had 700 troops. Under cover of night he led a party of seventeen men to a wooden bridge within earshot of the Yankees and ordered them to ride over it in circles for several hours. Convinced there were thousands about to attack him, the Union commander surrendered to McNelly the next morning. Unable to take a whole regiment in tow McNelly had to stall for time and send for help.[1] McNelly's phantom hit-and-run tactics became legendary. His troops wasted no ammunition and did not shoot until they were on top of an enemy. McNelly led dozens of raids against the Yankees but was wounded only once.

When Governor Davis first invited McNelly to help command the State Police he wanted no part of the "carpetbagger" regime but was eventually persuaded by friends to accept a commission. McNelly served with distinction as one of four State Police captains and was wounded in a jail-break by two prisoners on trial for murdering a Black man.[2] The Reconstruction police were disbanded in 1873. For most Texans it was good riddance but McNelly's popular image was untarnished by his association with the Davis government.

Capt. Leander H. McNelly

In January, 1874 Reconstruction came to an end in Texas with the electoral defeat of Edmund Davis by Democrat Richard Coke. Governor Coke promptly reinstated the Texas Rangers and on April 10 the Legislature authorized the raising of seven companies. These troops, the Frontier Battalion, were placed under Major John B. Jones and deployed in West Texas against the Comanches, Apaches and Lipans.

There was more unrest below Austin, Texas caused by the Sutton-Taylor feud in DeWitt County. To suppress the feud, another Ranger company was organized with McNelly as its captain. It was commissioned as the Washington County Volunteer Militia, Company A, and also known as the "Special Force." The Washington County Volunteers were so named because they were mustered into service at McNelly's farm near Burton in that county. The Special Force was detached from Major Jones's Frontier Battalion and McNelly reported directly to Adjutant General William Steele in Austin.

In Buena Vista, Georgia twenty-two-year-old Lawrence B. Wright heard about the rebirth of the Texas Rangers and knew of McNelly whose wartime feats were legendary in Georgia. The allure of joining the Rangers and serving under such a man was irresistible to the young farmer. In June he mounted up and headed for Austin 800 miles away. When he arrived in the Texas capital, a notice for new volunteers appeared.

> The members of Captain McNelly's company now in the city intend leaving for DeWitt County immediately upon the receipt of orders from the Captain, which are expected daily; anyone wishing to join can apply today at Dei's stable or at Cook's building, corner of Congress Avenue and Pecan Street.[3]

After enlisting in the Washington County Volunteers as a private, Lawrence rode to Burton where he and his companions were given rifles. From Burton they headed for Clinton in DeWitt County 75 miles southeast of Austin.[4]

On July 25 McNelly issued his first muster roll for the Special Force showing 47 troops present for duty. They wore no uniforms or badges and each Ranger supplied his own horse. If a horse was killed or lost the state paid the owner its appraised value. According to the muster roll Lawrence's horse was valued at $90.00 and his monthly salary was $25.00. Though the Rangers were a military unit, strict discipline was not enforced. Ranger captains led more by example than command. The source of McNelly's power over his men is revealed by an episode recounted by one of them over forty years later.

"Captain McNelly and a U.S. Captain were sitting on a wagon tongue when one of our ranger boys went up and sat down by Captain McNelly. The U.S. Captain jumped up and said, 'Captain McNelly, do you allow one of your privates to sit down by you?' 'Yes sir,' said Captain McNelly, 'I do at any time. I haven't a man in my company but what can lie down and sleep with me if he wishes to do so.' The U.S. Captain said, 'We don't allow privates that privilege with officers.' To this Captain McNelly replied, 'I would not have a man in my company that I didn't think was as good as I am.' That showed the kind of love Captain McNelly had for his men and he did not have a man in his company that wouldn't have stepped in between him and death. We all loved him like a father as well as a captain. He always said, 'Come boys,' he never said, 'Go boys.' He never sent us anywhere he would not go himself; he always went in front and told us to come and we always went."[5]

In appearance McNelly was no storybook lawman. He stood but five and a half feet tall and was a consumptive. The tuberculosis made his voice wheezy and barely audible. A long brown beard extended to the middle of his chest. In the field McNelly was a fastidious dresser who wore a flannel shirt with tie, jacket, duck pants, felt hat and white gauntlet gloves. His style was modest, direct and devoid of pretense. McNelly's written reports to General Steele were succinct. By contrast his second-in-command, Lieutenant Truxton Chanders ("Pidge") Robinson, was a poet and essayist. Robinson wrote prolifically about his experiences in the Rangers and his works regularly appeared in the Austin press.[6] One of Robinson's first pieces from Clinton was a humorous sketch of the company's departure from Burton.

"Capt. McNelly had about thirty men in camp and after drawing rifles we started for this place which we reached on the first ultimo; on the route the captain had us drawn up in double ranks, and was informing us of what our duties would consist when H---s, who is the most unfortunate man in the company, came charging down to take his place in ranks and was thrown clear over the line and lit on his head in front of the men much to their astonishment; some of them thought he had dropped from the clouds. The captain said he would shoot the first man who ran from the fight and I look upon my death-warrant as already signed and sealed. I am as good as dead already for my only hope is cut off."[7]

The Sutton-Taylor feud posed an enormous challenge for McNelly. The rivalry is said to have started in Alabama before both clans settled in DeWitt County. The Taylor gang included the notorious outlaw John Wesley Hardin who claimed to have killed over thirty men "not counting Mexicans or negroes."[8] Hardin would be brought to justice a few years later by one of McNelly's officers, Lieutenant John B. Armstrong. The citizens of DeWitt County regularly witnessed lynchings, shootings and intimidation of those who ran afoul of the clans. The authorities, including judges and prosecutors, were completely in the thrall of the feudists.

In August the Special Force saw its only armed action in the Sutton-Taylor affair. Sergeant John C. Middleton and three privates were escorting John Taylor from Yorktown to Clinton to testify in a murder trial. On the road to Clinton the Rangers were set upon by about two dozen men led by Captain Joseph Tumlinson, an old Indian fighter and chief of the Sutton faction. A Ranger private and three horses were wounded. Taylor escaped into the night but was recaptured the next day.

McNelly was more referee than lawman in Dewitt County. To his credit the violence ended without the loss of a single life. This was accomplished by the Rangers' credible show of force. In one of McNelly's first reports to General Steele he wrote, "You may rely on my not doing anything but what you will endorse or my orders permit.

I need Winchester rifles because these people are all armed with them and Tumlinson has from 40 to 75 armed men in town every day and if I am compelled to fight I don't want to get whipped."[9]

The next day McNelly again wrote of Tumlinson, "I saw him at the head of 75 well-armed men who have no interest but in obeying his orders, he is a man who has always righted his own wrongs and he tells me that the only way for this county to have peace is to kill off the Taylor party. He has never been made to feel that the civil law could and should be the supreme arbiter between man and man...I feel entirely able to whip Tumlinson with the men I have if it must be a fight but will need more men. Fifty men cannot over-awe these people; they have been in the habit of overriding the officers of the law so long that it will require more than I have to bluff them."[10]

Besides his precarious military situation in DeWitt County, McNelly had to contend with endless quarreling between pro and anti-Reconstruction factions. A stridently anti-Coke journal in San Antonio carried this editorial a month after McNelly's arrival in Clinton. "The Sutton-Taylor war in DeWitt county continues with unabated fury. We have just learned that Capt. McNelly, with his small company of Coke's State Police, finds himself powerless to quell the insurrection or to give any relief to the county. His company consisted, at first, of forty men, but five of these have deserted him, others are still leaving and he is unable to cope with the difficulties of the situation. He has called upon Gov. Coke to reinforce him with a hundred men..."

"Is it not strange, incomprehensible strange, that the Governor of a great State like Texas should allow a handful of desperadoes to hold a whole county in terror, to take helpless prisoners out of jail and hang them, and to hold possession of a county seat, and disperse the courts at their pleasure...He has a company of State Police between Corpus Christi and Brownsville that is doing only mischief among innocent Mexican citizens and another company on the Rio Grande that is equally useless. Why have they not long ago been sent to DeWitt County?...If a few negroes or Mexicans were even reported in arms the cohorts of 'Cokery' would be down on them at once. But Democratic desperadoes are to be treated very gently."[11]

There was some truth to the Republican diatribes against Governor Coke. Contrasted with his decisive action against the Indians in West Texas and Mexican bandits in the Rio Grande Valley, the DeWitt County feudists were handled with kid gloves. Unlike the Indians and bandits, the clansmen were Texans, which may have mattered little to their victims. Tumlinson, however, was too shrewd to fall into McNelly's clutches. Week after week the stalemate in DeWitt County persisted.

In late August, McNelly reported to Steele that the presence of his troops in DeWitt County was having a civilizing effect. But he added, "The action of the District Judge and state's attorney, or rather their inaction, has been the cause of trouble which might have otherwise been nipped in the bud. I am satisfied that if a judge and attorney of probity, ability and nerve were sent down to hold court in December, they could effectually prevent a continuation of disgraceful scenes in and out of the halls of Justice. With the present incumbents there is no hope."[12] In his next report a few days later, McNelly emphasized that the DeWitt County prosecutor "when sober is of no earthly account. Everyone curses him when they feel like doing so and he will resent nothing."[13] That fall, Tumlinson died of natural causes and a truce between the feudists followed.

In late 1874 Linton L. Wright and his teenage cousin, George P. Durham, left Georgia to join Lawrence and enlist with McNelly. George's father, John A. Durham, was an officer of the 49th Georgia Infantry Regiment during the Civil War. John Durham was promoted to major shortly before he was mortally wounded in the right thigh by a Minie ball on May 24, 1864 at Jericho Ford, Virginia. After the war his widow Mary Louisa Durham sent young George to stay with kin and he probably lived with her cousin John Wesley Wright before leaving Georgia.

On January 1, 1875 Linton Wright joined the Special Force as a private at Clinton. At first there was no opening in the company for George Durham. To bide his time he found work in Burton where he waited for an audience with McNelly, figuring the Captain would come home sooner or later. George recalled their first encounter at a soda shop.

> Everybody in the store, including my senorita sorta come to attention to wait on the little brown-haired feller and, as they all knowed I was hankering to see Captain McNelly, just see him, one of the men angled over to me and said, "That's him."
>
> "Who?" I asked.
>
> "McNelly," he said. "Captain McNelly--you been askin' about him."
>
> "But," I said, "I wanted the old Captain; the one that fit in the war; the one that was head of the Texas fighters in Louisiana."
>
> "Son," said the man, kinda solemn and respectful-like, "there ain't but one Cap'n McNelly. Thar never was but one of him. The Lord put all he had in that one batter."
>
> Well, I argued a while and let all that soak in; and by the time the little brown-haired feller had drunk his sody pop, I had nerve to walk up.
>
> "Are you Cap'n McNelly?" I asked. "I'm from Georgia," I said, "Durham is the name."
>
> "All right".
>
> "I jest wanted to meet you."
>
> "All right".
>
> There seemin' to be nothing else to say, I said it.

> And so did he. But, be dog, I never went through such a feeling. I wanted him to tell me to go over and ask the senorita to marry me and I'd a gone poppin' my heels. I wanted him to tell me to start shootin' down lights or killin' sody clerks. I wanted him to tell me to do something. There never was a fifteen-year old boy that wanted a man to tell him to do something like I wanted this soft-spoken, dreamy-eyed man to tell me.[14]

Uncertain of his continued purpose in DeWitt County, McNelly went to Austin in mid-January to meet with General Steele. By March he was back in Clinton begging for credit from local merchants who were also uneasy about the future of the Special Force. His instructions from Steele were less than reassuring. "You need not buy any more supplies than will do for immediate use, as in the event the Legislature refuses to make any appropriation for the purpose of keeping your Company in service, it will be disbanded at once."[15] Indeed, the company's payroll lapsed between February 24 and April 1, 1875.

Skepticism about the Special Force was eagerly fanned by the Republican newspapers. "The State troops, organized with such a flourish at the beginning of Coke's reign, are to be withdrawn soon and disbanded. The Legislature gets the credit for doing it because they failed to make the requisite appropriation to keep these troops in the field. During the winter there was little use for these troops on the frontier and Coke has used them as a kind of state police force to regulate some of his unruly partisans in DeWitt county and elsewhere..."[16]

But at the very moment this news was going to press, events unfolding to the south on the Nueces River were creating a new mission for the Washington County Volunteers, the kind for which McNelly's skills were perfectly suited.

"Dadblame if I didn't get dubs."

7
The Battle at Palo Alto Prairie

The Rio Grande valley lies along the cultural fault line that separates the United States and Latin America. Texas's war of independence from Mexico in 1836 left unresolved where would be the Lone Star State's southern border. Texans considered the Rio Grande to be their lower boundary. Mexico still claimed all lands below the Nueces River which flows 150 miles north of the Rio Grande. The dispute smoldered for the next nine years while Texas was an independent republic. In 1845 Texas became the 28th of the United States. Mexico had warned it would consider the annexation of Texas an act of war by the United States.

Several months after Texas joined the Union, President James K. Polk raised the ante and ordered United States troops and federalized Texas Rangers under General Zachary Taylor to march south from Corpus Christi to the north bank of the Rio Grande. Mexican President Antonio Lopez de Santa Anna accepted the challenge and so began the Mexican War. The first battle was fought on May 8, 1846 twelve miles north of Brownsville, Texas at a site called Palo Alto. It was a rout for the Mexicans but Palo Alto would see more clashes between armed men from opposite sides of the Rio Grande.

Like the Texan war of independence, the Mexican War also ended in the defeat and capture of Santa Anna, this time in his own capital of Mexico City. The war established the southern border of Texas as a political fact. In actuality the region between the Nueces and Rio Grande remained a no-man's land where settlers from the north ventured at great risk. The dangers on that frontier were heightened by near anarchy in the adjacent Mexican state of Tamaulipas. Beyond the arm of the central government in Mexico City, the region was a haven for outlaws and the dispossessed.

Tamaulipas was ripe for a strongman who could seize power and wealth by forging its desperate elements into a loyal body. Such a man was Juan Nepomuceno ("Cheno") Cortina. Cortina was born in 1824 in Camargo, Mexico to an aristocratic mother and illiterate father. As a youth he was incorrigible with an early aptitude for manipulating the lower classes. Cortina joined the Mexican army in 1845 and fought in the battles of Palo Alto and Resaca de la Palma in Texas. Cortina's war experience left him with an intense hatred of the Americans. He was said to have once remarked, "The sight of an American makes me feel like eating little kids."[1]

In 1859 Cortina shot the sheriff of Brownsville and took a Mexican prisoner from his custody. By this deed Cortina became a hero to many of his countrymen who longed to retake the lands they believed had been stolen from them. Cortina then organized raids along the Rio Grande. In one incident his men ambushed and killed three Texas Rangers near Palo Alto in retaliation for the lynching of a Cortinista.[2] The geographic coincidence must have pleased Cortina. After several skirmishes with federal troops and Texas Rangers led by Lieutenant Colonel Robert E. Lee and Major Samuel P. Heintzelman, Cortina's forces were driven out of Texas in 1860.[3] Despite his defeat on the field the "Cortina War" was a political bonanza for Cheno. He stood up to the enemies of Mexico and emerged as the undisputed warlord of Tamaulipas.

During the brief reign of Emperor Maximilian, Cortina was first allied with the resistance leader Benito Juarez in the patriotic struggle against Mexico's French invaders. Juarez made Cortina one of his rebel generals but when French forces captured Matamoros in 1864 Cortina declared for the Emperor and began exterminating his fellow Juaristas. When the Emperor's downfall appeared inevitable the chameleonlike Cortina changed colors and turned Juarista again. Cortina even participated in the capture and execution of Maximilian of which he often boasted. While the Civil War raged in the United States, Cortina continued to plague Texas by giving aid and intelligence to the Union outpost on Brazos Santiago Island at the mouth of the Rio Grande. Posing a chronic threat to Brownsville, Cortina helped the Federals distract Colonel John Salmon ("Rip") Ford's Confederate cavalry regiment.[4] Cheno's Yankee handlers were so enamored with him that some proposed making him a brigadier general in their army. More level heads up North squelched that idea.

The post-war Union occupation of South Texas brought only temporary relief from Cortina's heavy hand. After Sheridan's cavalry left Fort Brown, the Rio Grande valley was lightly defended by a small Federal detachment of 250 Black troops and white officers. Cortina's ruffians rode circles around this force and by the early 1870s South Texas was at his mercy. His brigands depredated with impunity below the Nueces River murdering, maiming and robbing Texans brown and white alike. It was estimated by United States and Texas authorities that from 1872 to 1875 bandit raids resulted in at least fifty-three murders, countless assaults and robberies, the theft of 300,000 cattle, 74,000 horses and other inestimable property losses.[5]

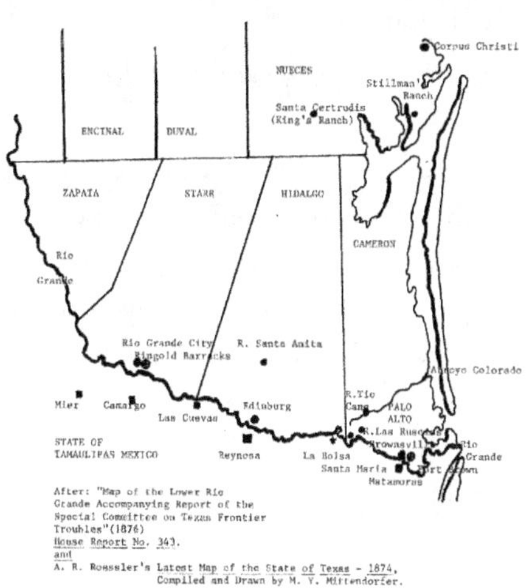

Map of the Lower Rio Grande

On Good Friday, March 26, 1875 dozens of Cortina's raiders swooped down on the settlement at Nuecestown twelve miles west of Corpus Christi. They killed, wounded and kidnapped several citizens and made off with the property of many more. The bandits robbed Thomas and Martha Noakes's general store and burned it to the ground after killing some of their customers. The Noakes family escaped with their lives but "Ma" Noakes was savagely quirted by a scar-faced bandit for refusing to tell where their cash was hidden. The Nuecestown raid could not be ignored by Governor Richard Coke and he swiftly responded to the call for action.

On March 31 the Special Force was reactivated at Austin and ordered by Governor Coke to proceed to Corpus Christi with all deliberate speed. The Governor gave Captain McNelly wide latitude to deal with Cortina's marauders. Unlike McNelly's peacekeeping assignment in DeWitt County this was to be a no-holds-barred contest. The Special Force was refitted and joined by some new recruits including George Durham who signed on as a private. George became the company prankster and was nicknamed "Josh." Before departing Austin, Lawrence and Linton Wright each drew $33.60 in back pay owed them from the end of February. The events in which the Wright brothers and their young Durham cousin would participate in the coming months were some of the most thrilling in the annals of the Texas Rangers.

Posterity is blessed with three richly detailed personal accounts of McNelly's South Texas campaign written by veterans of the Special Force. Two were authored by George Durham and William C. Callicott during their later years.[6] A third book was written in the 1890s by Napoleon A. Jennings.[7] The memoirs of Durham and Callicott are considered by historians to be reliable and accurate. Jennings's book must be read more cautiously. According to muster rolls he did not enlist in the company until May 26, 1876. Jennings, however, portrays himself as a participant in much earlier events. While writing his book Jennings interviewed Lawrence and Linton Wright shortly before their deaths.[8] Therefore, his references to them are probably factual.

The Special Force arrived in Corpus Christi in mid-April. At Sol Lichenstein's dry goods store the Rangers traded in their .30 caliber Winchester repeaters for .52 caliber Sharps carbines. Nicknamed the "needle gun," the Sharps fired a single hard-hitting round at long range with greater accuracy than the Winchester. This was a critical advantage on the open South Texas prairie. The carbine could be quickly reloaded by a mounted man on the move. The trigger guard lowered the breech block to open the rear of the barrel. A linen-wrapped cartridge was then inserted into the breech. By retracting the guard, the end of the cartridge was sheared off releasing its powder charge inside the barrel. With a percussion cap placed over the nipple the Sharps was ready to be cocked and fired. Each Ranger also carried two Colt .45 revolvers and a Bowie knife for use in close quarters.

The company rode west from Corpus Christi to the stage depot at Banquete. There McNelly was handed a package from Austin by William Woodson ("W6") Wright, a rancher and merchant from Oglethorpe County, Georgia. "W6" Wright had lost a team of horses and wagon to Cortina's gang in the Nuecestown raid and was eager to help the Special Force. Surveying McNelly's new recruits, "W6" wagered that several would not measure up to the task awaiting them in bandit country.[9] The package from General Steele contained copies of a list of over 5,000 wanted fugitives believed to be hiding in South Texas. The lists were handed to Lieutenant Pidge Robinson and Sergeant Lawrence Wright. After a brief session among "W6" Wright, McNelly and his officers, the company headed south for Captain Richard King's ranch at Santa Gertrudis. Captain King had lost thousands of beeves to Cortina's raiders.

On April 30 McNelly issued a muster roll at Santa Gertrudis listing Lawrence Wright as Fourth Sergeant and Linton Wright Fifth Sergeant of the company which numbered thirty-nine troops. The hazards facing McNelly's Rangers in South Texas were extreme. In northern Tamaulipas Cortina's bravos were organized by the hundreds as a mounted force that could be mobilized and massed on a moment's notice. They were aided by a sophisticated spy network on both sides of the Rio Grande that instantly relayed information on the location and movements of their enemies. Devoted to Cortina and his campaign of plunder, the bandits were skilled riders and ruthless killers.

In later testimony before a Congressional committee, McNelly described the fighting qualities of his foes. "If five hundred of the best troops we can get were to cross the river, go four miles into the interior and remain twenty-four hours in one place, I have not the remotest idea that they would ever return. I speak as a soldier. I served four years in the Confederate army. I have met some of these Mexicans out there and they are men who stand killing splendidly...The men are all mounted and very well armed...They gather rapidly and are very patriotic."[10] George Durham paid homage to the Cortinistas too. "I heard of folks say a Mexican can't fight. Well I've fought them and they're plenty damn good enough for me. I've never come out of a fight with them that I didn't have my belly chuck full of fightin' for the time being."[11]

The company continued south from the King Ranch. Along the way McNelly enlisted a Mexican rancher named Jesus ("Casuse") Sandoval as a guide and interpreter. Sandoval became one of McNelly's biggest assets. An implacable bandit-hater, Sandoval once had a horse ranch near Brownsville. He incurred Cortina's wrath when he caught four bandits on his land and hanged them. The Cortinistas retaliated by kidnapping Sandoval's wife and fourteen-year-old daughter. After defiling the women the bandits left them in a Matamoros convent. McNelly's arrival gave Sandoval a coveted chance for revenge.

The Nuecestown raid set off a rampage by roving white posses against innocent Mexican farmers. En route to Brownsville the Special Force encountered some of the vigilantes and disarmed them. It was McNelly's first step toward restoring law in South Texas. Though they were few the Rangers needed no help from a lynch mob.

The next morning McNelly warned his men, "We are headed right into the jaws of hell and any of you that can't take the gaff had better turn back now."[12] Five took his advice and collected discharges just as "W6" Wright had predicted.

The Special Force made its camp at Rancho de los Indios twenty miles north of Brownsville where McNelly began recruiting spies of his own. Selected locals were paid to report bandit activity and promised protection by the Rangers. Sergeant Lawrence Wright was in charge of morning roll calls. Private Jennings wrote of him. "I remember how surprised I was to note the youth of Lieutenant Wright[13] who, mounted on a sturdy little black stallion, rode at the head of the troop. He certainly was very young to be second in command. I don't think he could have been more than nineteen years old at the time; but his face was a determined one and he had a trick of drawing his eye-brows into a straight line and knitting his forehead above them which hardened his expression and made him seem older than he actually was. His straight, thin mouth and firm chin denoted much character and it did not take a very expert student of physiognomy to see that he was eminently fitted, despite his lack of years, to lead men into danger."[14]

One morning the company was roused and formed to break camp. George Durham recalled, "In quite a bit less than five minutes we had formed our line, mounted, with the sleep brushed from our eyes; alert, eager, tense. Lieutenant Wright formed us, counted us, soldier fashion, by twos. And, at his muffled command, 'forward, by twos, on right into line,' moved us off in double file--to where, what for, only one man knew and that was the Captain who wasn't talking."[15] The company shifted north to a new base near the El Sauz headquarters of the King Ranch (now Raymondville) and resumed reconnaissance patrols. Durham soon brought in a prisoner who turned out to be a young Mexican going to his wedding. McNelly, however, detained anyone encountered on patrol to prevent the company's position from being revealed. He further ordered that any prisoner attempting escape would be dealt with under "la Ley de Fugas," the old Spanish fugitive law. In other words, he would be shot. From El Sauz the Special Force moved south again and then west along the Rio Grande encamping at Rancho Las Rucias near Edinburgh.

Meanwhile, Cortina's terror shifted to the Mexican side of the border. A prominent rancher near Reynosa, Don Manuel Trevino, caught some of Cortina's bandits stealing his cattle. Don Trevino killed one bandit, wounded another and took a third prisoner who was turned over to the local alcalde. When Cortina learned of this he gathered 135 men and rode to see the alcalde demanding the prisoner. When the alcalde failed to comply, Cortina hung him and shot Don Trevino dead. After the Trevino incident Mexican President Sebastian Lerdo de Tejada timidly moved against Cortina by ordering him to Mexico City for military duty. Bemused, Cortina sent Lerdo his resignation from the Mexican army. Cheno's henchmen cheered his insubordination and continued their raids.[16]

At Las Rucias, McNelly enlisted another scout, Herman S. Rock. Rock was a deputy customs inspector at Brownsville and an ex-Union soldier. Like many bluecoats sent to Texas after the Civil War, Rock made his home in the Rio Grande Valley. McNelly's spies were constantly reporting bandit crossings into Texas but no raiders had been caught. McNelly infiltrated First Sergeant George A. Hall, into Mexico where he got work on the docks at Bagdad near Matamoros. Hall kept a watch on stolen stock being loaded onto ships for sale in Cuba. On June 11 McNelly got a message from Hall that Cortina had received a big Cuban order for beeves. George Durham remembered that day well.

"It was Friday, June 11, when Jesus arrived in camp excited and went to the captain. A few minutes later, in rode Old Rock and they went into a conference in the Captain's shelter. Besides the guard, there was sixteen of us in camp then ready for duty. In a moment Lieutenant Wright come from the captain and told us to mount and get ready for the trail. 'Pull your cinches in tight now,' he said, 'there'll be no stops.' There was something in the air that made me know we was goin' against the real thing now. McNelly had calmed down and spit out his cigar. They busted open more boxes of ammunition and Old Dad Smith issued us two hundred rounds each."[17] McNelly asked for volunteers and got them. The Wrights and George Durham stepped forward. So did 16-year-old Benjamin ("Sonny") Smith, son of the company quartermaster, D.R. ("Dad") Smith. Sonny's father begged him not to go but McNelly admired the boy's pluck and let him join.

From Las Rucias the Rangers headed northeast to the Arroyo Colorado 20 miles above Brownsville. At the Arroyo the patrol made a shocking discovery. A few days earlier a school-teacher named William F. McMahon had been riding alone to his class near the Stillman Ranch when he encountered some bandits. One recognized McMahon as a former Brownsville deputy sheriff who once arrested him. The gang murdered McMahon, dismembered him and stacked his severed parts in a pile on the road. Bandit Librado Mendez recalled that after McMahon's feet were hacked off he was forced to dance on the stumps of his legs before being finished with a bullet to the head.[18] McMahon left a Mexican wife and two small children. The Rangers buried the teacher's remains in a blanket and rode on hell bent for vengeance.

Before sundown the squad took a prisoner who turned out to be a bandit scout. According to Durham, "He hablad and waved a lot of arms and stuff and said he knowed nothing. But he was riding one of them Dick Heye saddles that had been took from Dad Noakes. When Captain McNelly saw this he pointed to a limb on a fairly good sized cypress and told us to see if the gentleman didn't want to change his mind about talking. Adams cast his riata over a limb and looped the captive's neck and we hoisted him off the ground. But he was stubborn and made no sign he wanted to talk; just puffed out his cheek and fought for air. Then Adams swung on his feet... When we let him down he told the interpreter that he was ridin' ahead for a gang. 'How many's in the outfit?' Captain asked. He said about fifty men...Then he named over the bandits and there was some Americans."[19] After the prisoner spilled all he was handed over to Jesus Sandoval for disposal. A while later "Casuse" happily reported, "He come backy no more."[20]

The bandits had boldly raided all the way up to the La Parra Ranch on Baffin Bay nearly ninety miles north of Brownsville. They were returning along the old Zachary Taylor Trail with a big stolen herd. As night fell McNelly picked up the bandits' tracks above the Arroyo Colorado but could not follow them in the dark. To help his men recognize each other if they came upon the bandits, McNelly took Bill Callicott's white shirt and cut it into strips. A piece of shirt was given to each Ranger to tie around an arm. At sunrise on Saturday, June 12 the bandit trail was found again and followed south along the Laguna Madre. Another bandit scout was soon captured and interrogated by Sandoval in similar fashion. He confessed his cohorts were nearby and knew they were being followed. McNelly was in his glory. "Boys," he said, "we will overhaul them poco pronto. Now, all I want you to do is stay ten paces behind me and do exactly as I say."[21]

Bill Callicott remembered the Captain's orders. "I will order you all in line of battle and when I order you to charge them, I want you to charge them in line. Do not go ahead of each other and get mixed up with the bandits. If you do you will be apt to kill our men instead of the bandits. Don't pay any attention to the battle. The bandit spy tells me that there are 17 Mexicans and one white man and that they are old General Cortina's picked men. If we can only overhaul them in an open part of the country we will teach them a lesson they will never forget. And when we overhaul them, if they should stampede, pick you out one that is nearest to you and keep him in front of you. Get as close to him as you can before you shoot. It makes no difference in what direction he goes, stay with him to a finish and don't get mixed up with them. That is all I have to say."[22]

With Rock in the lead the company continued a few miles on a southwesterly course. At 7 o'clock in the morning Rock suddenly halted and signaled with his right hand indicating the bandits were in sight. They were riding hard for the border with their rustled herd. As soon as the bandits were spied, McNelly took over. Durham recalled, "McNelly was ten or so paces to the head of our column. When Rock raised his hand, Captain McNelly buried the rowels of his spurs in the sleek flanks of the strawberry roan, half circled his right arm above his head in the signal to put on speed and ride like hell. We whizzed by Old Rock with that barrel chested, cat limbed horse of the Captain's throwing hardpan fifty foot back. I got a glimpse of Captain as I flogged my horse for more speed; Captain had his pistol out twirling the chamber. His brown hair was trailing behind his hat; his silky beard was parted behind him."[23]

The bandits crossed the west end of the Bahia Grande, herded the stolen cattle onto a small island and forted themselves on the south side of the lagoon fourteen miles northeast of Brownsville. The inlet was 600 yards wide with mud hock deep to the horses. For the Rangers to try crossing it under fire would be sheer madness. At least the bandits thought so. The Cortinistas, however, made a fatal mistake. They believed the hazy figures on the opposite bank were federal cavalry from Fort Brown. Regulars would never dare charge them across the muddy flat. Sixteen bandits chose to make a stand. They settled in along the five-foot high bank expecting to trade a few long shots with their pursuers.

Looking south across Bahia Grande toward the Palo Alto battlefield

On his side of the lagoon McNelly gathered his men for one more pep talk. "Boys, across this resaca are some outlaws that claim they're bigger than the law--bigger than Washington law, bigger than Texas law. Right now we'll find out if they're right or if they're wrong."

"This won't be a standoff or a dogfall. We'll either win completely or we'll lose completely. Those cut-throats have plundered and raided and murdered at will. They've mistreated our women and carried off some into slavery. You will follow me in a skirmish line spaced at five-pace intervals. Don't fire a shot until I do. Don't shoot either to your right or left. Shoot only at the target directly in front." McNelly further cautioned, "And don't walk upon no wounded man. A man that's down will kill you."[24] Durham remembered McNelly was smiling and "cool as a dry norther."

The combatants were evenly matched. The Rangers were Captain Lee McNelly, Lieutenant Pidge Robinson, Sergeants R.P. Orrill, Lawrence and Linton Wright, Corporals M.H. Williams and W.L. Rudd, Privates S.A. Adams, William C. Callicott, George P. Durham, Matt Fleming, Horace Maben, Tom McGovern, H.J. ("Deaf") Rector, Jesus Sandoval, Sonny Smith and Jim Wofford. On McNelly's command the Rangers waded into the mire. Across the water the bandits crouched behind their mounts. Using saddles as gunrests they began rapid firing at the apocalyptic horsemen slowly splashing toward them. As the Rangers drew closer bullets whizzed and spattered the water around them. A hundred yards from the south bank horses began to rear and fall as they were hit by bandit slugs.

First Deaf Rector's, then Sergeant Orrill's, Sonny Smith's, Corporal Rudd's and George Durham's horses went down. The riders plunged into the muck, rose and kept coming. To the bandits they must have seemed impervious to the barrage. Still the Rangers held their fire waiting for McNelly's order, wondering if it would ever come. Durham recalled what it was like crossing that lagoon. "I'll venture to say that at least one half the lead being throwed was aimed at Captain who was ten paces in front, smiling, cool, deadly as hell and paying no attention so far as you could learn. I wanted to shoot. We all wanted to shoot. We could see the bandits darting from cover to cover and firing. I wanted to answer that fire...I prayed. I was scared. If I could just start shootin' that would let off some steam and relieve the feelings.

But it is plumb hell to walk right up to gun muzzles and not shoot or not flinch, or not stop. Just do nothing but proceed. Try it once and see."[25]

Thoroughly unnerved by McNelly's procession the bandits began to panic. As he neared the south bank the Captain saw several raiders bolt for some live oaks. He motioned Sergeant Lawrence Wright and a handful of his riders to cut them off. When the bandits saw the Rangers between them and the woods they halted and stood their ground. As McNelly reached the bank he raised an arm to signal and fired his Colt revolver, claiming the first bandit less than ten yards away. Every Sharps in the company rang out and more bandits fell. Josh Durham's first target was the scar-faced villain who had whipped "Ma" Noakes in the Nuecestown raid. Sonny Smith was the next to drop a bandit. He was the leader of the pack, Camilo Lerma. Tragically, young Smith forgot McNelly's warning in the heat of the moment. As the boy approached Lerma the downed bandit rolled over and fired back killing him instantly. Smith was the only Ranger fatality that day.

It was Lawrence Wright's turn to engage the raiders. After firing his carbine at the bandits Lawrence made an extraordinary pistol shot while chasing them on his black stallion. With some discrepancy in detail it was described by all three of his comrades who wrote about Palo Alto. According to Durham, "Two of them had mounted one horse and were spurring away when Lieutenant Wright got in a good carbine shot. One rolled from the saddle, the other tumbled twenty paces farther on. Lieutenant Wright grinned wide. 'Dadblame if I didn't get dubs,' he said. 'Captain only ordered us to get one with each shot. Reckon he'll charge me for that?'"[26] From then on Lawrence was called "Dubs" by the others.

Callicott and Jennings attested that Lawrence made the shot with his revolver while the bandits were fleeing for the Rio Grande.[27] Callicott wrote, "During the running fight that morning, a bandit's horse was killed from under him and another bandit came by him and he jumped up behind him and a Ranger named Lonnie Right ran up as close to them as he could get and fired a shot with his pistol killing them both with one shot. The ball passed through both at once and both fell from the horse dead at the same time."[28] Jennings gave a similar version based on his interview with Lawrence. "Lieutenant Wright, during the running fight, killed two men with one shot from his revolver. The men were riding on one horse when he killed them both and both were shooting back at him."[29]

One of the tandem bandits survived long enough to plead for last rites. Durham wrote, "Lieutenant Wright was close to the first one he had shot from behind the saddle. He motioned Captain. 'He's asking for a chaplain,' Wright said. 'He must be a war veteran. He wants a chaplain before he goes out.' The old outlaw had taken that Sharps right below the rib cage and was bad torn up and going out fast. Captain asked no questions. He dismounted, holstered his pistol, and took a testament from his jacket pocket. He came up to the dying outlaw, not as the Captain of a Texas Ranger outfit but as a Virginia minister. He was bent over reading the Scripture to him when the man went out."[30]

The running fight took place over a five-mile stretch of prairie east of the old Palo Alto battlefield. It was a series of man-to-man pursuits in which the remaining bandits were successively overtaken and unsaddled at close range. The last bandit to die was the most feared of all, Jose Maria Olguin, alias "La Aguja"(The Needle). Olguin earned his sobriquet by sneaking into Texan homes at night and murdering their sleeping residents with his knife. As told by Bill Callicott, Olguin's end was a fitting one.

"The last one that we killed was riding the best horse in the Mexican bandits' crowd and kept away ahead of the rest of them. Captain and 3 or 4 of us were after him. We killed his horse from under him near a little Spanish dagger thicket. He ran into it on foot."

"Holding back one shell was one of McNelly's tricks. And it was good."

"We rode up to it. The Captain ordered us to surround it and in case we saw the bandit not to shoot at him, that he would dismount and go in after him and if we were to shoot we might kill him instead of the bandit. The Captain got down off his horse, took his pistol out of the scabbard. He started in on the right side of the thicket, the bandit was coming around on the left hand side. They met face to face with each other about 6 or 8 feet apart. The bandit had emptied his pistol and Captain had only one ball left in his. The bandit drew his bowie knife with a grin on his face and started to Captain McNelly, saying as he came: 'Me gotta you now, me gotta you.' The Captain leveled his pistol, the last shot he had, placing the ball between the bandit's teeth the same as if he had placed it there with his fingers."[31] Durham claimed McNelly lured "The Needle" into the open by pretending his pistol was empty and calling out in Spanish for more ammunition. He quipped, "Holding back one shell was one of McNelly's tricks. And it was good."[32]

In his report to General Steele on the engagement at Palo Alto, McNelly declared, "I have never seen men fight with such desperation. Many of them, after being shot from their horses and severely wounded three or four times, would rise up on their elbows and empty their pistols at us with their dying breath."[33] Only one of the bandits escaped from Palo Alto by feigning death and crawling away after the battle. He later died from his wounds in Matamoros according to some reports.

After the fight McNelly had the bandits' bodies hauled to Brownsville for identification. He would not allow his men to handle the corpses, however, and sent for civilian help. The fifteen dead bandits were part of Cortina's personal bodyguard. They were Camilo Lerma, Captain Jorge Jimenez, Lieutenant Pancho Lopez, Cecilio Benavides, Telesforo Diaz, Guadalupe Espinosa, Tibutio Fuentes, Casimiro Garcia, Encarnacion Garcia, Manuel Garcia, Juan El Guarache, Jose Maria Olguin, Rafael Salinas, Jacinto Ximenas and an American outlaw named Jack Ellis.[34] One of the ex-bandits was found wearing a new suit belonging to the slain teacher William McMahon.[35]

Sonny Smith's body was lashed to a horse by Bill Callicott and taken to Fort Brown. He was buried the next day with military honors. Callicott wrote, "At half past three P.M. Lieutenant Robinson and old Casuse and the balance of us marched up to the undertaker's where we found the hearse ready with two big fine black horses hitched to it, two U.S. bands of music and two companies of U.S. Regulars to march with us to the cemetery. We marched by a church and took him in and had his funeral preached. We then marched to a cemetery that was but a little distance off. There people had gathered from far and near to see the last of our 16-year-old Ranger boy laid to rest in the northwest corner of the Brownsville Cemetery, June 13, 1875. The U.S. Regulars fired the farewell shot over his grave and body and today our 16-year-old Ranger boy sleeps in an unknown grave on the Texas side of the Rio Grande."[36]

Returning to Brownsville, McNelly set up headquarters in the Miller Hotel with Sergeants Lawrence Wright, John B. Armstrong and R.P. Orrill. He ordered Sergeant Wright to fetch the U.S. Marshal and brand inspector so that the captured cattle could be returned to their owners. Lawrence then raced to Las Rucias to fetch the rest of the company. McNelly had every reason to expect Cortina to retaliate against Brownsville. George Durham insisted the Rangers were ready for him. "The Brownsville air that night of June 12, 1875 was heavy with fight. The Cortinistas had taken their worst licking in their history and a licking is something a bandit leader can't take without striking back quick. But not a one of us McNellys was jittery. We had us a boss who we now knew wouldn't let us go into a fight we couldn't win."[37]

Concern about how Cortina would react to his humiliation at the hands of the Special Force reached the highest levels of the U.S. Government. On June 14 General William Tecumseh Sherman's Assistant Adjutant in St. Louis, Missouri, General William D. Whipple, telegraphed the War Department in Washington, D.C., "Captain McNelly, commanding company of Texas troops, had an engagement June 12 near Palo Alto, about fourteen miles from Fort Brown, with Mexican cattle-thieves... Report says party crossed to rescue that attacked by Captain McNelly and a company sent from Brown to cut it off...General Ord says infantry may be needed from New Orleans if Cortina crosses. General Sheridan advises the Government to send a vessel of war to mouth of Rio Grande and also a good swift tug to patrol the Rio Grande."[38]

The danger of a war with Mexico stemming from the Palo Alto incident was cited on June 16 by General Edward O.C. Ord in a telegram to Secretary of War William W. Belknap. "Cortina is arming followers and threatens to revenge those killed by McNelly's company. Colonel Potter [at Fort Brown] wants more troops... Colonel Taylor has ordered to Brown three more companies of cavalry and one of infantry, increasing his garrison to six companies of infantry and five of cavalry, enough, unless as may be expected, the Texas troops drive the Mexican rancheros from our side of the river to Cortina, who will be tempted to use them in a border war."[39] General Ord somehow got the strange idea that after dealing with the bandits, McNelly would then attack Mexican ranchers and turn them into Cortinistas!

General Philip Sheridan endorsed the plan to beef up Fort Brown and he wired Sherman the same day. "The seemingly well-authenticated fear that Cortina may organize a force to retaliate on account of the just punishment administered a few days ago to the Mexican band of marauders has caused General Ord to increase the garrison at Fort Brown...This, it is thought, will be enough to meet all the wants of the service in and about Matamoros."[40] On June 17 President Ulysses S. Grant authorized stationing of two naval vessels on the Rio Grande to prevent crossings by Cortina's raiders.

Little did the Washington brass know that Cortina was in no position to even think about retaliation. His fortunes were rapidly waning. The annihilation of his bravos at Palo Alto was the beginning of his end. Three weeks later Cortina was arrested by President Lerdo and brought to Mexico City for trial. The wily Cheno, however, slipped away from his jailers and made his way back to Matamoros where he joined the movement of General Porfirio Diaz against Lerdo in early 1876. In the competition to become Diaz's commander of the Rio Bravo Line, Cortina lost out to a bitter rival, General Servando Canales. Canales was an ex-Juarista officer who had not forgotten Cortina's treachery in the war against the French. At his first opportunity Canales had the turncoat re-arrested and imprisoned in Matamoros. Cheno was court martialed and condemned to death.

Incredibly, Canales was dissuaded from executing Cortina by ex-Confederate Colonel John "Rip" Ford, another of the bandit's old adversaries and a former Texas Ranger. From Brownsville Ford wrote to Canales across the river, "It is known to everyone that yourself and Gen. Cortina are deadly personal enemies. If you approve of the proceedings of the court-martial by which he was tried, and he is shot, it will be said that personal ill feeling actuated your approval. It will, in my opinion, be a stain on your memory for all time to come."[41] Cortina's death sentence was commuted and he was brought back to Mexico City where he could molest Texans and their cattle no more. Denied martyrdom, the bandit chief was kept under house arrest till he died eighteen years later.

For more than half a century after the final battle at Palo Alto, George Durham was solicited by the curious to guide them to the site where Cortina's raiders met their doom. Durham always declined these requests. He explained Captain McNelly was highly superstitious and used to admonish his men never to return to the scene of a fight. Obedient to the end, Durham would not go back to the place where he had escaped the "jaws of hell." McNelly's phrase brings to mind these immortal lines:

> Half a league, half a league,
> Half a league onward,
> All in the valley of Death...
>
> Stormed at with shot and shell,
> Boldly they rode and well,
> Into the jaws of Death,
> Into the mouth of hell...
>
> Stormed at with shot and shell,
> While horse and hero fell,
> They that had fought so well
> Came through the jaws of Death,
> Back from the mouth of hell,
> All that was left of them...
>
> When can their glory fade?
> O the wild charge they made!...[42]

"Give my compliments to the Secretary of War and tell him to go to hell."

8 The Raid on Las Cuevas

Palo Alto had a chilling effect on the raiding in South Texas but did not end it. With Juan Cortina deposed, other gangs vied for control of the lucrative traffic in stolen cattle. In the late summer of 1875 McNelly's spies reported more crossings from Mexico and a few small parties were intercepted by Special Force patrols. McNelly wanted another sensational punishment, but the bandits moved upriver to avoid him. McNelly wrote to Adjutant General William Steele from Brownsville, "There has been no determined attempt at driving off cattle since you were here and no crossing below my camp. The Mexicans won't ride across Palo Alto after dark. Most of the leading spirits have gone up to Camargo and above."[1]

Camargo is about ninety miles upriver on the Rio Grande from Brownsville. Twenty miles downstream from Camargo was the Las Cuevas ranch, headquarters of bandit chieftain General Juan Flores Salinas. Las Cuevas (the dens) was well-named. It was ringed by a stockade guarded by heavily armed bandits whose raids into South Texas filled the general's coffers. Flores's influence with the provincial government of Tamaulipas ensured that his operations went unhampered by the authorities. Indeed, regular troops were garrisoned nearby to support the general and his private army.

One of those listed in McNelly's book of 5,100 wanted outlaws was Pete Marsele, a renegade Frenchman who was among the denizens of Las Cuevas. McNelly recruited Marsele to inform on the Cuevians. With this intelligence, the Rangers planned to ambush the bandits in

Texas. In early August, Marsele tipped McNelly off to a big raid in the works at General Flores's ranch. George Durham wrote, "Old Rock was over talking to Captain when Pete rode in late and joined them. While they were still talking Lieutenant Wright told us to catch up our mounts and to saddle and draw a heavy supply of shells."[2]

The company left Las Rucias and rode north to the edge of the "Big Sands" country where they hid in a motte of trees. According to Marsele the bandits would pass near there on their way back to Las Cuevas. McNelly kept his men out of sight and no fires were allowed. On the fourth day Jesus Sandoval rode up with news that the bandits had struck all the way up in Nueces County and were safely back in Mexico. McNelly was infuriated at being double-crossed and put Marsele back on the wanted list.

McNelly's health worsened in October and he went home to Burton. The company was turned over to Lieutenant Pidge Robinson. Like McNelly, Robinson was a Virginian, but he was not a professional soldier. Though Robinson was a capable officer his true talents were literary. Most of McNelly's troops were young men who had never taken human life before Palo Alto. Robinson's writings suggest he was haunted for weeks by the bloody incident on the Bahia Grande. That fall an Austin paper published a poem by Robinson entitled "Rio Grande--1875:"

By night he sought the ranger's camp.
Admitted by the sentinel--
"Pass weary stranger--all is well:
Go in, the midnight dew is damp."
Beneath the canvass well he stood,
That ancient man so stern and gray:
"Stranger, when I have said my say,
You'll learn that aye avenged is blood."

The pallid ghost of one I slew,
In former years, has followed me
Around the world, by land, by sea--
The sun itself was not more true.
O'er Afric's sand, through desert waste,
I bent my steps--'twas with me still;
Through Polar snows, Siberian blasts--
The form of him I could not kill.
Four days ago I looked upon
The Rio Bravo, rolling wide,
And for the last time by my side
Appeared the shade, with hollow groan:
"Live here in peace; henceforth thou'rt free:
Thy suffering's o'er, thy penance done."
I've driven thee from many a land
Have followed fast and followed well,
But I had rather live in h-ll
Than anchor on the Rio Grande.[3]

McNelly returned in late October with secret orders from U.S. Army General Ord and Adjutant General Steele. The plan called for a Ranger invasion of Mexico with federal troop support to recover stolen livestock and deal the bandits a blow on their own territory. There were three federal posts along the lower Rio Grande manned by the 8th Cavalry and 24th Infantry Regiments. Fort Brown was commanded by Colonel Joseph H. Potter, Edinburgh was headquarters for Major D.R. Clendenin and Captain James F. Randlett and Ringgold Barracks at Rio Grande City was commanded by Major A.J. Alexander. The Special Force was at Las Rucias near Edinburgh.

Adjutant General William Steele
The Library of Congress

McNelly itched for another match with the bandits and was confident of getting Army backing if he had to go into Mexico after them. He advised Steele, "Major Alexander says that he will instruct his men to follow raiders anywhere I will go. I hope to be able to put them to the test in a few days as I have learned that the parties who buy most of the stolen cattle have contracted to deliver 18,000 head in Monterrey within the next ninety days. I should think myself in bad luck if I don't find some one of their parties on this or the other side of the river."[4] The Rangers would soon discover how much the Government's promises were worth.

On November 18 Lieutenant Robinson received a telegram from McNelly ordering the company to meet him at the river across from Las Cuevas. The Rangers broke camp at Las Rucias and made a forced march covering fifty-five miles in only six hours. The day before, bandits crossing stolen cattle were surprised by Captain Randlett's cavalry but the Cuevians got away. When the Rangers arrived Randlett was waiting for orders. He refused to follow McNelly into Mexico without approval from Colonel Potter. George Durham described what followed.

"Captain was starched up as neat as any military officer. His britches were fresh ironed and washed, and so was his brush jacket. His beard was trimmed, and he even had on a little black necktie. He looked every inch the boss ... 'Men', he said, 'these Las Cuevas bandits crossed a herd of 250 beeves yesterday. I'm going to bring those beeves back to Texas...We'll be on our own. I can't guarantee to bring you back. All I can guarantee is to lead you up to a dang good scrap. I won't send you--I'll lead you. If you don't volunteer it won't be held against you or show on your record. It's squarely up to you. Take all the time you need to make up your mind. If any decide to go, step across this trail to this side.' As well as I recollect, Deaf Rector was the first one to step across, then Charley Nichols, then Sergeant Armstrong and Orrill and Lieutenant Wright. Then the balance of us. Besides Captain there were twenty-nine of us."[5]

At one o'clock the next morning the Rangers began fording the Rio Grande in groups of three in a leaky rowboat piloted by a Mexican guide. Sandoval and four others swam over with their horses. By four o'clock all were ashore in Mexico awaiting McNelly's direction. Under cover of a thick fog the Rangers followed the guide up a cattle trail into the brush. McNelly split the company in half directing Lieutenant Robinson to angle to the right with a patrol and meet him at Las Cuevas. At daybreak McNelly came to a ranch about three miles from the river. Believing he was at Las Cuevas, McNelly gathered his men and looked them over. The Captain sneered, "Boys, I like your looks all right--you are the palest set of men I ever looked at. That is a sign that you are going to do good fighting. In the Confederate army I noticed that just before battle all men get pale."[6]

As he unlatched the gates of the ranch McNelly exclaimed, "Stand to one side, boys, let old Casuse wake them up."[7] With a Comanche war yell Sandoval led the mounted men into the bandit camp blazing as they went. When they reached the middle of the camp the riders veered out of the way to avoid the fire of those on foot behind them. Just then Lieutenant Robinson's squad arrived amid the shooting and confusion. Sergeant Linton Wright was among them. In the fog Robinson's troops could not tell McNelly's party from the bandits. Linton's quick action prevented his men from firing on the other Rangers.[8]

Bill Callicott resumes his narrative. "The Captain had said kill all except old men, women and children. Many of the men were on their woodpiles cutting wood while their wives were cooking breakfast out doors. Not one of them moved a muscle. We shot them down on their wood piles and wherever we saw one we killed him till we killed all we saw in the ranch. After we had them all killed, the pilot told the Captain that he had made a mistake in the ranch, that this was the Cachattus [Las Cucharas] Ranch, that the Las Cuevas ranch was half a mile up the trail. The Captain said, 'Well, you have given my surprise away; take me to the Las Cuevas ranch as fast as possible.'"[9]

Las Cucharas was merely an outpost of Las Cuevas, a decoy for General Flores. As the Rangers drew within sight of Las Cuevas a force of 250 Mexican regulars dashed into the stockade. The soldiers and bandits then brought up artillery. McNelly saw the futility of trying to storm the fort and kept his men hidden in the brush. Mounted troops soon ventured out of the gates. George Durham recalled the reception the Rangers gave them. "We all had our targets and had the hammers down on our Sharps. We were only waiting for Captain to open fire. When he did he got one of the scouts. Amongst us we got the other three almost as one shot. Then we leveled off on the bunched outfit that was still milling close together. It was fairly long shooting but in the range of our Sharps and our first round tore them to pieces. Every shot seemed to bring down either a horse or rider."[10] Minutes later more defenders poured out of the stockade. George Durham and Lawrence Wright were lying on the ground next to McNelly to keep from being spotted by snipers inside the ranch.

"'Take your time, boys,' Captain McNelly warned as he saw the corral gate throwed back. 'Pick off your men carefully. And remember--don't waste no ammunition! Here's what I mean,' the Captain said as the column poured out. He raised his carbine slowly, took careful aim; and when the hammer dropped the leader tumbled from his saddle. 'That way,' Captain said. I done as near like the Captain as I could. I shoot left-handed. I remembered his orders to shoot only at a man in front of you; so I was watching a space not more than ten feet wide. And when a rider showed there I took a careful squint down my barrel and didn't shoot until I had a bead. But I reckon I was doing pretty good, because once when I was throwing a shell into my chamber I looked at Captain and he was watching me and smiling. And I heard him say to Lieutenant Wright by his side, 'That damn kid's all right.'"[11]

George P. Durham
Western History Collections, University of Oklahoma

General Flores intervened to take personal command of the troops and bandits. Not knowing how few were his enemies, Flores divided his force and began flanking the Rangers. McNelly ordered the company to fall back to the river. The mounted Mexicans made easy targets while the Rangers had the advantage of the fog and brush. The Rangers reached the river bank and took cover behind it. McNelly shouted, "Randlett, for God's sake come over and help us."[12] Captain Randlett and forty of his troopers shed their uniforms and plunged into the Rio Grande.

General Flores was meeting no resistance as he approached the river and thought the invaders were swimming back to Texas for their lives. When the Mexicans appeared, McNelly sprung his trap. Bill Callicott recalled, "The Captain said, 'Charge them, boys!' We ran up a cow trail to the top of the bank. The Captain said, 'Open up on them boys, as fast as you can.' We opened fire on them and they broke and ran back to the thicket as far as they could run on horseback. It only took a second to make the 150 yard run into the thicket towards the Las Cuevas ranch; we fired on them until they got into the thicket. General Flores fell dead from his horse in 75 yards of the thicket with his pistol in his hand with two needle gun bullets through his body...The Captain stooped down and picked up the pistol. It was a Smith & Wesson plated with gold and silver, the finest I ever saw."[13]

General Flores and his party were caught in a cross-fire between the Rangers' Sharps and one of Captain Randlett's Gatling guns manned by Sergeant Leahy on the north bank. Ranger Lieutenant Robinson wrote, "[O]n the Texas side were some of the Eighth Cavalry and a Gatling gun and just here I would like to remark that if there is an inanimate object in this whole world for which I have a pure and unadulterated veneration, respect and love, that object is the Gatling gun; if Mr. Gatling has a daughter I would marry her tomorrow, if she would have me, for the sake of her father--and the gun. The Rangers, the Regulars and the Gatling opened on the Mexicans simultaneously and they did not stay much longer...[14]

The Rangers next sought better ground along the river to stand off further attacks. Some of the men were out of Sharps ammunition and only had their pistols. McNelly chose a spot where the bank was four feet high with a clear view up and down the river. He assured them, "If they charge us they will have to come across that open field for 150 yards and we can stand here and mow them down with little danger of ever getting hit with a bullet, unless it is in the head and then the pain won't last long."[15]

Hundreds of Mexican soldiers, bandits and civilians were massing for a charge on the Rangers and U.S. troops. McNelly was ready to return to his side of the border when a truce party appeared under a white flag. The delegation was led by the Mayor of Camargo, Don Diego Garcia. Surprisingly, Garcia offered to turn the stolen cattle over to McNelly the next day and arrest the bandits if the Americans would leave Mexico at once. Sensing the Mexicans' reluctance to attack, McNelly and Randlett decided to stay a while longer. McNelly replied that he would not leave without the cattle. With typical bravado he agreed to give the Mexicans an hour's notice before attacking them!

At sunset Major Alexander arrived from Ringgold Barracks and ordered Captain Randlett to evacuate his men leaving the thirty

Rangers to face a force that had grown to about 400.[16] The next morning Colonel Potter sent a telegram to Major Alexander advising of Secretary of War Belknap's demand that McNelly immediately quit Mexico. Potter ordered Alexander not to aid McNelly if he was attacked on Mexican territory.[17] After reading Potter's message McNelly sent him a reply, "I shall remain in Mexico with my rangers... and will cross back at my own discretion...Give my compliments to the Secretary of War and tell him and the United States soldiers to go to hell."[18]

McNelly and his twenty-nine now faced nearly twenty times their number. Worse still, advance columns of a Mexican army brigade from Monterrey were marching into Camargo as McNelly played out his bluff. Even under these circumstances his audacity was matchless. At four o'clock in the afternoon on November 20 he served notice on Mayor Garcia that the Rangers would strike in one hour if the stolen cattle were not in his hands! The ultimatum prompted the appearance of another truce party led by Dr. Alexander ("Doc") Headley, an American who was on the list of 5,100 wanted. Headley tried to engage McNelly and Robinson in small talk but they shrugged him off. Suddenly, Lawrence Wright shouted, "They're closing in on you, Captain."[19] Headley turned to ride away and was instantly covered with Sharps muzzles. The bandits were ready to negotiate.

"Doc" Headley promised McNelly the stolen beeves would be brought to him the next morning at Rio Grande City. The Rangers withdrew to their side of the river and proceeded to Ringgold Barracks. On the morning of November 21, however, McNelly was given a message from Camargo that the stock had to be inspected and, it being Sunday, the custodians could not exert themselves on the Sabbath. The cattle would not be ready until Monday. McNelly took 10 men, boarded a ferry and crossed the Rio Grande again. He was confronted by twenty-five armed men. Bill Callicott wrote of the encounter.

"The Captain told Tom Sullivan to tell them that the Presidente promised to deliver the cattle on the Texas bank. The boss shook his head and said not until they were inspected. The Captain told Tom to tell him they were stolen from Texas without being inspected and they certainly could be driven back without it...The Captain motioned Lieutenant Robinson and he ordered us to fall in ranks. We fell in. Instantly we loaded our guns and covered the Mexicans. The Captain then told Tom to tell the son-of-a-bitch that if he didn't deliver the cattle across the river in less than five minutes we would kill all of them and he would have done it too for he had his red feather raised. If ever you saw cattle put across the river in a hurry those Mexicans did it--and in less than five minutes."[20]

Major A.J. Alexander's troops en route to Rio Grande to support McNelly's raid on Las Cuevas. The Library of Congress

Thirty-five head bearing the King Ranch brand were cut from the herd and given a Ranger escort back to Santa Gertrudis where they were delivered to Captain King. Bill Callicott remembered the cattleman's greeting:

> "Well, boys, I am glad to see you all and glad you all are still alive...How many men did the Captain have with him over in Mexico?" We told him 29.
>
> "What, only 29 men to invade Mexico with?"
>
> "Yes, sir..."

"And the ranches you all attacked were the Cachattus and Las Cuevas. Those are the two worst ranches in Mexico...It was settled by General Flores and I understand he still owns it."

We said, "No Captain, the other feller owns it. We killed the General..."

"Well," said Old Captain King, "there is not another Captain on earth like Captain McNelly who could invade a foreign country with only 29 men and stay three days and three nights and all get back alive."[21]

Back in Texas without a single casualty McNelly gathered his partisans to reflect on their second escape from the "jaws of hell." "I went into the Confederate army at sixteen and at seventeen I was made captain of a company. I have been in many tight places where it seemed that neither I nor my men could get out, but I always got out with part of them. When we went into Mexico with only thirty men three miles from the river with no hope of getting help was one time when there seemed little chance of escape. If the pilot had not made a mistake, and we had dashed into Las Cuevas instead of Cachattus we wouldn't be here tonight. Of course we could have taken the ranch, but the 250 Mexicans would have surrounded us and we would have had little show. If we had gone into the houses to protect ourselves they would have killed us with the artillery. That U.S. Captain never would have come over to help us. God pity such a captain. I claim that to be the tightest place I was ever in for all of us to get out alive."[22]

The foreign threat to Texas was contained but the Rangers still had plenty of badmen to reckon with at home.

"This court is now opened. At the first sign of any disturbance, you Rangers will shoot to kill."

Keeping the Peace in Nueces Country

In eight months the Washington County Volunteers did what no other Ranger or federal force could do. They brought the bandit raids to a virtual halt. In January, 1876 Captain Lee McNelly and Sergeants Lawrence B. Wright and John B. Armstrong rode to Ringgold Barracks at Rio Grande City. There McNelly telegraphed the War Department requesting troop support for more cross-border attacks on the bandits. After his barbed message to Secretary of War Belknap during the Las Cuevas mission, McNelly could not have been surprised when no help came.

McNelly went to Washington, D.C. that month to testify before the Congressional Special Committee on Texas Frontier Troubles which was investigating the depredations in the Rio Grande Valley. McNelly had been to the capital three years earlier to confer with President Ulysses S. Grant about the bandit raids. A veteran of the Mexican War and the Battle of Palo Alto, Grant was an astute observer of events on the Texas border. At their first meeting, McNelly was typically irreverent toward the former Union commander. When Grant asked him, "Haven't I seen you before?" McNelly shot back, "If you did, you looked back over your shoulder. Because the only time we met in Louisiana I licked hell out of you and you was running when you saw me."[1]

After several weeks of testimony by McNelly and other influential Texans the Committee passed a resolution authorizing the President to station two regiments of cavalry and as much infantry as necessary between Brownsville and Laredo to prevent raiding. Mindful of McNelly's successful attack on Las Cuevas the Committee resolved, "The President is hereby authorized to order the troops when in close pursuit of the robbers with their booty, to cross the Rio Grande, and use such means as they may find necessary for recovering the stolen property and checking the raids, guarding, however, in all cases against any unnecessary injury to peaceable inhabitants of Mexico."[2]

While McNelly was away the Special Force criss-crossed Cameron County on patrol. The Rangers were bothered by the refusal of many Mexicans to cooperate with them. There were still quite a few Cortinistas in the valley. The cold-shoulder treatment inspired a Robinson satire on how new Ranger recruits were trained to cope with it.

"Did you ever hear of quien sabe? We have heard nothing else for a year; it is the everlasting and never failing response to all inquiries as to distance, routes, directions, forage, water, weather, state of the country, characters of people, soil, climate, and productions. A person who remains here six months will have the tiresome old phrase stereotyped on his brain until he seems to breathe a perfect atmosphere of quien sabe. Its literal translation is 'who knows' and it is the general opinion of the whole population; description conveys but a faint idea of its comprehensiveness, the expressive gestures which accompany the quien sabe are dreadful to contemplate, especially when one has lost his way or is very hungry.

"When we receive recruits, they are always informed of what they will suffer from the quien sabe, and its nameless horrors are generally unfolded to them, otherwise they would desert the service or commit suicide. The third sergeant [Lawrence B. Wright][3] is relieved from all duty in order to prepare the new men for the terrible ordeal through which they are to pass. He drills them in what is termed 'Instructions in the quien sabe' and relieves it of some of its horrors by teaching the recruits retaliation on the Mexicans."

"The men are formed in single rank, without carbines, the instructor commands: 1. Squad. 2. Quien. 3. Sabe. At the first command, carry the toes of both feet outward at an angle of 185 degrees; (two) bring the hands in front of the body as high and as opposite to the shoulders, fingers extended as wide as possible; (three) make a frightful grimace at the same time elevating the right shoulder and depressing the left; look as much like an idiot as possible. The recruits resume the position of the soldier at the remark, 'What a lot of d--d fools!'"[4]

McNelly returned to Brownsville in mid-March in time to see neighboring Matamoros captured by General Porfirio Diaz. Diaz's seizure of power from President Lerdo was supported by many Texans who hoped he would suppress the bandits. On May 17 the Rangers caught a gang crossing stolen cattle five miles upriver from Edinburgh and shot three raiders within hailing distance of Diaz's troops. The next morning McNelly sent a letter to the mayor of Reynosa asking him to return the cattle and arrest the thieves but to no avail.[5]

In late May, McNelly moved his company from Laredo to the region along the Nueces River which was infested with outlaws. He divided the Special Force into squads and stationed them along the Nueces, using Fort Ewell as his headquarters. Lawrence Wright remarked years later, "Each Ranger was a little standing army in himself."[6] Thus, the Washington County Volunteers became 46 standing armies each armed with a new Winchester repeater. En route to the Nueces country the Rangers arrested the most notorious outlaw in South Texas, John King Fisher. King Fisher ruled over a band of criminals who terrorized the area between Eagle Pass and Castroville. Fisher got rich by sending his minions into Mexico to steal horses and livestock from bandits. When business was slow in Mexico he plundered in Dimmit and Maverick Counties and killed anyone who got in his way. On the way to his ranch there was a sign, "This is King Fisher's Road--Take the Other."

Ranger Napoleon Jennings gives a colorful description of King Fisher. "Fisher was about twenty-five years old at that time and the most perfect specimen of a frontier dandy and desperado I ever met. He was tall, beautifully proportioned and exceedingly handsome. He wore the finest clothing procurable, but all of the picturesque, border, dime-novel kind. His broad-brimmed white Mexican sombrero was profusely ornamented with gold and silver lace and had a golden snake for a band...A brilliant crimson sash was wound about his waist and his legs were hidden by a wonderful pair of chaparejos, or 'chaps', as the cowboys called them. These chaparejos were made of the skin of a royal Bengal tiger [that] had been procured by Fisher at a circus in Northern Texas. He and some of his fellows had literally captured the circus, killed the tiger and skinned it, just because the desperado chief fancied he'd like to have a pair of tiger-skin 'chaps'...He was an expert revolver-shot and could handle his six shooters quite as well with his left hand as with his right."[7]

On June 1 the Rangers left Carrizo Springs to get King Fisher. McNelly's men approached his house with orders to let the outlaws have the first shot. When the Rangers identified themselves, the outlaws waived the privilege. McNelly confronted Fisher at the front door and took him with eight of his men into custody. McNelly, Sergeant Lawrence Wright and six Rangers took the prisoners to Eagle Pass. The Captain, though, had neglected to gather witnesses and evidence against Fisher. His name was not on the wanted list and there were no warrants for his arrest. When the Rangers brought the prisoners to the Maverick County sheriff, they were met by Fisher's lawyer. George Durham recalled:

> We followed Captain to the door of the sheriff's office. He went inside. "My name's McNelly," he said. "I'm a Ranger--Texas Ranger. I got nine prisoners I want to deliver."
>
> A man wearing a badge got up from behind a desk.

"My name's Vale," he said, "I'm chief deputy of Maverick County. I'm happy to know you, Captain. You are Captain McNelly of the Rangers?"

"That's right."

"All right, Captain. You have some prisoners you want me to hold for you?"

"That's right. Nine of them."

"Very well, Captain. I see you've got Mr. Fisher."

"I've got King Fisher, yes."

"What charge, Captain?"

"He's no stranger to you. He's a damn bandit and killer."

The lawyer spoke up. "That's an opinion, Captain--not a charge under Texas law. You must name his bandit victims and produce them as witnesses. You must produce the bodies of his homicide victims, with proper witnesses."

Captain's fire was burning mighty low...He seemed mighty short of breath. He was whipped...

Captain turned to Lieutenant Wright and ordered, "Give these men back their guns and release them."

Captain ordered Lieutenant Wright to take us hands back to camp on the Carrizo and that he'd come in a day or so.

Wright told us, "Captain ain't doing too well. There's a doc here he wants to see."[8]

The Rangers and King Fisher would meet again. That spring Lieutenant Pidge Robinson returned home to Virginia and was killed in a duel. Lawrence Wright, McNelly's choice to replace Robinson, was put in charge of the Ranger post at Oakville. On his next trip to

Austin, McNelly handed Adjutant General Steele his recommendation for Lawrence's promotion.

Austin, July 8, 1876

Gen. Wm. Steele

Sir:

I respectfully recommend that Sergt. L.B. Wright be appointed First Lieutenant of my company for gallant & meritorious conduct on the field & in camp.

Very respectfully,
L.H. McNelly

P.S. If the Governor appoints the second officer would be glad that you would have him report at once as we will need him more at first than at any other time.

L.H.M.

McNelly to Steele, July 8, 1876, recommending L.B. Wright's promotion to First Lieutenant

In the summer of 1876 cattlemen in Goliad and San Patricio Counties hired roughnecks to drive away squatters. On July 27 some of the gunmen shot the ex-Sheriff of San Patricio as he stood in a church doorway. McNelly dispatched Sergeant John B. Armstrong to investigate the crime. When Armstrong arrived the county coroner had already conducted an inquest and decided there was no evidence to link anyone to the killing. Lieutenant Wright reported the murder to General Steele.

Oakville, Texas
Aug. 3rd, 1876

Genl. Wm Steele,
Austin, Texas

Sir:

I have the honor to report that on the night of the 27th inst. Captain McNelly learned that a man named Ed Garner, ex-sheriff of San Patricio Co. had been killed at church in San Patricio Co. and that the murderers were defying the authorities. He at once ordered Sergt. J.B. Armstrong with a detachment to the disturbed point. On his arrival the next day he found that the accused parties had been arrested and that the coroner after a lame investigation found no evidence sufficient to justify the retention of anyone; everything else being quiet in that section. Sergt. Armstrong returned to camp.

Lieut. Hall reports everything quiet in the neighborhood of Goliad. All quiet in this county.

Very respectfully,
L.B. Wright
1st Lieut., State Troops

P.S. Am I required to make a report like the foregoing while Capt. McNelly is with the company, our reports being then merely duplicates?

McNelly was certain he knew who killed Sheriff Garner and advised Steele, "I privately sent the Meanses word that the governor had sent me down here to stop all such things and that the next man they killed in that quarrel, or in that manner, I would come down direct and shoot them in less than two hours."[9] A month later Lieutenant Wright reported another unsolved murder.

Oakville, Texas
Sept. 10, 1876

Gen. Wm Steele,
Austin, Texas

Sir:

I have the honor to report that on the night of the 4th inst. a man arrived in camp stating that a murder had been committed that afternoon at a sheep ranch about twelve miles from here. Capt. McNelly immediately sent Sergt. Orrill with a detachment to the place. On his arrival with the sheriff he found two or three Mexicans employed on the ranch who could give no explanation in regard to the murder, stating that they were not present at the time. The coroner at his investigation found it necessary to order the arrest of a Mexican woman who was present at time of the murder but who refused to give any satisfactory information in regard to it. She was brought to the county jail at Oakville. Sergt. Orrill not being able to find any clue to the murderer, returned the next day.

I have been on duty with the company since its arrival at Oakville.

Very respectfully,
L.B. Wright
1st Lieut., State Troops

Two days later Lawrence Wright took his oath of office as a first lieutenant before Live Oak County Judge G.W. Jones.

I L.B. Wright do solemnly swear that I will faithfully and impartially discharge and perform all the duties incumbent upon me as First Lieutenant in Special State Troops of Texas for the period of six months, unless sooner discharged, according to the best of my skill and ability agreeably to the Constitution and laws of the United States and of this State; and I do further solemnly swear, that since the adoption of the Constitution of this State, I being citizen of this State, have not fought a duel with deadly weapons, within this State, nor out of it; nor have I sent or accepted a challenge to fight a duel with deadly weapons; nor have I acted as second in carrying out a challenge, or aided, advised, or assisted any person thus offending. And I furthermore solemnly swear that I have not directly nor indirectly paid, offered or promised to pay, contributed, nor promised to contribute any money, or valuable thing, or promised any office, or employment as a reward to secure my appointment, so help me God.

L.B. Wright

Sworn to and subscribed
before me this 12th day
of September, AD 1876.

G.W. Jones
County Judge
L.O.C.

With his promotion, Lawrence Wright's pay was raised from $50.00 to $130.00 per month. Lieutenant Wright's next report to General Steele told of more violence.

Oakville, Texas
Sept. 17, 1876

Genl. Wm. Steele
Austin, Tex.

Sir:

I have the honor to report that on Monday, the 8th inst. Capt. McNelly placed at the request of the sheriff a guard in Oakville for the purpose of keeping the peace during the session of the District Court. The guard was on duty day and night during the week. No disturbance occurred. A man was killed in McMullen Co. last week. The Grand Jury has probably formed an indictment against the supposed murderer; if so, Capt. McNelly will have him arrested.

It has been reported that two men, John Dern, one of the supposed murderers of Lawrence in Oakville, and Jesse Coe, were killed by the sheriff of Duval Co. while resisting arrest for disturbing the peace in San Diego last Tuesday night. Capt. McNelly has sent a detachment to investigate the matter.

Very respectfully,
L.B. Wright
1st Lt., State Troops

Later that month Lieutenant Wright informed General Steele that the Rangers were after King Fisher again.

Oakville, Texas
Sept. 25th, 1876

Genl. Wm. Steele
Austin, Texas

Sir:

I have the honor to report that on the 21st inst. Capt. McNelly sent a scout of twenty men to the Coriza [Carrizo], Dimmitt Co., for the purpose of arresting King Fisher and his band of thieves and others who are supposed to be in that section.

No disturbance has occurred in this county during the last week. I am on duty with the company at Oakville.

Very respectfully,
L.B. Wright
1st Lieut., State Troops

* * * * * * *

Oakville, Texas
Oct. 1st, 1876

Genl. Wm. Steele
Austin, Texas

Sir:

I have the honor to report that not the slightest disturbance has occurred in this County during the last week. The scout sent to Coriza not yet been heard from at this place.

I report on duty with the company at Oakville.

Very respectfully,
L.B. Wright
1st Lieut., Comd. State Troops

The Rangers' presence guaranteed tranquility in Live Oak County but neighboring DeWitt County was unsettled by a murder according to Lieutenant Wright's next report.

Oakville, Texas
Oct. 8th, 1876

Genl. Wm. Steele
Austin, Texas

Sir:

I have the honor to report that this section of the country has been very quiet during the last week. Not the slightest disturbance of the peace has occurred in this county. Fugitives from justice seem to have left this county and are making other places their headquarters for the time being.

Martin King of Clinton DeWitt Co., one of the best citizens of the county, was killed in Clinton on last

Sunday night. The murderer, a worthless vagabond, was arrested and lodged in jail. King was unarmed and it is said that the murder was altogether unprovoked.

Very respectfully,
L.B. Wright
1st Lieut. Comdg State Troops

In October Dr. Philip Brazzell and his 12-year-old son were killed by members of the Sutton gang in Dewitt County. Lieutenant J.E. (Lee) Hall and several Rangers entered the home of a suspect in the midst of a wedding party and arrested several revellers. The Sutton men were taken to Clinton to stand trial before Judge Henry Clay Pleasants. To prevent interference with the trial Judge Pleasants requested the Rangers to guard his courtroom. McNelly did not disarm the spectators, as if to dare anyone to disrupt the proceedings. As soon as the court was filled, McNelly announced, "This court is now opened. At the first sign of any disturbance from the audience, you Rangers will shoot and shoot to kill."[10]

After bringing the Brazzell killers to justice the Rangers left the Nueces country. At the end of October the Special Force was transferred to San Antonio where McNelly made his headquarters at the Menger Hotel. Lieutenant Wright's last two reports from Oakville indicate the situation was in hand.

Oakville Texas
Oct. 8th 1876

Genl. Wm Steele
Austin Texas

Sir,

I have the honor to report that this section of country has been very quiet during the past week. Not the slightest disturbance of the peace has occurred in this county. Fugitives from justice seem to have left this county, and are making other places their head-quarters, for the time being.

Martin King of Clinton DeWitt Co. one of the best citizens of the county, was killed in Clinton on last Sunday night. The murderer, a worthless vagabond, was arrested and lodged in jail. King was unarmed, and it is said that the murder was altogether unprovoked.

Very respectfully
L.B. Wright
1st Lieut Comd. State Troops

479

L.B. Wright to Steele, Oct. 8, 1876, reporting the murder of Martin King

Oakville, Texas
Oct. 15th, 1876

Genl. Wm. Steele
Austin, Texas

Sir:

I have the honor to report that on the 9th inst. Lt. Hall arrested at Mission Refugio one Charlie Fox alias Cas Jones charged at Pleasanton with attempt to murder. I immediately sent him to Pleasanton jail.

This county continues to be quiet, not the slightest disturbance having taken place during the last month.

Sergt. Armstrong has not yet returned from the Coriza settlement. I have heard nothing from him recently.

Very respectfully,
L.B. Wright
Lieut. Comdg., State Troops

* * * * * * *

Oakville, Texas
Oct. 22, 1876

Genl. Wm. Steele
Austin, Texas

Sir:

I have the honor to report that on Friday, the 20th inst. Sergt. Armstrong and detachment arrived in Oakville from twenty days scout. I have received orders from Capt. McNelly to move with the company to San Antonio for the purpose of establishing headquarters there. Will probably leave Oakville tomorrow. Everything quiet in this section.

Very respectfully,
L.B. Wright
1st Lt., State Troops
per N.A. Jennings, Jr.,
Co. Clerk

In his next missive to General Steele, Lieutenant Wright applied for one of the perquisites of his rank.

San Antonio, Tex., Nov. 8, 1876

Genl. Wm. Steele
Austin, Texas

Sir:

I have the honor to inform you that I have not had a servant since the date of my commission. Please inform me if I am allowed to employ one at the expense of the State?

Very respectfully,
L.B. Wright
1st Lt., Special State Troops

Several days later McNelly ordered Lawrence Wright to ride from San Antonio to Eagle Pass and join a Frontier Battalion detachment that was tracking bank robbers. McNelly advised General Steele, "I have not heard from Lt. Wright since he left for the west. Suppose he is near Eagle Pass now. I have to get two men who were implicated in the Goliad bank robbery out about Eagle Pass."[11] Two days later Lawrence wrote:

Eagle Pass, Nov. 20th/76
Genl. Wm. Steele

Austin, Texas

Sir:

I have the honor to report on detached service with frontier men for the purpose of scouting through the Coriza and Pendencia settlements. I also intend to scout through Uvalde County and will probably go up through the Nueces Valley to the Llano as I have heard something of a stolen herd of cattle taken from below this place.

Very respectfully,
L.B. Wright
Lt. Comdg detachment
State Troops

Unable to catch the Goliad robbers, Lieutenant Wright was called back from Eagle Pass. McNelly reported, "Received a dispatch from Lt. Wright today from Eagle Pass. He reports that he can do nothing & I have ordered him in. I have located several parties that I will have him arrest on his way back. I think from all reports that the Fisher gang are for the time pretty well broken up."[12]

On December 7 Lieutenant Wright sent Sergeant John B. Armstrong and Private T.W. Deggs to Wilson County to arrest a murderer named John Mayfield. When they arrived at Mayfield's farm he refused to surrender and shot at Armstrong from the corral. Deggs returned fire wounding Mayfield who continued shooting at Deggs until Armstrong killed the fugitive. As the smoke cleared the Rangers saw several heavily armed friends of Mayfield approaching and quickly retreated. They returned to the corral a few hours later with Lawrence Wright and ten other Rangers but Mayfield's body was gone.[13] Wright reported to General Steele.

San Antonio, Dec. 10, 1876
Genl. Wm. Steele

Austin, Texas

Sir:

I have the honor to report that on the 7th inst. I sent Sergt. Armstrong and Private Deggs to arrest one Jno. Mayfield sentenced to death for murder, from Parker Co. Mayfield resisted and they were obliged to kill him in self defense. Mayfield fired two shots at Armstrong and Deggs.

On the 8th inst. the Sheriff of Guadalupe Co. applied to me for a few men. I sent the men who on the 9th inst. arrested in Medina Co. one Gage McDonald charged with murder in Guadalupe Co.

After the killing of Mayfield, hearing that the prevailing sentiment in the County was not favorable to this Company, I took a few men with me and went to investigate the matter. I learned from the sheriff, county attorney, District Clerk, and some of the best citizens that the affair was heartily indorsed by the good people of the County.

Very respectfully,
L.B. Wright
1st Lt., State Troops

The weeks before Christmas were extremely dismal. Half the company was bed-ridden with illness according to Lieutenant Wright's final report to Austin for the year.

San Antonio
Dec. 17/76

Genl. Wm. Steele
Austin, Texas

Sir:

During the last week I have sent out several scouts, but have failed to make any arrests. I have in camp thirteen men including teamsters, but have only seven able for duty. There has been considerable sickness in the camp the past two weeks.

Very respectfully,
L.B. Wright
Lt. Comdg. Company

From San Antonio the Rangers moved to Victoria. There Lieutenant Wright was plagued by state property losses that had to be explained. He must have winced while posting these affidavits to General Steele.

Victoria, Texas
Jan. 25/77

I hereby certify that on or about the 5th Nov., 1876 two company mules ran off from the herd while being herded into the brush, and I further certify that immediate and diligent search was made for said mules. I further certify that I sent out men frequently afterwards for the purpose of recovering said mules without effect so far. And I further certify that the loss of said mules at the above mentioned time and place could not have been avoided.

L.B. Wright

Sworn to and subscribed before
me this 25th day of January A.D.

1877 at Victoria, Texas.
Eugene Sibley
N.P.V.Co.

* * * * * * *

I hereby certify that on or about the 18th Jan. 1877 there was stolen from the camp two pistols belonging to the State and that it could not have been avoided at the time.

L.B. Wright

Sworn to and subscribed before
me this 26th day of January A.D.
1877 at Victoria, Texas.
Eugene Sibley
Notary Public V.Co.

* * * * * * *

I hereby certify that Capt. L.H. McNelly placed me in charge of all the arms and ammunition of said L.H. McNelly's company, this was last July 25th 1876 & that I know of but fifty pistols and forty six carbines which are accounted for. If I ever had any others they were stolen. I have at all times kept a strict watch over the arms of the State.

L.B. Wright

Sworn to and subscribed before
me this 26th day of January A.D.
1877 at Victoria, Texas.
Eugene Sibley
Notary Public V.Co.

On January 25 the Special Force was reorganized at Victoria under Second Lieutenant Lee Hall and Sergeant John B. Armstrong. On February 1 Linton and Lawrence Wright resigned from the Rangers with honorable discharges. McNelly's farewell to the Wright brothers was one of his final acts as Captain of the Special Force. He returned home to Burton where his tuberculosis overtook him a few months later at age thirty-three. Despite his years of faithful service to Texas as one of its most illustrious soldiers and lawmen, McNelly was abandoned on his deathbed and received no financial assistance from

Special Force encamped at Victoria, Texas in 1877. McNelly seated in foreground

Austin.

After leaving the Rangers Lawrence Wright entered the College of Medicine at Nashville, Tennessee. He had saved enough of his Lieutenant's salary to pay for his education. Nineteenth century medical schooling was practical and brief. Lawrence graduated five months later on July 5, 1877 as class valedictorian and was awarded a prize in physiology.[14]

Two weeks after his discharge Linton Wright reenlisted in the Rangers on February 15, 1877. Lee Hall's company was trimmed from fifty-five to thirty-one troops reflecting the need for a leaner, cheaper Ranger force in South Texas. Linton rejoined the ranks at $40.00 per month as a private but quickly rose again to corporal. In the spring Hall's company was transferred to Cuero. Linton soon regained his old rank of third sergeant and $50.00 monthly salary. On October 21 Lieutenant Armstrong reported to General Steele, "Sent Sergt. Wright with five men to Indianola to remain during court." Hall was promoted from first lieutenant to captain on December 1.

Linton Wright was soon joined by his nineteen-year-old brother Harry who enlisted as a private on Christmas Day, 1877 at Cuero. Harry wrote of his first assignment. "I was immediately added to the guard that was guarding the jail that contained the Sutton-Taylor feudists who murdered Dr. Brazzell and who were on trial before the Hon. Clay Pleasants, Judge. This was an entirely new experience for a farmer boy like myself, then under twenty years of age, to be thrust into such a responsible and trying experience as to guard the jail which contained probably the most desperate gang of outlaws that ever depredated any part of Texas. The friends of the gang had served notice on Judge Pleasants that if he undertook to hold the trial of that case they would overpower the jail and rescue the prisoners. I will say in passing that Judge Pleasants was one of the most elegant gentlemen that I have ever known and probably the most fearless judge of his day...

"After remaining with the guard above mentioned for three or four days, I was ordered to report to Corpus Christi, Texas. I arrived at Corpus Christi on January 1, 1878 and remained there with a squad of Rangers under the direction of my brother, Linton L. Wright, who was the sergeant in charge of the squad for some time. I was transferred to camp at Banquete, Texas which was made headquarters of the squad for a short time. During this time we were sent out in pursuit of murderers, thieves, criminals of almost all classes that infested that country during those troublesome years."[15]

Linton Wright's mission to Banquete was reported by Captain

Hall to General Steele. "I sent a detachment of nine men under Sergt. Wright to Banquete, the terminus of the narrow gauge R.R. from this place West, where I will establish a camp for the winter as a large number of Mexican trains are constantly loading and unloading at this place and have recently been fired into by white men of this County. I have also directed Sergt. Wright to make a short scout in the direction of San Diego to try and arrest two murderers who are said to be located near that place, one from Victoria County, the other from Grimes."[16]

Nashville College of Medicine. Tennessee State Museum Tennessee Historical Society Collection

On February 1, 1878 Lawrence reenlisted in the Special Force at Corpus Christi. He was the company's physician during his second stint with the Rangers but only received a private's monthly pay of $40.00. For the next seven months Lawrence, Linton and Harry all served together in Hall's company.

In mid-May Captain Hall sent a squad to Gonzalez to stand guard at the execution of Brown Bowen, a member of the Taylor faction. Bowen was sentenced to hang for the murder of Thomas Haldeman. The motive for the killing was said to be Bowen's suspicion that Haldeman was a spy for the Sutton clan. Bowen went to the gallows protesting that the crime was actually committed by his infamous brother-in-law, John Wesley Hardin. Subsequently discovered evidence suggests Bowen's innocence.[17]

Sergeant Linton Wright was among the Texas Rangers and 5,000 spectators who watched as the trap door was sprung beneath Bowen sending him to his death on Friday, May 17, 1878 at 2:55 pm. If he was innocent, Bowen was nevertheless stoic at his moment of reckoning. According to a journalist present, the condemned man "looked over the crowd with a stern, fixed gaze, as if he were searching for somebody in the crowd."[18]

Several days later Linton Wright wrote to Sheriff Robert C. Houston in nearby Wilson County requesting a warrant for the arrest of a seventy-two-year-old murderer and forger by the name of Ben Goodwin. Goodwin was captured by Captain Neal Coldwell's Rangers a month before near Comfort but he escaped from jail. Despite his years the grizzled outlaw was described as "hale and hearty."[19]

Gonzalez, Texas
May 22nd, 1878

Sheriff Wilson Co., Tex.

Dear Sir:

I wrote to you some time ago to send me warrant for Ben Goodwin, but never received a reply. I know where this man Goodwin is and am on my way there now. Will you please forward immediately a capias with a copy of indictment to the Governor, so that in case he is found out of the state a requisition can be made for him. By complying with the above you will oblige.

L.L. Wright
Hall's Co., S.S. Troops

(N.B. I am on my way now to see the Gov. with regard to the above matter. L.L.W.)

Sheriff Houston was eager to assist in recapturing Goodwin and replied.

Floresville, Wilson Co.
May 28th, 1878

L.L. Wright, Esq.
Care of Gov. of State
Austin, Tx

I forwarded to you by return mail a capias for Ben Goodwin at yr. former request. The Grand Jury has never been in session since Volrath was murdered consequently can not send you a copy of the indictment. The Co. Judge has taken cognizance of the offence however & capias [will be] issued [by] Dist. Ct. next week after which I will be able to furnish you with any papers desired.

Total amt. of reward for Goodwin is $850. God grant you success in capturing him as his case has caused me a great deal of trouble, besides he should be brought to Justice. I have & am still doing all in my power to do so.

Respectfully,
R.C. Houston
Shff. Wilson Co.

Captain J.E. (Lee) Hall
Scribner's Magazine, 1873

Goodwin was finally apprehended over a year later in Montgomery County.[20]

By the end of that summer Dr. Lawrence Wright was ready to start his medical practice. Hall's muster roll, dated August 31, 1878, records that Dr. Wright was discharged from the company at Corpus Christi at his own request. Linton and Harry Wright remained in the Rangers a while longer. That fall Linton scouted between Corpus Christi and San Diego.

In late September Captain Hall dispatched Linton Wright to recover a herd of stolen cattle. "Sent a detachment of four men under Sergt. Wright to the lower part of Live Oak & San Patricio counties. They assisted the stock men in recovering from the cattle thieves about 500 head of stolen cattle. None of the thieves was arrested, however, as the owners of the stock refused to prosecute them, stating it was impossible to get a conviction. The health of my company has been exceedingly bad for the past month, at times there being more sick than well men in camp."[21]

A week later the Galveston press reported more Ranger activity. "Sergeant Wright of Hall's command brought in from Collins [now Alice] on Monday evening's train a Mexican who had nearly decapitated a fellow countryman with an ax...Between Collins and Banquette, as the train was coming toward Corpus, three men were espied at a distance who were suspected to be deserters from the United States cavalry company stationed at San Diego. The speed of the train was slackened and Lieut. Pond, U.S.A., Capt. Hall and Sergt. McMurray got off to investigate. A few shots were fired, whereupon two of the men surrendered and proved to be deserters sure enough. The third continued on his flight, but was fired upon and wounded--his finger carried away by a Winchester ball. Mr. Tom McComb, a brakeman on the train, joined in the pursuit and captured the man."[22]

Captain Hall's report for October, 1878 reported the arrest in Nueces County of Antonio Garcia who was probably the ax-wielder collared by Linton. Hall noted, "Sent Sergt. Wright & 4 men to Live Oak, McMullen & San Patricio and they captured 400 head of blotched [brand] cattle and delivered them to the owners." At the end of October more budget cuts forced Hall to demote Sergeants Linton Wright and S.A. McMurray to the rank of private. Hall was also ordered to discharge his twelve most junior privates including Harry Wright.

Two months later Linton Wright was honorably discharged from the Special State Troops on December 30 at Cuero not far from where he had joined McNelly's company exactly four years earlier. His discharge certificate recites that $12.00 was deducted from his pay for the purchase of a pistol. He would need it as the next Sheriff of Duval County. More than sixty years later Harry wrote admiringly of Captain Lee Hall and sadly recounted a killing he witnessed while serving in Hall's company.

"Captain Hall was a very dashing and daring officer and led his men into many desperate encounters and, in fact, so far as I know, he and his men were successful in bringing to justice the law-breakers for whom they were looking. Many encounters were had between the Rangers and desperadoes; but while I served in the company only one of our men was shot down. This was more in the nature of a frame-up by the enemies of the Rangers who brought about a personal difficulty between one of the Rangers and one of the civilians. The Ranger who was shot also killed the civilian. It was all done so speedily that it was over in less time than I have spent in trying to tell you about it. The man who was killed by the Ranger fell right at my feet and the life-blood ebbed out and left him a lifeless form as a result of the tragedy.

"It was very much regretted by all our men and also by the family of the deceased. I make this observation advisedly because the Ranger that did the killing was let out on bond and left the country. Twenty-six years later he was arrested and tried for the murder and out of the venire that was summoned to try the case was the son of the deceased who was a baby in his mother's arms when the killing had taken place. When he met me he apologized to me in the most elegant manner that a gentleman could and told me he had no malice against the man who had done the killing or against any of the Rangers; that he had known nothing of it as a child; but that he regretted that his father had gone out that way and that of course he could not serve in the jury under the circumstances."[23]

Following Harry Wright's discharge from Hall's company he was hired as a deputy by Nueces County Sheriff Thomas Beynon. The skills he acquired as a Ranger continued to serve him well. In the summer of 1880 he received a plaudit from the Corpus Christi press for capturing a fugitive.

"One by one the jail birds forsake their brushy restricts and return to the iron grated bower of Nueces county, commonly called a jail. Thursday night John Brown, relying upon the darkness of the night and the similarity of his color thereto visited the house of Jane Owens, nearer brown than Brown himself. Jane's house is just beyond the railroad bridge. Deputy sheriff Harry Wright had a vision the night before that John Brown had been there. With Martin Hinohosa as assistant he kept watch until Friday morning about one o'clock, when he was rewarded for his trouble by the capture of the veritable jail breaker. He was well dressed, had plenty of provisions, a six shooter and a rope. None knew better than John of the trouble with which he had to contend of getting out of this country, consequently he was preparing himself prior to departure. His course will probably be changing towards Huntsville."[24]

Capt. Thomas L. Oglesby

Harry Wright's notoriety may have upstaged his boss for he was soon seeking new employment. The press tersely announced, "Sheriff Beynon has relieved Harry Wright of his commission."[25]

Two months later Harry Wright re-enlisted at San Diego for a final three-month stint in the Special State Troops. On August 31 he signed on as a private with Captain Thomas L. Oglesby. Oglesby's muster roll listed Harry as 21 years old, five feet and eleven and a half inches tall with dark hair, blue eyes and fair complexion. His first assignment was to ride to Carrizo Springs to arrest King Fisher. The encounter with Fisher is best told in Harry's own words.

"After a time, I left Corpus Christi and went to San Diego, Texas and again enlisted in the Rangers under Captain Oglesby who took us on a scout trip to Carrizo Springs where we went into camp to await reports from our undercover men who were reconnoitering to locate a very much wanted outlaw by the name of King Fisher. I was detailed to hold the camp against all assaults while the others in the squad went in pursuit of King. They returned the next day with him in chains. Supper was ordered, King was chained to me and all the men save the sentinel, who had orders to kill the prisoner in case an attempt was made by his friends to rescue him, retired for the night with the earth for mattresses and saddles for pillows, the sky for cover.

"So we spent the night and when we woke King looked at me and said, 'Wright, what are you going to do when you quit the Rangers?' I replied, 'I do not know, look for a job I guess.' King Fisher then said, 'I would like to have you on my ranch and if you will go there with me I will give you an interest in it and make you rich. I like your looks and want you to accept.' During the day the Captain ordered me to take the team to San Diego and the rest of the squad to take King Fisher to San Antonio to jail. I never saw King after that. He was acquitted of his many indictments for murder and else and years later was killed in San Antonio. He was a very handsome man looking more like a Sunday School teacher than an outlaw."

On November 30, 1880 Harry Wright collected $90.00 in pay and received an honorable discharge from the Special Force. The Wright brothers' service in the Rangers spanned six and a half years in which South Texas was freed from a legion of criminals. Linton, Lawrence and Harry contributed to that struggle and helped make life possible in a land once uninhabitable by civilized people.

"When I saw Lonnie Wright's blue eyes, I knew he was the one."

10 Gone to Texas

While Lawrence and Linton Wright ranged the Rio Grande Valley their father, John Wesley, prepared to move the rest of the family to Texas. Their exodus from Georgia is told by Harry Wright in his memoirs. To save enough to pay for the family's transportation, sixteen-year-old Harry worked as a ploughman for $10.00 a month. For ten months he toiled from four o'clock in the morning to nine o' clock at night managing to save $90.00 of the $100.00 he earned. With Harry's wages his father booked passage to Galveston. Their route likely took them overland from Buena Vista to nearby Columbus for a voyage down the Chattahoochee River to Apalachicola, Florida and thence by steamer to Galveston.

The Wrights landed at Galveston in late September, 1875 several days after a hurricane struck the Texas coast. When John and his children disembarked at Galveston they beheld devastation. From September 15 to 17, high winds and ten-foot waves pounded Galveston leaving countless dead and extensive property damage. The Galveston press reported, "The people are suffering for food and clothing and the beach for twenty miles is strewn with dead bodies...The whole country for miles in the interior was submerged, houses swept away and the rescued men report that there must be great loss of life."[1]

Survival in Texas was a struggle. The Wrights first boarded in Galveston where Harry and John, Jr. attended school in a one-room structure two miles away. Harry walked to class each day with a cold lunch and chopped wood along the way to heat the schoolhouse. At age

17 his lessons were from the speller "McGuffy's Reader." After a few months the family moved to Waverly about fifty miles north of Galveston. There John, Harry and John, Jr. eked out a living by farming. In late 1876 Harry and John, Jr. found jobs as saw mill hands in Willis where they worked for a year until Harry left for Cuero to join Linton and Lee Hall's Ranger company.[2] Sixteen-year-old John, Jr. got work with the International & Great Northern Railroad Company based in Palestine, Texas. In 1880 John, Jr. was a railroad night watchman living in a boarding house in Huntsville.[3] In 1884 John, Jr. was back in Galveston employed as a fire engineer with the I.& G.N. and living in the home of Mrs. Jane Lyons.[4]

After Dr. Lawrence Wright was discharged from Hall's company at Corpus Christi he established a medical practice in San Diego, Texas. Four months later Linton received his final discharge from the Rangers and also took up residence in San Diego. From 1878 to 1880 Linton was a Duval County Deputy Sheriff under Sheriff Eugene A. Glover.[5]

As Sheriff Glover was also the County Tax Collector, Deputy Wright had early knowledge of foreclosures. Under deeds, dated May 10, 1879, he bought two tracts in San Diego for $35.20 at public auction. The lots were owned by Caballero Crisostorno and Asuncion Naranjo until their tax payments fell into arrears. The deeds recite that Linton took title to the lots in fee simple with the condition that the prior owners could redeem them within two years by paying their back taxes. In late 1880 Linton was elected as Sheriff with an annual salary of $300.00.

Dr. Wright probably came to San Diego soon after leaving the Rangers in the fall of 1878. In 1879 he began receiving Duval County "warrants" for services rendered to the county.[6] San Diego must have held good prospects for a young doctor. When he arrived, construction of the Texas-Mexican Railway line between Corpus Christi and San Diego had just been completed and the link from San Diego to Laredo was finished two years later. San Diego's location between the two cities boded well for its growth and the town had very few doctors. Still, Lawrence was not one to leave job security to chance.

In early 1880 Dr. Wright requested the Duval Commissioners' Court to designate him as the county physician. The Court's minutes for February 14 recite, "The petition of L.B. Wright, M.D. asking to be appointed County Physician was heard, considered and respectfully declined as no necessity existed for the appointment." Dr. Wright's status was never officialized but his medical services to the county continued for the next twelve years. The Court's minutes for June 19 and 29 record that Dr. Wright was paid $14.00 by the County for "attending prisoners" and $30.00 for a postmortem examination.

On June 4 an agent of the United States Census Bureau took inventory of San Diego's citizens. He found Dr. Wright living in the home of the German widow Elizabeth Martinet and her three daughters. Linton Wright lived in a rooming house nearby with five other tenants.[7] On June 7 the enumerator for Milam County found John Wesley Wright and thirteen-year-old Richmond residing in Rockdale thirty miles northeast of Austin where John worked as a store clerk.[8] They lived with John's newlywed nineteen-year-old daughter Frances Wright McLeod and her thirty-two-year-old husband, Daniel, a railroad engineer from Mississippi. In the early 1900s the McLeods lived in Palestine where Daniel was a railroad superindent.[9]

In 1879 or early 1880 Dr. Wright met his future wife, Mary Anne Hickey. Mary recollected they first met on a train between Corpus Christi and Kingsville, Texas. For her it was love at first sight. She said, "When I saw Lonnie Wright's blue eyes I knew he was the one."[10] Lawrence was a Methodist and Mary a Roman Catholic but religion was only a minor impediment. Dr. Wright did not convert to his wife's faith but permitted her to raise their children as Catholics.

Bishop Dominic Manucy granted the couple a dispensation to be married in the Roman Church and he performed the nuptial ceremony on October 13, 1880. The marriage was announced a few days later. "At the residence of Mr. Thomas Hickey, brother of the bride, on Wednesday night, by Rev. Bishop Manucy, Dr. L.B. Wright of San Diego, to Miss Mary A. Hickey of this City. The happy pair will leave for their home in San Diego tomorrow and will take with them the congratulations and good wishes of their friends."[11] Captain Richard King presented the couple with a pewter pitcher as a wedding gift.

Mary Hickey and L.B. Wright on their wedding day, Oct. 13, 1880

Mary Hickey's parents were Daniel Hickey, born in 1815 in Gowran, Ireland, and Elizabeth Dargan, born in 1811 in Goresbridge, Ireland. Daniel and Elizabeth were married in Goresbridge on February 21, 1841. Daniel was a civil engineer for the British government. His death in 1865 prompted Elizabeth to leave Ireland for Texas with her younger children. One of Elizabeth's brothers was William Dargan who was responsible for the construction of Ireland's first railroad, the Dublin & Kingstown. For his services to the Crown, William was offered a knighthood by Queen Victoria and Prince Albert but he declined the title. According to Hickey lore William privately confessed, "I would rather be an Irish gentleman than an English lord."

Like the Wrights, the Hickeys journied piecemeal to Texas. Another of Elizabeth Dargan Hickey's brothers, Philip, left Ireland for the Texas Republic in 1842 and fought in the Mexican War. Her eldest son, Thomas A. Hickey, left Ireland in 1859 at age seventeen and settled in Brazoria fifty miles southwest of Galveston. In 1862 Thomas enlisted as a private in the 13th Texas Infantry Regiment of the Confederate States Army, also known as the Brazoria Coast Regiment. He served in Captain McMaster's 2nd Company G.[12]

Soon after the Civil War Elizabeth Dargan Hickey and six of her younger children sailed from Ireland in 1865 and arrived at Galveston to join Thomas. By 1870 Thomas was prospering in Brazoria as a produce merchant with assets valued at $4,750.00. He resided with his mother Elizabeth, sisters Kate and Mary Anne, brothers Philip and Michael and two servants.[13] The Hickeys moved from Brazoria to Corpus Christi in 1878.

In 1880 Thomas's household included his wife Mary, children James and Kate, mother Elizabeth, sister Mary Anne, brothers Patrick and Philip, a cousin James Dargan and three servants.[14] Thomas was active in Corpus Christi Democratic politics and co-founded the Corpus Christi National Bank of which he was a manager. His brother James was a partner in the produce firm of Hickey & Hawley in Galveston. Patrick D. Hickey settled in Cotulla, Texas where he was the Lasalle County Clerk. Philip Hickey resided in San Diego and was a Customs official.

Michael Hickey attended St. Mary's University in Galveston where he won several prizes for oratory. After graduating Michael studied law with the Galveston firm of Ballinger, Jack & Mott. On the heels of his admission to the Texas bar Michael's mettle was put to the test when he was appointed by a Brazoria judge to defend a Black man accused of killing a white man, an unenviable assignment in the climate of those times. After a mistrial the case was tried again, dismissed and the defendant lived in Brazoria undisturbed for the rest of his life. Michael later served as Brazoria County Attorney and a District Court Judge of Fort Bend County.[15]

Daniel Hickey, Jr. remained in Europe and received his education at Catholic seminaries in Paris and Rome. He was a theologian of great erudition and conducted mass in several languages. He was the personal confessor of the King of Portugal and the Queen Regent of Spain. From 1864 until his death in 1897 in Lisbon, Portugal, Daniel maintained correspondence with his brother Thomas in Texas. Daniel's letters contain many eloquent and insightful commentaries on nineteenth century events.

By 1880 Linton Wright was also courting his wife-to-be, Laura Savage. They most likely met in Corpus Christi where Laura lived with her older brother, Robert R. Savage, and his family.[16] The Savages hailed from Choctaw County, Mississippi and came to Texas in 1870. Robert entered the livestock business in Corpus Christi with Major J.S. Smith. In the 1870s Smith and Savage drove herds from Nueces County to markets in Iowa and Wyoming. In 1881 Robert began ranching in Nueces and Duval Counties. The Savages were loyal Democrats and devout Presbyterians.[17]

Linton and Laura Wright were married in Corpus Christi on February 1, 1881. Their union was reported in the local press. "Yesterday morning at 7 o'clock invited guests and relatives of Mr. L.L. Wright, of San Diego, and Miss Laura Savage, of the City, congregated at the Presbyterian Church to witness their marriage, Rev. J. R. Jacobs officiating. The Bride was dressed in a traveling suit and after the ceremony accompanied her husband to the depot where the cars were taken for San Diego, the future home of the young couple. We tender them our congratulations."[18]

No children were born to Linton and Laura Wright. Lawrence and Mary had five sons and a daughter. They were James Lawrence (b. 1881), Elizabeth Lucile (b. 1883), Linton LaFayette (b. 1885), Edwin Daniel (b. 1887), John Thomas (b. 1889), and Philip

Thomas (b. 1892). Within five years the Wrights escaped the poverty and despair of Reconstruction Georgia and established themselves as industrious and respected Texans. The next decade would bring them acclaim in their new community.

Laura Savage and Linton Wright on their wedding day, Feb. 1, 1881.

"The animal carried Gonzalez about thirty yards on his horns...
Dr. L.B. Wright performed the necessary surgical operations..."

The San Diego Years

The Duval County region was first colonized in the early 1800s by settlers from Camargo and Mier, Mexico who received land grants from the Spanish Crown. The area encompassing the grants was partitioned into San Diego de Arriba and San Diego de Abajo on the north side of the San Diego Creek and the San Leandro Grant on the south bank. A permanent settlement, Perezville, was established on the San Diego Creek by Pablo Perez of Mier. The village was renamed San Diego in 1852. Duval County was organized in 1858 and named for Captain Burr H. Duval who was among those massacred at Goliad in the Texas war of independence.

Once part of a larger Nueces County, San Diego was incorporated into Duval County as its seat in 1876. Until the end of the Civil War Duval and Nueces counties were sheep ranching country. After the war Australian competition shrunk the demand for South Texas wool. In the mid-1880s disease decimated the sheep herds but a decade later South Texas rebounded in cattle production. The discovery of oil and gas after the turn of the century brought more prosperity.

From periodicals, Duval County records and oral history passed along by Mary Hickey Wright to her children and grandchildren we can savor life in San Diego the way it was in the late 1800s. As now, San Diego's population was overwhelmingly Mexican and the Wrights were one of few Anglo families. There is no evidence that this was a problem for the Wrights. On the contrary, they assimilated well and adopted the Spanish language as their own. San Diego was center stage for most local events and the Wrights were often in the news.

In 1880 Dr. Lawrence B. Wright was a physician for the U.S. 8th Cavalry Regiment on the San Leandro Grant. "Dr. Wright is acting camp surgeon, filling vacancy in that position caused by the revocation of the order by which Dr. Bagget was assigned to this post. Dr. Carter of Fort Concho, a regular commissioned officer, will soon take his place."[1] At that time Dr. Wright also tended Captain Thomas L. Oglesby's Ranger company which was stationed in San Diego.

On October 4, 1880, a few days before his wedding, Dr. Wright petitioned for membership in Corpus Christi's Masonic Lodge No. 189 which is still active. According to the Lodge's minutes he was elected to receive an Entered Apprentice degree on November 15. Unable to attend the next meeting on December 20, he sent a message that was read to those gathered.[2] Dr. Wright received his Entered Apprentice degree on July 18, 1881.[3]

In January, 1883 the Corpus Christi Weekly Caller began publishing. The Caller covered San Diego news and over the next few years the Wrights often figured in it. After his second stint with the Texas Rangers ended in late 1880 Harry Wright became a Duval County Deputy Sheriff under his brother Linton. One of Harry's duties was guarding prisoners being transferred between the county jails in San Diego and Corpus Christi. The Caller reported, "Harry Wright, deputy sheriff of Duval county, brought in a prisoner from San Diego last week, remaining in the city a couple of days."[4]

Dr. Wright's services were in demand when calamity struck. In September, 1883 a train wreck occurred on the Texas-Mexican Railroad line between San Diego and Corpus Christi. The doctor was at the scene. "Dr. Wright, of San Diego, and J.S. Elliff of Banquete arrived in [Corpus Christi] early Wednesday morning, having been out most of the night with the wrecked train. Speaking of the late rise in the San Diego creek, Mr. Wright said it was the biggest the people had there for over ten years."[5]

On September 15 Drs. Wright and T.C. Hannelly acquired Dr. William Taylor's practice which they continued as "Wright & Hannelly." The partnership lasted four years until Dr. Hannelly's death. The venture was announced by The Caller's correspondent in San Diego. "Dr. Taylor, our popular druggist, who is quite an authority on antediluvian relics, has sold out to Drs. Wright and Hannelly. The latter gentlemen, both of whom are favorably known in this county, have formed a partnership as doctors and druggists. Dr. Wright imparts dignity to the new firm, while the jovial Hannelly believes in and is a substantial proof of the old adage, 'laugh and grow fat.'"[6]

The lease for the drug store stipulated that Wright & Hannelly would pay $18.00 per month in rent. The store stood on the northwest corner of the present intersection of Dunlap Highway and St. Joseph Street in San Diego. Dr. Taylor further agreed that at the buyers' option he would sell them the land and store for $1,250.00. Wright & Hannelly knew how to drive a bargain. Dr. Taylor sold out to them only three months later for $975.00.

Dr. Wright dispensed his cures with pragmatism and humor. He was once visited by a San Diegan with an insufferable body odor. Unable to get near his patient, the doctor prescribed sugar pills and three consecutive daily baths for the man and told him to return after finishing that dosage. On another occasion his help was sought by a man bent on suicide. He asked Dr. Wright for a lethal elixir but, instead, was given a powerful laxative which had the desired effect. He was back the next day begging the doctor to save his life.[7]

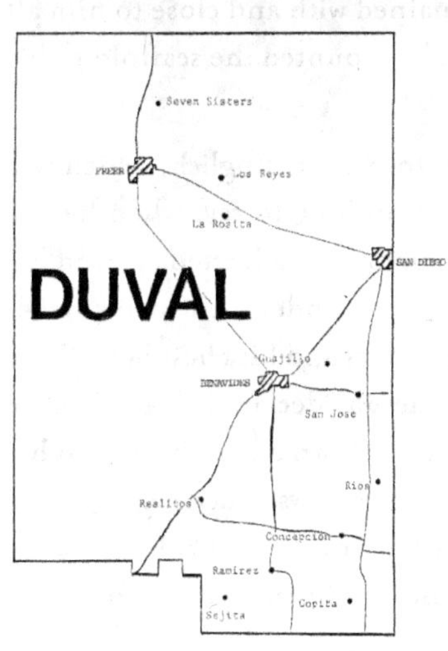

Map of Duval County, Texas

In the early 1880s John Wesley Wright left his daughter's home in Rockdale to spend his remaining years in San Diego. By then he was about 60 years old and decided to join his elder sons after his youngest son Dick left home. In 1884 John made his debut as a public figure in Duval County. The County Commissioners' minutes for April 8 recite, "A vacancy appearing to exist in the office of Justice of the Peace of Precinct No. 4 Duval County on account of the failure of A.J. Ayers to qualify within the time prescribed by law, J.W. Wright is hereby appointed to fill the said vacancy and the Clerk instructed to notify him of his appointment." John was well qualified to be a Justice of the Peace, having held that office in Georgia for more than twenty years.

On June 6, 1884 Refugio Gomez was hanged in San Diego for murder. Predictably, the event drew a big crowd. Doctor and Sheriff Wright attended in their official capacities. "The execution of Refugio Gomez for the murder of Estefan Dimas a year or more ago occurred this evening between twelve and one o'clock. At 12:15 the San Diego Gun Club marched into the jail yard and took position around the scaffold. The murderer was then brought out accompanied by Father Bard, the priest in attendance, who remained with and close to him all the time.[8] The irons were removed and he mounted the scaffold to his doom.

"The sheriff read the sentence to him in English, which was translated into Spanish. He said he had nothing to say, when he was rebound, the black cap put on and the fatal noose adjusted around his neck. At 12:20 the drop fell, breaking the condemned man's neck. He made a few convulsive motions with his legs and his chest heaved for some time. Twenty five minutes after he was declared dead by Drs. Wright and Hannelly, when his body was cut down and delivered to his friends for interment."[9] Gomez's walk to the gallows ended a prodigious criminal career that included eight murders, numerous robberies, six jail breaks and the torching of a San Antonio brothel after one of its employees displeased him.

On October 11 Dr. Wright was summoned to the aid of Monico Basques who was shot in a violent encounter with J.R. Jenson. A Nueces County Justice of the Peace gave an account of the altercation. "In reference to the shooting of the Mexican Monico Basques at the Tranquiles on Saturday the 11th inst. by Mr. J.R. Jenson, I desire to say that the evidence that I have is that the Mexican attacked Jenson, striking him over the head with a whip and drawing his knife, when Jenson drew his pistol and shot in self-defense. Jenson at once came and delivered himself up to me. Bob McCoy who accompanied him made a statement that showed that Jenson acted solely in self-defense. Another of the parties present, Manuel Mindreto, says that he did not see anything.

"Mr. Miller who was present and saw it all gives the same statement as that made by McCoy. I let Mr. Jenson go, on hearing the testimony of the above parties, on his own recognizance to wait for the result of the shot. Yesterday a relative of Basques' came to see me and asked me to let the matter drop as the wounded man acknowledged that he was in fault and made the assault on Jenson. Mr. Jenson at once sent for Doctor Wright of San Diego. The Doctor is now attending the sufferer who has a fair chance of recovering. Hoping this will give satisfaction to all, I remain, yours truly, John Fitch, J.P.P. No. 4, N.C."[10]

The next month Duval County's elections coincided with the national election of Democrat Grover Cleveland as President. Cleveland was originally from New Jersey but his candidacy was supported by a majority of Southerners who were stalwart Democrats. Cleveland was the only Democrat to occupy the White House during the 44-year interval between the end of Andrew Johnson's administration in 1869 and the inauguration of Woodrow Wilson in 1913.

On November 4 John Wesley and Linton L. Wright celebrated their own elections as Justice of the Peace and Sheriff, respectively. The Caller reported, "Can not send you the results of election in this county as the county judge will not allow any body to look at the lists...The following county officers were elected: Judge-J.W. Moses, Sheriff-L.L. Wright, District & County Clerk-R.B. Glover, Treasurer-Geo. Bodet, Surveyor-J.J. Dix, Assessor-Jno. Buckley, Chamberlain-J.J. Dix, C.F. Stillman, Justice of the Peace, precinct no. 1-J.W. Wright."[11]

Duval County records and newspaper articles indicate that John Wesley Wright's duties as Justice of the Peace were diverse. He performed marriages, conducted coroner's inquests and functioned as a magistrate in processing those arrested for crimes. For the Wrights, criminal justice was a family business. Linton arrested perpetrators and delivered them to his father for arraignment. Lawrence tended to the prisoners' medical needs and occasionally attested to their victims' causes of death.

By the mid-1880s Dr. Wright's growing family needed permanent quarters. Under a deed, dated April 8, 1885, he bought the parcel located at Lot 3-Block 54 from Trinidad Flores y Peres. There he built a single story house just a few yards north of his drug store. The

Mary and Lawrence B. Wright (c.1890)

house was kept in the Wright family for seventy-five years until it was sold in 1960 by Dr. Wright's daughter, Lucile, to the Perez family which still lives there.

For the rest of 1885 and 1886 the local press and county records were mute on the Wrights. When The Caller resumed its attention to their affairs in early 1887 it was to report the death of Linton's wife, Laura, at age twenty-seven. "From the Presbyterian Sunday school at Corpus Christi, Texas: Again the angel of death has visited our number and has taken from us Mrs. L.L. Wright, ending a life so full of bright promise of true Christian womanhood. While we bow with meek submission to the inscrutable decrees of an all-wise Being, we deeply lament the death of our sister which occurred at San Diego on the 15th day of March, 1887.

"In 1877 she moved from her native State of Mississippi, and located here with her brother, R.R. Savage, and resided here until her marriage in February, 1881, to Mr. L.L. Wright, since which time she was a constant attendant of our Sunday school, either as a pupil or teacher. As a pupil she was courteous, respectful and deferential to her teacher and kind, generous and agreeable to her classmates; as a teacher she was prompt and efficient, and by her tenderness and love, always maintained the respect and high esteem of her pupils. She was an earnest Christian and steadfast friend.

"We extend our heartfelt sympathy to her bereaved husband, brother and family in this, their hour of afflication. The evidences of a Christian life assure us that she is now happy in the 'mansions above prepared for those that love Him.' In behalf of our Sunday school we record this our tribute to her memory."[12]

A month after Laura's death The Caller mentioned a visit by Linton to Corpus Christi. "Sheriff L.L. Wright and Joseph Shaw of San Diego were perambulating our streets Wednesday. They report a good rain in San Diego Sunday..."[13] In May, The Caller had more news about Sheriff Wright. "The number of prisoners in the county jail in San Diego is fourteen. Some of them, it is said, are from other counties. Sheriff Wright is certainly the Wright man in the Wright place and the law breakers must stop their deviltry or they will be in jeopardy."[14]

Sheriff Wright's duties did not endear him to everyone. Late one night his house on the corner of Bexar and St. Charles Streets in San Diego was the target of an assailant who rode by on horseback firing several shots through the windows. The shooter escaped and Linton was unharmed. Whether it was an assassination attempt or random "deviltry" was never determined. The Meek family's home across the street was also penetrated by a bullet that lodged in the headboard of their bed narrowly missing them as they slept.[15] For many years a legend persisted that the mysterious gunman was the lone bandit who escaped from the Palo Alto fight. According to Duval lore the bandit crossed the Rio Grande one last time to avenge his dead comrades.[16]

That summer was a busy one for the Wrights. Collecting more laurels from The Caller, Linton was commended for timely settling tax accounts with the State of Texas. "Our worthy sheriff L.L. Wright has just got a full receipt from the comptroller and a letter congratulating him for his prompt settlement with the State under the new law, being square to date. The letter also says that the comptroller takes pleasure in informing him that he is among the first to comply with the law and that such acts are appreciated by the department. Duval county is proud of her sheriff and she ought to be."[17] A week later Linton gave state's evidence against a pair of horse thieves. "Sheriff Wright, deputy sheriff Lino Cuellar, Juan Gonger and Ramon Gonzales all went to Floresville as witnesses in the horse-theft cases against Guerra and Martinez arrested some months ago in this county."[18]

The community's high regard for Judge John Wesley Wright was exemplified in an item that appeared in The Caller in May, 1887. "Judge J.W. Wright returned from his visit Saturday, and immediately began to hold court, to replenish [prisoner] stock of course. Not many fairer, more impartial justices of the peace, however, can be found in Texas."[19]

There was no "revolving-door" justice when Judge Wright was on the bench. "Judge Wright bound Pancho Bain over to the grand jury on a charge of stealing a pair of boots, and he failing to give bond went to jail. This, I believe, makes sixteen in the county jail for court."[20] The Caller carried another report of his gaveling a week later. "The West end row Saturday night wound up with one party bound over for five hundred dollars, charged with assault to murder, two for unlawfully carrying arms and one fined for assault by Judge Wright on yesterday. 'The way of the transgressor is hard.' Sheriff Wright with deputies have been on the ride all week getting ready for District court, and has his business all up ready as usual. Nothing is left by him for tomorrow what he can do today. The big deputy has been on the ride too."[21]

The most gratifying experience for a physician is to save the life of a child. Dr. Wright did so at least once in his brief career. "Dr. L.B. Wright was called to Mr. Jas. Bryden's house last Monday to attend Mr. Bryden's little boy who had been bitten by a rattlesnake. The Doctor went in a hurry but succeeded in bringing the boy around all right."[22] A few weeks after Dr. Wright saved the boy Donald Bryden, Mary gave birth to another son. In August, The Caller announced the birth of Edwin Daniel Wright, the writer's grandfather. "We understand Dr. L.B. Wright has a little stranger at his house 'whose influence and presence is greatly to be praised' and 'who is chief among ten thousand and altogether lovely.'"[23]

In October The Caller carried two lengthy articles from San Diego under the banner "From Duval's Capital." The first described Dr. Wright's efforts to save a vaquero who suffered a horrible fate. "Margarito Gonzales, Mexican who has been for some time working at Shoener's ranch on this side of the Nueces river, just across the line into McMullen county, met with a serious accident last Monday and was brought here for medical attention. It appears that while Gonzales and other parties were branding cattle one of the brutes became infuriated and running at Gonzales, struck him with its horns, one of which entered his neck, under the chin, passing up through the head and coming out just over the eye, breaking the jawbone. The animal carried Gonzales about thirty yards on his horns when one of the party present coming to his assistance, the animal turning, threw Gonzales down, the horn coming out where it had entered. Dr. L.B. Wright performed the necessary surgical operations, setting the jaw, etc. Gonzales at this writing is in a precarious condition with little hopes of recovery."[24]

The other piece showed a more genteel side of San Diego life. "Tuesday night at the house of Wright and Glover or 'Bachelor hall' in this city, there was 'begun and holden' a meeting of the following gentlemen and citizens of this city: W.B. Croft, W.H. Simmons, J.O. Luby, J.W. Wright, C. Tiblier, Frank Feuille, L.L. Wright, C.K. Gravis, C.L. Coyner, George Bodet, R.B. Glover, J.W. Shaw, and L.B. Wright, a full baker's dozen as charter members, who organized themselves into a social or literary club...A literary club is always beneficial, no matter how little is done. Debates, essays, speeches, readings, declarations, no matter from whom, brings out dormant ideas, creates new ones, and imparts and retains those already obtained. Go ahead gentlemen, and if we can't be with you, we certainly will not be against you...There is good material in San Diego for a good literary club. Set the ship properly afloat and the fair wind will keep her on her way."[25] This was the first and last bulletin on the San Diego literary club.

Judge John W. Wright was soon riding the wedding circuit. "Deputy county clerk, J.W. Wright, left Tuesday for San Antonio to be absent two weeks. It is rumored amongst his friends that he carried off a marriage license with him. The matrimonial market has been dull for some time, but we have been informed that one of San Diego's handsome young men will shortly join the 'benedicts' and take unto

Duval County Sheriff Linton L. Wright

himself the belle of Duval. Success to you, young man, but look out for dynamite if her Benavides beau catches you in his neighborhood."[26]

While Judge Wright was away, Sheriff Wright was on his stalking horse. "The masher of Duval county, our delicate, though handsome sheriff, L.L. Wright, went up the road last Monday on official business and judging from the shotguns, carbines and pistols that he took and his general equipage we thought he meant business. He says he doesn't want any kidnapers to take him in for $4,000 or $5,000. Well, if they tie the sheriff the rope will have to be very thick and strong or it will dry up before the sheriff does."[27]

That Christmas John W. Wright, Jr. made a visit to San Diego which did not go unnoticed by The Caller's gossip-monger. "Mr. John Wright of Palestine, Texas, brother of the Doctor and the Sheriff, and son of Judge Wright of this place, is on a visit to our city. While Don Juan is of lighter weight than his two brothers and father he is exceedingly fine looking and strikes one favorably at sight. If you have any more fine looking boys Judge, call them in."[28]

The Wrights' political activities in 1888 were followed by The Caller. The journal reported the election of Duval County Democratic delegates on May 17 to the upcoming state convention. "The Democracy of Duval county met at the court house last Thursday evening and in the absence of the Chairman, Mr. F.C. Gravis, were called to order by the Secretary, Mr. A.R. Valls. Mr. J.W. Wright being called to the chair the following delegates were selected to cast the vote of Duval county at Fort Worth, on the 22nd of this month; Messrs.

L.L. Wright, N.G. Collins, George Bodet and John D. Cleary."[29]

In July The Caller announced the election of Democratic delegates at Fort Worth to another state convention to be held in August. "At the Democratic county convention the following parties were sent to the coming conventions to represent our county; State Convention August 14, 1888--George Bodet, N.G. Collins, F.K. Ridder and L.L. Wright; Representative convention to be called by chairman John Buckley--J.J. Dix, E.N. Gray, J.W. Wright, E. Corkill, L. Levy, John Buckley, John Puig and F.C. Gravis. At said convention Cleveland's administration, Senator Richard Coke and Congressman W.H. Crain's course in congress and Governor Ross's administration and other State officers were indorsed by resolutions offered by Charles L. Coyner and seconded by F.C. Gravis, who made some appropriate remarks covering the same. J.W. Wright was elected Democratic Executive Chairman of Duval county for the next two years and George Bodet, secretary."[30]

Dr. Lawrence Wright was then a member of an academic review board that evaluated teachers for tenure. The Caller announced, "Prof. Littleton stood an examination before the examining board last Monday, composed of Dr. L.B. Wright, Miss Addie Feuille and Prof. Coningham and obtained a first-class certificate, and commenced school at the academy the next day."[31] The Caller soon gave an update on Judge Wright's dispensation of due process. "Judge Wright bound over to district court a man and his wife for burglary last Saturday and the parties failing to give bond went to jail. There are now five or six in jail awaiting the action of the grand jury."[32]

San Diego may have been a sleepy hamlet but its citizens were well-attuned to national and world affairs. During the 1880s and 1890s, relations between the United States and England were strained. On August 10, 1888 the execution of an Englishman named Hugh M. Brooks, alias "Maxwell," for murder in St. Louis, Missouri became a cause celebre. The day before his appointment with the hangman

Maxwell issued a statement claiming a frame-up by the prosecutors. The British government requested a stay of Maxwell's execution which was denied by Missouri Governor Albert P. Moorehouse.[33]

The day after the execution The Caller published a tongue-in-cheek account of Dr. Wright's reaction to Maxwell's demise. "I learn that Dr. L.B. Wright will raise a company of rangers if the United States goes into war with John Bull on account of the Maxwell case in St. Louis.[34] Your correspondent would like to enlist as a high private of the rear rank and is already rubbing up his 'pepper box.'"[35]

In October the Wright men were involved in the aftermath of

The author's grandfather, Edwin Daniel Wright and his dog "Old Red" (c.1905)

a killing in San Diego. The Caller carried a lengthy article on the shooting of the tailor Atanacio Gomez. "About sun down last Saturday night our quiet little town was thrown into excitement by the fact becoming known that the Mexican tailor Atanacio Gomez was shot and killed. Our Justice of the Peace, J.W. Wright, called upon county attorney Coyner to assist him and proceeded to hold an inquest upon the body of the deceased who was found by Judge Wright lying dead upon the floor of Encarnacion Ysaguerra's barber shop.

"The inquest was commenced and postponed until Sunday morning when it was closed. The following facts as near as can be given were established by William L. Rogers, Ignacio Gouna, Manuel Padron, barber, Deputy Lino Cuellar and Dr. L.B. Wright, the first three witnesses being present when the killing occurred and Cuellar being the officer who arrested the party charged with the killing and Dr. Wright as an expert to show what caused the death.

"W.L. Rogers testified in substance that he was in the barber shop named above, Francisco P. Gonzales had been shaved and was putting on his coat when deceased, Atanacio Gomez came in the shop and made the remark that he could not understand why Mexicans in San Diego were allowed to carry pistols. Gonzales told Gomez to report him, deceased said he would not disgrace himself by so doing. Gonzales remarked that he lived amongst a people that would not disgrace themselves by reporting others, was why he carried a pistol.

"Deceased said 'you scared my boy last night, I wish I had been there so you could have scared me' and further that he was unarmed and opened his vest to show me he had no pistol, that he would fight Gonzales a fist fight. Gonzales said he did not want to fight, that this was not a place to settle the matter and both started for the door. At the door Gonzales stopped, turned round and drew his pistol, and backed up towards the other door, being in the shop, and then they clinched, when Gomez struck Gonzales in the face and grabbed at the pistol with the other hand when the shot was fired.

"The deceased and Gonzales were close to each other and scuffling, when Rogers jumped and grabbed Gonzales by the hand that held the pistol. Gonzales said, 'let me go,' Rogers said 'I will not.' Gonzales said 'let me go or I will shoot you.' Then Deputy Sheriff

Lino Cuellar came in and took the pistol from Gonzales and arrested him and carried him off. After the shot was fired the deceased never said another word, sank down upon the floor of the barber shop and in about five minutes was dead.

"Deceased struck the first blow. There was only one shot fired. The pistol was taken away from Gonzales by Cuellar and shown witness was recognized to be the pistol by which deceased was killed. This happened about sun down Saturday evening October 28th, 1888, in Encarnacion Ysaguerra's barber shop in San Diego, Duval county, Texas. Dr. Wright examined the body and stated that deceased was dead, that he came to his death by a gunshot or pistol shot wound, that the ball had entered the heart of deceased.

"The body was turned over by Judge Wright to his relatives and deputy sheriff Lino Cuellar ordered to arrest Francisco Gonzales and keep him in custody. On the next morning complaint was filed before J.W. Wright, and Monday morning set for examination of defendant Francisco J. Gonzales, for the murder of Atanacio Gomez, at which time county judge James O. Luby, counsel for defendant, asked until Wednesday at 2 o'clock to prepare the defense, which was granted by the court...

"Sheriff Wright, who was in the country, was sent for, arrived at San Diego about 10 o'clock and found all quiet, though some further trouble was expected on account of Gonzales being a Guarache and Gomez a Bota but when the facts showed that politics had nothing to do with it the excitement abated.[36] Deputy sheriff Cuellar deserves credit for his prompt action in the whole matter. Sheriff Wright also deserves credit for his forethought and precaution in the matter since as it was rumored that Gonzales would be lynched, he had a posse of men besides the jail guard in waiting on Saturday night ready for an emergency."[37]

Several weeks later, Sheriff and Dr. Wright appeared in The Caller under the rubric "San Diego Sprinklings." "Our Sheriff has been summoning grand and petit juries for next Monday when court is expected to open up full blast. While out, he captured a horse thief, one Caterino Gonzales, who will have a hearing as soon as the witness can be brought down from Laredo where the horses were sold...Juan Garcia Pefia who was mysteriously cut and robbed is under the kind attention of Dr. Wright. He is able to sit up and converse but can throw no light on the subject. The Houston Post reports the death in San Diego of Juan G. Pefia who was stabbed last week. Just hear Dr. Wright laugh, 'I am glad the Post informed us of the fact. I was conversing with Pefia this morning.'"[38]

November of 1888 brought a reversal of the political fortunes of the Wrights and their Democratic Party. President Grover Cleveland was narrowly defeated by Republican Benjamin Harrison despite Cleveland winning a majority of the popular vote. Duval County's elections were held on Tuesday, November 6. The Caller reported John Wesley and Linton Wright were reelected to their respective offices. "Wright for Sheriff 419 over Buckley 330. Wright for JP Precinct #1 254 over Diaz 156. Judge Wright has been sick for several days but is on the street once again."[39]

After Judge John W. Wright won re-election as Justice of the Peace for Precinct No. 1, the Duval County Attorney filed a misdemeanor charge against his challenger Manuel Garza Diaz. Diaz had resigned as the Precinct No. 5 Justice of the Peace before the election and moved to San Diego to run against Judge Wright. The problem was former Judge Diaz continued acting as a justice in Precinct No. 5 without legal authority after resigning that office. Diaz was arraigned before his opponent Judge Wright.

According to the local press, the defendant's "indignation knew no bounds when brought before the very dignified and judge like justice of the peace of precinct No. 1. The ex-judge demanded an interpreter at the start. The court remarked with surprise, 'What! You a justice of the peace for two years and want an interpreter!'" Diaz chose to represent himself and pleaded not guilty, but after four witnesses testified against him, he agreed to pay a fine and turn over his official books and seal. [40]

In the race for Sheriff and Tax Collector, Linton Wright's contender was Tax Assessor John W. Buckley. Like the Wrights, Buckley was a newcomer to San Diego. He was born in Hamilton, Ontario and came to Texas after the Civil War. Buckley was reputed to have been physically powerful, an excellent marksman and a man of few words.[41] His grandsons include the television commentator and journalist William F. Buckley and former U.S. Senator and Federal Circuit Court of Appeals Judge James L. Buckley.

What would become a two-year legal duel between Linton Wright and John Buckley began with certain irregularities in the election returns from two of Duval County's precincts. On November 13 the Duval County Commissioners' Court convened to address the problem. The returns from San Diego, Concepcion, Pena and Realitos were found to be correctly tallied. The ballot boxes from Benavides and Los Julios, however, were untallied. Commissioners Edward Corkill, F.K. Ridder and Judge James O. Luby voted against estimating the returns from Benavides and Los Julios based on the untallied ballots. Commissioners William Hebbron and Pedro Eznal voted in favor of estimating the ballots. Thus, in a three to two vote by the precinct commissioners, Linton's third term as Sheriff seemed assured.

John Buckley probably had substantial support from the Mexican-Americans of Duval County because he championed them in their occasional conflicts with the Texas Rangers. Buckley's relationship with the Rangers was so strained that they had criminal charges brought against him. The charges were eventually dismissed.[42]

Less than two months after the election Linton Wright was named in a lawsuit brought by John Buckley to secure the office of Duval County Sheriff. On January 3, 1889 Buckley filed an action styled "The State of Texas by James S. Hogg on the Relation of John

Buckley v. L.L. Wright" in the Duval County District Court. James S. Hogg was the Attorney General of Texas and joined Buckley as a co-plaintiff. Buckley hired the law firm of Nicholson and Dodd to plead his case. Sheriff Wright was represented by the King Ranch's lawyers, Wells, Stayton and Kleberg. On Buckley's motion venue was transferred to the Nueces County District Court in Corpus Christi. The case was tried in early 1890 without a jury before Judge John C. Russell who ordered the Duval County Commissioners to install John Buckley as Sheriff.[43]

In essence the case turned on the admissibility of incomplete ballots from Benavides and vote tally sheets from Los Julios. Linton Wright's lawyers objected to the admission of these records on the grounds that some ballots and tallies were unsigned or signed by unauthorized individuals and that these documents were never delivered to the Duval County Clerk. Buckley's lawyers also introduced a vote tally sheet from Realitos although the ballots from that precinct were properly counted.

The plaintiff called as a witness Linton Wright's brother-in-law, Robert R. Savage, who was one of the Realitos election managers. Savage testified that he had seen the tally sheet from Realitos and believed it to be an accurate record of the votes cast there. The Realitos tally sheet was admitted into evidence by Judge Russell to establish seventy-four votes for Linton Wright and twenty-eight for John Buckley. The tally did not benefit Buckley's case but the theatrical effect of having one of the Sheriff's kin testify for the plaintiff was reason enough to make an issue of it.

Savage was not the Sheriff's only relative used against him. John Buckley testified that only two weeks before the trial he went to the Duval County Clerk's office where he encountered Justice of the Peace John Wesley Wright. When Buckley asked Judge Wright to provide him with certified copies of the returns and poll lists, the Judge replied he had forgotten the combination to the safe where these papers were kept and that County Clerk Rufus B. Glover was home sick. The suggestion of family collusion in suppressing evidence provided more courtroom drama.

Judge Russell's rulings on the votes cast by aliens from Los Julios must have galled the defense. On one hand the Judge ruled that the alleged admission by one Pedro Ochoa to John Buckley that he was a citizen of Mexico and had voted for Linton Wright was admissible as evidence of an illegal vote for the Sheriff. On the other hand the Judge excluded as hearsay a similar confession allegedly made by one Felix Espinosa to Sheriff Wright and Deputy Lino Cuellar that Espinosa was a non-citizen who had voted for Buckley. The Judge's refusal to deduct Espinosa's vote from Buckley's count was all the more perplexing after he admitted into evidence Espinosa's conviction of the crime of illegal voting.

Linton Wright argued that even if all illegal votes received by both candidates in Los Julios were deducted, his vote still exceeded John Buckley's. Judge Russell disagreed. He struck eleven illegal votes from Linton Wright's count but none from John Buckley's. The failure of the defense to have illegal votes stricken from Buckley's count is inexplicable. During the trial the Sheriff's lawyers filed an amended answer to Buckley's petition. The answer identified fifteen persons who were alleged to have unlawfully voted for Buckley but no proof was produced as to those votes.

One of John Buckley's witnesses, County Commissioner Pedro Eznal, testified that some of the Los Julios returns had been discarded because they were signed only by Captain E.N. Gray.[44] Eznal did not mention how many ballots were thus lost or for whom they were cast. Despite the facts that some of the Los Julios ballots produced by John Buckley lacked required election manager signatures and the Los Julios tally sheet was also unsigned, Judge Russell admitted the ballots into evidence. The vote count from Los Julios as determined by the court was ninety-nine for Buckley and eighty-eight for Wright.

The coup d'grace for Sheriff Wright's case was the court's ruling with respect to the voting in Benavides. Without objection from either side the ballot box from Benavides was opened in the courtroom and tallied by the court clerks. The total of 120 votes for John Buckley and ninety-three for Linton Wright was initially accepted by both sides. That count still gave Linton Wright a slim 554 to 549 lead over John Buckley. Three days later, however, Buckley's attorneys moved to strike the count and offered to prove that the ballot box had been tampered with after it was delivered to the Duval County Clerk. The Sheriff's attorneys objected that no such allegation had been made in Buckley's pleadings. Still the judge allowed the plaintiff to develop his surprise argument.

John Buckley moved to exclude the Benavides ballots on the ground that thirty-two had been scratched out obliterating the names of the candidates. When, where or by whom these ballots were altered was not established. No evidence was produced to show that the Benavides ballot box had ever been in the possession of the Duval County Clerk. By raising the spectre of ballot tampering Buckley persuaded Judge Russell to disregard the 120-93 ballot count in favor of the tally estimate made by the Benavides election managers. The estimate gave John Buckley a much larger 161-84 lead over Linton Wright. The adjusted Benavides vote tipped the election in Buckley's favor. When Judge Russell concluded his evidentiary rulings and factual findings, the Sheriff's original 419 to 330 victory became a 590 to 555 defeat.

On April 19, 1890 an appeal was filed on behalf of Linton Wright in the Texas Supreme Court. On June 27 John Buckley's counsel filed a motion to dismiss the appeal. They argued the defense improperly withheld the transcript of the trial after receiving it from the District Court. The next day the Supreme Court dismissed the appeal without opinion. Nothing in the record suggests that either candidate engaged in any electoral fraud. John Buckley served ably as Duval County Sheriff from 1890 to 1896 and the suit did not leave lasting ill feelings between the litigants' families. Linton's niece,

Lucile, maintained a lifelong friendship with the Buckleys.[45]

After Linton Wright's departure from office, Judge John Wesley Wright continued for a while as Justice of the Peace and Deputy County Clerk. In late 1890 Judge Wright's career drew to an end. The last document bearing his official signature is a certificate of a marriage he performed on October 7. He died a month later on November 7. His obituary was telegraphed from San Diego to the San Antonio Daily Express.

"Judge J.W. Wright died at the residence of his son, ex-Sheriff L.L. Wright, in this place last night at 7 o'clock. The deceased was sick but a short time, and was during his last illness attended by his son, Doctor L.B. Wright, who did all that could be done to relieve the suffering of his much lamented father, but the fiat had gone forth and the venerable gentleman is at rest. Judge J.W. Wright was a native of Georgia and was 67 years of age at the time of his demise. He had been for several years a resident of San Diego, Duval county, and was highly respected by every one of this community. His two sons in this place and his children in other parts of Texas have the sympathy of our people."[46]

The Caller's references to Linton and Lawrence Wright during 1891 indicate that both suffered from poor health. In April it was reported, "Dr. Arthur E. Spohn came up Monday to visit Dr. Wright and two of his children. The father is suffering with dengue, the daughter pneumonia and son bronchitis.[47] May they speedily recover is the earnest hope of all their friends."[48] Two months later Linton was said to be infirm and trying to liquidate his property holdings. "Mr. L.L. Wright, who has been under the weather is again up and about, ready to sell a lot or 50 acre garden patch, just as the customer desires."[49]

By the summer of 1891 Dr. Wright was well enough to travel to Corpus Christi. "Dr. Wright and Messrs. Bodet and Shaw of San Diego are on a visit to the bluff city. Mr. Bodet has not been in Corpus for four years and of course noted many changes."[50] A few days later Lawrence, Linton and some cronies went to a boxing match on the coast. "L.L. Wright, L.B. Wright and James Chapel and a few light weights go down to Rockport via Corpus to attend the pugilistic encounter to take place in the city tomorrow night."[51]

A drought descended on South Texas that summer threatening ranchers large and small alike. The manager of the King Ranch, Robert J. Kleberg, was a man with imagination and a scientific bent who devised a sensational scheme for making rain. Kleberg believed precipitation could be induced by creating a concussion in the skies thirty miles northwest of the ranch. With the assistance of the Department of Agriculture and U.S. Army, Kleberg loaded seventeen gas balloons with 1600 sticks of dynamite, 250 cannon charges and 100 mortar bombs. The balloons were lofted into the air and detonated over San Diego on October 16, 1891.

Kleberg's experiment produced none of the intended results but provided San Diegans with spectacular entertainment. The bombardment was repeated the next day and at four o' clock in the morning on October 18 a downpour fell on San Diego. Unfortunately, little rain reached the King Ranch. Similar experiments were continued by the Government but later abandoned after no causal relation between the explosions and rainfall could be proved.[52]

Dr. Wright's youngest child, Philip Thomas, was born on New Year's Day in 1892. "Dr. L.B. Wright had a handsome new years present given him, a bouncing 12 pound boy. The doctor is doing fairly well and says he feels a great deal better. Mother and child in good health."[53]

In the early 1890s South Texas was again the scene of clashes between United States forces and guerrilla bands. The leader of the insurgents was Catarino Erasmo Garza, a Mexican-born journalist and revolutionary who married the daughter of a prominent rancher in Palito Blanco, Duval County.[54] In 1885 Garza began publishing a newspaper in Eagle Pass, Texas devoted to vehement criticism of the Mexican dictator Porfirio Diaz.

In the summer of 1891 Garza recruited 200 men to make raids into Mexico using his father-in-law's ranch at Palito Blanco as a base.

Garza's campaign against Diaz, though ineffectual, was an embarrassment to the United States which was bound by neutrality laws not to harbor anti-Diaz rebels. As Garza was not violating any Texas laws, however, the new Governor was at first indifferent to him. The Governor was Linton Wright's nemesis, former Attorney General James S. Hogg.[55]

On December 22, U.S. cavalry intercepted some of Garza's men returning from Mexico and a skirmish occurred at La Grulla, Starr County in which an American soldier was killed. The incident made Garza and his followers fugitives under Texas law. Governor Hogg now ordered two Ranger companies to join with federal troops in rounding up the Garzaists.[56] On January 5, 1892 Garza was routed by cavalry in a fight at La Joya in Hidalgo County. La Joya broke up the Garzaists but did not end their activities. The guerrillas continued to operate in cells and were supported by the poor rancheros who spied for them and offered sanctuary as troops and Rangers closed in.[57]

During the mop-up Linton Wright's friends, former County Clerk Rufus B. Glover and ex-deputy Lino Cuellar, enlisted as scouts for U.S. troops encamped at the Sweden Ranch in Duval County. On February 1 Glover, Cuellar and another scout, Juan Moreno, were trailing Garza 17 miles north of Benavides near the Soledad Well when they were ambushed. A volley of nearly one hundred shots was fired at the scouting party. Glover fell dead from his saddle and Moreno's horse was killed but Cuellar and Moreno escaped back to the Sweden Ranch.[58] Glover's death set off a furor. A correspondent to the San Antonio Daily Express reported, "Excitement over the killing of Glover does not abate. The murdered man leaves a wife and family of little children whose bereavement has awakened a sentiment throughout this entire section which will never rest short of purging the country of an element so direful as that which now troubles it."[59]

As a former Ranger and Sheriff, Linton Wright's views on the sensational Garza affair were sought by The Caller. Still smarting from Hogg's alliance with John Buckley, Linton seized the golden opportunity to impugn the Governor.

"Everything is quiet out our way and there is nothing new in Garza circles," remarked Mr. L.L. Wright, who came in last night from San Diego, to a Caller representative.

"Are the troops and rangers still beating the brush for Garza men?" asked the news rustler.

"Yes, and they capture an occasional would-be revolutionist but so far have not caught up with any of the Glover murderers.

"What reply did Governor Hogg make to the petition sent him by Capt. Dix, asking for rangers to help enforce your county laws?

"I understand that he told Capt. Dix that he would have the laws enforced in our county if it took every ranger in the state to do it. As yet, however, he has done nothing, and this is one instance where delay is surely dangerous.

"What about the report telegraphed from San Antonio that Garza was in Cuba and that his wife had gone to him?

"I have no idea whatever that Garza is in Cuba and as far as his wife is concerned, I have not heard of her leaving Palito Blanco. I guess the report is only a newspaper sensation, and about as truthful as many similar sensations that have been telegraphed the newspapers by the correspondents who have given Garza his great notoriety.

"Do you think Garza's men are pretty well scattered?

"Oh, yes, and that makes them harder to find. As long as they stayed together, they were not calculated to do so much harm as they are in bands of two and three and this also makes it a harder matter to locate them. However, the rangers and their guides know many of them and, with the assistance of United States troops, are hunting them high and low and causing them to hug the bushes like rabbits."

> Mr. Wright thinks that if the Governor will do as he promised and station a sufficient number of rangers in Duval, with full power to disarm all armed persons, that the scattered revolutionists will soon return to their jacals or seek a new field in which to carry on their war against the people of the United States.[60]

Garza eventually fled Texas and was believed to have been killed around 1905 in Bluefields, Nicaragua while engaged in another insurgency.[61] Diaz's long-lived regime was finally unseated in 1911. Soon after The Caller's interview with Linton he left San Diego and moved to Silver City, New Mexico. It is not known what work he procured there. The loss of his wife and career must have prompted him to leave San Diego.

According to the Duval County deeds registry the last of Dr. Wright's land purchases was on February 13, 1892. He bought several parcels in San Diego from Trinidad Flores, the same Flores from whom he acquired the lot on which his home was built. Two deeds filed on February 16 recite that Dr. Wright paid Flores $340.00 for ten lots. Considering the size of his family and the real value of $340.00 in those days, these records are ample evidence that his medical practice and drug store were prospering.

Influenza was then sweeping South Texas. The epidemic placed an enormous burden on Dr. Wright who had to tend the sick without respite. One rainy evening in late February he left home on horseback to make his rounds. When he failed to return, Mary went to the door to look for him and saw him lying face down in the front yard. He had collapsed after finishing his night's work.[62] Mary brought her husband indoors and put him to bed but the combination of illness and exposure had damaged him beyond repair. Dr. Wright died on February 29, a week before his fortieth birthday. The Caller described his passing.

"The shadow of death has darkened our community and cast a gloom over our little city in the loss of our old friend and physician, Dr. L.B. Wright, who departed this life at noon today from paralysis of the heart. Deceased had been complaining of a pain in the back of his head for several days but nothing serious was thought of it at the time. He retired, as usual, last night, feeling very well. Mrs. Wright awoke at 2 o'clock this morning and went to his bed and found him resting easy and at 5 o'clock she again went to him and this time found him breathing hard. She tried to arouse him, but in vain, and at once called Mr. John Cleary, who rendered all assistance possible and wired Mr. Thomas Hickey of your city, brother of Mrs. Wright, and also Dr. A.E. Spohn who came up on the morning train, and did all that could be done but to no avail. Deceased leaves a wife, several children and a large circle of relatives and friends to mourn his untimely death. Dr. L.B. Wright has for many years practiced medicine in this county and won for himself a host of warm friends who tender the bereaved family their deepest sympathies in the dark hour of their bereavement."[63]

Lawrence's death was noted as far away as San Antonio. The Daily Express reported, "At 12 o'clock today Dr. L.B. Wright died at his resident of apoplexy. The doctor was unconscious for some eight or ten hours previous to his death. He had been suffering with la grippe for some two months or more. Being the only physician in town, his services were in constant demand, never having time to recover from this dreaded malady. Our town is thus placed in mourning for our sad loss. He leaves a wife and six children to mourn his untimely death."[64]

Linton rushed from Silver City to San Diego when he received news of Lawrence's death. A week later Linton too was stricken with an infectious illness. Compounding the tragedy besetting the Wright family, Linton died at the Savage home in Corpus Christi on March 9 at age forty-two. The Caller published a poignant obituary.

"There were many sad hearts this week over the very unexpected announcement of the death of Linton L. Wright, which sad event occurred a few minutes past 3 o'clock Wednesday evening at the resident of Mr. R.R. Savage in this city. Only a few short weeks ago The Caller announced the departure for New Mexico of Mr. Wright who expected to make his home in that faroff country. Hardly had he become settled there, however, when he was called back to San Diego, where he had made his home for many years past, by the sudden death of his brother, the lamented Dr. L.B. Wright. On his arrival in San Diego he was taken ill with erysipelas in the face and head and he continued to grow worse until Sunday evening last when it was deemed advisable to bring him to this city for medical treatment and he arrived here on Sunday night's train.[65]

"He was taken to the residence of his brother-in-law, Mr. R.R. Savage, and seemed to be doing very nicely, retaining all his faculties, until Tuesday night about 10 o'clock when he suddenly became delirious which was but the flaring up of the candle just before it goes out forever. After his first moments of delirium he sunk rapidly nor did he regain consciousness again, death coming as gently as though he had fallen into a peaceful sleep. The remains will be taken to San Diego Thursday morning and laid in their eternal rest beside his loving wife who has gone before to wait for him in that beautiful 'Home of the Soul.'

"It is surely hard to realize that genial, generous and noble Linton Wright is no more. A man of splendid physique, he was just in the prime of life when the spoiler came and swept that life away. Generous to a fault, manly and honorable in every walk of life, he was ever the friend of the oppressed and never faltered to raise his arm in defense of the right. Long will it be ere we shall gaze 'upon his like again' and many will be the tears today that will moisten the sod that will close forever upon all that was mortal of him of whom we write."[66]

As did Lawrence's death, Linton's made news far from the small community where he had lived. The Galveston Daily News reported, "Linton L. Wright, ex-sheriff of Duval county, a man highly respected for his many noble traits of character, died here last night. About one month ago he took up residence at Silver City, N.M. and only returned here last week on account of the death of his brother Dr. Wright. Linton Wright's death has cast a gloom over this section of the county where he was esteemed by all who knew him."[67]

With its two eldest men suddenly gone, there was a void in the

Wright family that would take a generation to fill. Mary Wright was left with six young children to raise alone. Dr. Wright's drug store continued in business for a time after his death under the name L.B. Wright & Co. The Duval County Commissioners' minutes for June 13, 1892 record that a warrant for $9.50 was issued to L.B. Wright & Co. as payment for "medicine for Co. prisoner." Before Dr. Wright's death the store was managed by Bruno Rios. Afterwards, Rios took over the business and for nearly a century his name was visible above the storefront.

Bruno Rios Drugstore (c.1908)
UTSA Institute of Texan Cultures

In 1900 Mary and her six children lived in the family home which she owned. Lucile, age 16, assisted her mother at home. Lafayette, age 15, worked as a salesman. Lawrence, age 18, Edwin, age 12, and John, age 10, attended school. Philip, age 8, was not yet in school.[68] As the five brothers and their sister grew up they remained close knit and protective of one another and their mother. While Lucile and Lafayette never married, their brothers did and all spent their lives in or near San Diego.

Standing: John Thomas and Philip Thomas Wright
Seated: Lawrence, "Fett" and Edwin Daniel Wright (c.1915)

James Lawrence Wright worked for the Texas-Mexican Railway in Alice and served on the school board there. He married Rosa Adami in 1910 and they had four children; James Lawrence, Jr., Roger E., Mary Jeanette and Howard Francis Wright. Lucile Wright lived in the family home in San Diego from her infancy until 1960 when she sold the house and moved to Corpus Christi. Lucile left no descendants and is fondly remembered by those who knew her.

Linton Lafayette ("Fett") Wright began his career in the title abstract business in 1900 in the office of W.W. McCampbell in San Diego. In 1909 Lafayette started his own firm, Wright & Wright Abstract Co., with his brother Philip. Lafayette was its senior partner for thirty-five years until his death in 1944. Lafayette and Philip claimed most of the abstract business in Duval County and were also engaged in real estate and lending.[69] Lafayette is remembered by his nieces and nephews as tall, quiet and an avid reader of Shakespeare.

Edwin Daniel Wright worked as a cowboy in his youth and enjoyed hunting with his dog "Old Red." Edwin was a graceful dancer and when he went to a Mexican fandango others would clear the floor to watch him. Although he did not much exceed 100 pounds and five and a half feet, he was an expert pugilist and was often forced to practice his art on larger men who had the misfortune of underestimating him.

In 1920 Edwin married Katherine Smith, a red-haired telephone operator from Missouri. After their marriage, Edwin was employed as a clerk with the H.E.B. Food Company and Katie worked for the telephone company as a supervisor for nearly fifty years. Edwin and Katie lived the entirety of their married lives in Robstown and had two sons, Edwin Daniel, Jr. and Robert Franklin Wright. Like all of Mary Wright's children, Edwin was devoutly Catholic. During the 1920s and 30s his faith brought him persecution by Ku Klux Klan hooligans who threatened and harassed him at work and even while his family walked to church, yet he never once yielded to them. Edwin was blind and housebound during his last decade but his stories about his father and youth in San Diego sowed the seeds of this book.

John Thomas Wright left San Diego and moved to Alice, Texas in his early adulthood. He married Bonnie Dale Mitchell in 1913 and they had two children, Evelyn and John T. Wright, Jr. From 1917 to 1923 John was the city secretary of Alice. In 1923 his family moved to Corpus Christi and in 1928 he participated in the organization of the Citizens Industrial Bank, later the Citizens State Bank, as one of its first stockholders. From 1923 to 1929 John was the city secretary of Corpus Christi.[70]

While Corpus Christi secretary, John honed his political skills as a campaigner and coalition builder. Though often urged he never ran for elected office himself. Self-taught in the law and an orator in English and Spanish, John was instrumental in the elections of Texas Governors Daniel J. Moody and James V. Allred as well as the elections of Corpus Christi mayors Perry G. Lovenskiold and William Shaffer.[71] The long list of Corpus Christi civic organizations to which John devoted his energies included the Housing Authority, Chamber of Commerce, Community Chest (now United Way), Lions Club and Boy Scouts. He was also a financial advisor to Bishop E.B. Ledvina.[72]

Mention any civic enterprise in South Texas and you will find that John T. Wright is interested in it and probably has served as a director or officer. He was born in San Diego and came here 17 years ago. He was city secretary from 1925 until 1929, going from that position to president of the Citizens Industrial Bank a year after its organization. He has held that position since. He headed the Community Chest for a year and still is a director and is also past president of the Lions Club and chamber of commerce. He is president of the Isaac Walton League but says he is an "enthusiastic fisherman who doesn't fish much." His many duties prevent much leisure time. He is a forceful public speaker and never fails to say exactly what he thinks regardless.

Reprinted with permission from the Corpus Christi Times, Aug. 25, 1939

Philip Thomas Wright lived in San Diego for most of his life and began working at age eleven after finishing the third grade. He got his first job on the stage coach in San Diego and later was a Spanish interpreter at the Duval County courthouse. Philip's courthouse work introduced him to the title abstract business which he entered in 1906 at age fourteen. As a principal of Wright & Wright Abstract Co., Philip developed a specialty in oil and gas leases.[73]

Philip married Elizabeth Leila Gravis in 1917 and they had four children; Philip Thomas Jr., Charles Lawrence, Helen Frances and Joyce Elizabeth Wright. During World War I Philip was the General Director of Publicity for the Red Cross in Duval County. He was also a director of the Chamber of Commerce, a member of the Texas Abstractors Association and the American Association of Title Men and active in the Catholic Church.[74] Philip is remembered by his daughters as humorous, fun-loving and a tenor who enjoyed singing in a quartet with his brothers on special occasions.

On March 4, 1917 Congress passed the Indian Wars Act which provided pensions to "the surviving officers and enlisted men of the Texas volunteers who served in defense of the frontier of that State against Indian depredations" from 1859 to 1877. The Act also granted pensions to the widows of qualified soldiers. Veterans of the Ranger Frontier Battalion were generally eligible for pensions. Some who served in the Special Force checking banditry on the Rio Grande believed they were entitled to benefits under the Act.

John T. Wright, Sr. and Philip T. Wright, Sr. (1940)

On August 3, 1917 Mary Wright sent a "Declaration of Widow for Service Pension" to the Secretary of the Interior in Washington, D.C. In her application Mary advised that her husband, Lawrence Baker Wright, served in Captain L.H. McNelly's company of the Texas militia from July 25, 1874 until February 28, 1877 and again as a physician in Captain Lee Hall's company. She described him as five feet, nine inches tall with fair complexion, gray eyes and black hair. Mary's application stated that Lawrence had fought "Mexican marauders."

After many months of inaction by the Interior Department, Philip T. Wright wrote to the agency concerning his mother's application, "Will you please advise the present status of this claim as it seems that it has hung up for quite awhile with no results. We understood that payment was to be made promptly, but nothing has been received to this day."[75] Eight months later Commissioner G.M. Saltzguber sent Mary a letter informing her that her claim was "rejected on the ground that [L.B. Wright's] service in Capt. L.H. McNelly's Co., Texas State Troops...was rendered against Mexican bandits, cattle thieves and robbers, and not in defense of the Texas frontier against Indian depredations, and, therefore, is not pensionable..."[76]

The legal distinction between bandits and hostile Indians must have escaped Mary Wright and others who were denied pensions. Paradoxically, under an 1882 Act of Congress, Texas was reimbursed by the federal government for monies paid to Ranger units engaged in defense against Indian as well as bandit raids. Thus, the Indian Wars Act's exclusion of bandit fighting from pensionable duty seemed incongruous to some.

Mary's pension claim was a raw nerve in the family for years. In 1932 Philip, still indignant over the denial of his mother's claim, wrote to Congressman Richard M. Kleberg of Corpus Christi. Kleberg forwarded Philip's letter on to Congressional House Speaker John Nance Garner who also happened to be a South Texan.[77] Garner sent a letter of inquiry to General Frank T. Hines of the Veterans Administration.[78]

Veterans Administration's Director of Pensions, E.W. Morgan, replied to Garner in a letter repeating almost verbatim the rejection letter that Commissioner Saltzguber had sent to Mary 13 years earlier. Morgan, however, generously added, "If Mrs. Wright desires to file a claim for pension under the Act of March 3, 1927, she is at liberty to use the enclosed blank form of declaration for that purpose."[79] So went the Government's shell game.

The Wright ladies: Katherine, Leila, Lucile, Rosa and Bonnie (c. 1930)

Mary lived 17 years without a pension. She passed away on July 7, 1934 in San Diego. A Benavides newspaper noted, "Mrs. Mary H. Wright, pioneer San Diego resident, died at her home in San Diego Saturday evening at 7:30 o'clock. The end followed a short illness of several weeks' duration. Mrs. Wright, who was 75 years old, was a native of Ireland. For the past 54 years she had resided in San Diego, having lived at the same homesite the entire time..."[80]

Mary was the last of the first generation of Wrights who settled in San Diego.

Building the Santa Fe Railroad line.

HARRY LEE WRIGHT AND JOHN W. WRIGHT, JR.

HARRY LEE WRIGHT.

Henry ("Harry") Lee Wright was the keystone of his parents' children. Agewise, he was in the middle of the brood and it was his hard work that enabled his father to save enough money to bring the younger children to Texas. After the deaths of Lawrence and Linton, Harry became the family elder. We know much about Harry from his memoirs written in 1940 several years before his death.

After mustering out of the Texas Rangers in November, 1880, Harry signed on with a group of engineers surveying the Texas-Mexican Railway line between San Diego and Laredo. He was handed an axe and put to work clearing brush. It was then that he first had the idea of becoming an engineer himself. For another year he worked on a cattle ranch near Corpus Christi before returning to San Diego as Linton's deputy.

In San Diego, Harry met state senator Norman G. Collins who recognized him as a young man with promise. Collins urged Harry on to higher education at the Texas Agricultural and Mechanical College. Harry resisted the idea because he believed his elementary schooling was deficient. With more prodding, he enrolled in October, 1883. Harry's academic records prove his fear of inadequacy was unfounded.

In his first year at A&M, Harry ranked second in a class of fifty-two from which thirty-three students were dismissed or resigned. He received Honors in Spanish and the rank of cadet corporal by the end of the year. In his second year Harry ranked fifth in a class of twenty-five from which another ten students dropped out and was promoted to sergeant major. On June 1, 1886, Harry graduated third in a class of eleven with a grade point average of 86 and the rank of quartermaster. Texas A&M's 1881 alumni roster shows that Harry was awarded a degree in civil engineering and graduated without a single demerit.

With diploma in hand Harry joined a team of Sante Fe Railroad Company engineers surveying the line between Dallas and Cleburne, Texas. He next worked for the Missouri-Pacific Railroad Company and the International & Great Northern Railroad Company overseeing construction of rail lines linking Hillsboro, Dangerfield, Texarkana, Longview, San Marcos, Lockhart and Houston, Texas.

A recession stalled railroad construction in late 1887 and Harry was transferred to the I.&G.N. Railroad's Engineering Department in Palestine, Texas. That position was also lost at the end of the year. Harry was moved to the I.&G.N.'s Wood, Tie and Timber Department in Little Rock, Arkansas where he worked for several months until he was sent back to Palestine. Months later Harry was waiting in the Palestine railroad station for a train when he was approached by Colonel G.W. Burkett who owned a real estate company. Burkett asked Harry if he could keep accounts. He replied he could and Burkett gave him a job. Harry readily adapted from field to office work.

Colonel Burkett arrived penniless in Texas from Ireland and built a fortune as a railroad contractor and realtor. He belonged to the Republican party which dominated the Texas insurance industry. After returning from a political convention, Burkett introduced Harry to a friend who was looking for a Palestine agent for his insurance company. Burkett asked Harry whether he was interested in that line of work. Harry confessed he knew nothing about insurance but Burkett prevailed on him. On February 4, 1889 Harry established an agency for two insurers.

Those two companies were increased to fifteen, most of which underwrote fire coverage. Near the end of his career Harry recalled with pride that in fifty years he never had a disputed claim and paid out a total of about $250,000 in claims, a modest figure by today's standards. In an interview with a Palestine journalist, Harry said he disliked the life insurance business because, "I do not like to buttonhole a man on the street and try to get his name on the dotted line."[1]

Harry Lee Wright (c. 1900)

On returning to Palestine from Little Rock in 1888, Harry made his residence in the home of Mrs. Harriet ("Attie") Gooch Wood. Attie was widowed by the death of her first husband, Samuel, from diphtheria. Samuel and Attie had three children, Fannie, Jessie and Gideon. Fannie and Gideon died in childhood leaving Jessie as Attie's only surviving child by her first marriage. To support Jessie and herself Attie took in boarders. Jessie recalled that Harry began courting her mother by playing dominoes with the girl in the front parlor. Harry's domino strategy worked. He and Attie were married on May 9, 1889. A year later Elizabeth Gooch Wright was born to them.

Elizabeth wrote of her birth, "It all began a long time ago on a rainy April night. My mother wakened my father and told him to go for the doctor. There were no cars or telephones and we did not have a horse and buggy. My father walked the two miles to the home of the doctor who hitched his horse to the buggy, dressed and offered my father a ride home. When they arrived at our house they found Mother lying very still so she would not injure the little girl who arrived without any help from anyone. I suppose even then I hated to wait to get things done." Jessie was adopted by Harry and nicknamed "Sisso" by her younger sister.

Harry left Colonel Burkett's company on June 14, 1892 and for the next few years he worked for the Palestine Water and Power Company as its manager. Under his management, the company's physical plant was overhauled with new pumps, mains and hydrants. About that time Harry was hired by a company from Lowell, Massachusetts to supervise the installation of Palestine's first sewer system. Harry oversaw the Palestine Water and Power Company and the sewer system along with his insurance agency for seven years. In 1900 Harry and Attie lived at 2 May Street with Jessie, Elizabeth and Attie's sister, Fannie Gooch. Elizabeth was attending school. Harry's occupation was "Life and Fire Insurance Agent."[2]

Harry's social calendar was always full. He was a Sunday school teacher at the First Methodist Church in Palestine; a trustee of the Texas Methodist Conference; founder of the Palestine YMCA; member of Masonic Lodge 31 and the Knights Templar; secretary of the Anderson County Farm and Loan Association; income tax advisor and Spanish interpreter for the Missouri Pacific Railroad Company.[3]

On September 17, 1909 Harry was appointed to the three-member Texas State Fire Insurance Rating Board in Austin. The Board regulated fire insurance rates charged by insurers and prevented rate discrimination. The Board was headed by the State Commissioner of Insurance and Banking, Frederick C. von Rosenberg, one of Harry's classmates at Texas A&M. Harry was appointed to the Fire Insurance Rating Board by Governor Thomas M. Campbell, himself a Palestine man. Harry's tenure on the Board coincided with an increase in the regulation of insurance in Texas due to discriminatory rating, unlawful claims practices and financial instability of some insurers.

After a year on the Fire Insurance Rating Board, Harry was appointed to the State Insurance Board on December 16, 1910. While

Harry and his family lived in Austin, Jessie and Elizabeth attended the University of Texas and both graduated in 1910. When Harry's government stint ended that year, he accepted a position as vice-president of the Rio Grande Fire Insurance Company in San Antonio. He lived in San Antonio for three years until 1914 and went back to Palestine to resume his own insurance business.

Harry Lee Wright with Sunday school class at the first Methodist Church, Palestine, Texas (1906)

After Harry returned to Palestine he was notified that his brother Richmond had died at the St. Anthony Hotel in San Antonio. Little is known about Dick after the family moved to Texas. Harry's grandchildren recall that Dick was said to have been a railroad man who often traveled in the company of shady women and carried diamonds sewn into his clothing. As the story goes, Dick was with one of his lady friends when he died. When Harry got the news he caught the next train to San Antonio to claim Dick's body and account for his belongings. At the hotel Harry discovered that Dick's "femme fatale" had made off with all but three of his gems. These Harry had set in rings which he gave to his wife and daughters.

On April 26, 1917 Harry filed for a pension under the 1917 Indian Wars Act. In his application Harry stated he had served in Captain Lee Hall's Special State Troops from December 25, 1877 until November 1, 1878 and again for four months in 1880 in Captain Thomas L. Oglesby's company. He described himself as five feet, eleven and a half inches tall, 186 pounds, with blue eyes, black hair and no scars. On March 21, 1918 Harry's application was denied by the Interior Department's Pension Bureau because he did not prove military service against Indians.

Harry was not about to give up without a fight. On March 3, 1927, Congress passed an amendment to the Indian Wars Act extending the period of pensionable duty beyond 1877. On May 13, Harry filed another application which was also rejected. The denial of Harry's second application was affirmed by the Secretary of the Interior on August 7, 1928. Harry appealed to the Veterans Administration's Board of Appeals demonstrating he was both imaginative and dogged in pursuit of his rights.

On appeal Harry argued that during his Ranger service most of Texas was subject to Indian attacks and, thus, constituted a "zone" of hostility within the meaning of the 1927 amendment. By analogy Harry argued that veterans who served in the Spanish-American War and World War I were eligible for pensions whether or not they saw battlefield duty. On July 11, 1932 the Board of Appeals ruled to the contrary and held that a "zone" meant an immediate area of combat and not an entire state. The Board distinguished between state militia service in Indian campaigns and suppression of outlaws and bandits. Only the former service was pensionable under the Indian Wars Act.

Harry's fifteen-year battle with the Veteran's Administration to win a pension for his 14 months of service with the Texas Rangers is a tribute to his tenacity. For years he was ribbed about it by his business partner, Willis C. Kendall. Kendall was one of the few Republicans in Palestine and delighted in telling Harry that he would have easily qualified for a military pension from Herbert Hoover's administration if he was a Republican. But Harry remained a "militant Roosevelt Democrat" to the end.[4]

Attie and Harry Wright at home in Palestine, Texas (c. 1945)

Harry's golden years were as productive than those of his youth. His insurance agency prospered through the 1920s and 30s and he was joined in his business for a while by his grandson Edward R. Stanford, Jr. before Edward enlisted in the Navy in 1941. On May 9, 1940 Harry finished his memoirs in which he revealed his recipe for success.

"For success these three things are very essential: satisfied clients, loyal cooperative employees and satisfactory relationships with the companies that an agency represents. One unpleasant business dealing with a client can greatly demoralize a well-regulated agency. I have also been extremely fortunate in securing men and women to work for me who were loyal and faithful to the principals of the agency. I have endeavored at all times to give the companies I represented the benefit of my best judgment and cheerful and sympathetic cooperation, and the result has been that invariably the companies have gone 'all the way' with me whenever I have asked them to do so."

Harry's achievements were commended by a local journal. "Harry Wright's ability and integrity quickly won for him the confidence of older and influential men who sought his services and assistance in many matters, both practical and technical. He was a close personal friend of many outstanding men in the state. He holds a warm spot in his heart for the memory of his first employer, Col. Burkett."[5]

Harry Lee Wright retired in 1944 at age eighty-six. On November 12, 1947 he died in Palestine at age eighty-nine.[6] Attie passed away several months later in May, 1948. Few can lay claim to a more colorful career than that of Harry who made his way for seventy years as a ploughman, sawyer, Texas Ranger, deputy sheriff, surveyor, railroad engineer, accountant, insurance agent and public official.

John Wesley Wright, Jr.

JOHN WESLEY WRIGHT, JR.

John Wesley Wright, Jr. spent his early years working as a laborer when the family moved to Texas. He farmed with his father in Waverly after they arrived in Galveston in 1875. After a year of farming John and Harry left Waverly for Willis where they worked in a sawmill for another year. In December, 1877 Harry and John parted company when Harry joined the Rangers in Cuero. John then went to work for the International & Great Northern Railroad Company as a night watchman and engineer.

On June 15, 1892, John married Lucy Walton Royall, a daughter of the family that operated the Royall National Bank of

Palestine. John and Lucy had two daughters, Ann (b. 1893) and Dorothy (b. 1895). After his marriage John became a banker and in 1899 he organized the Citizens National Bank in Tyler, Texas over which he presided for the next ten years.

In 1909 John moved to Dallas where he was President of the Commonwealth National Bank. He served on a committee of bankers that founded the Federal Reserve Bank in Dallas and continued as a banker until he retired in the early 1920s. After retiring he remained a vice president of the Royall National Bank and lived in Dallas, Florida and New York. John died in Dallas on January 20, 1929 at age sixty-eight.[7]

He was survived for many years by Lucy who passed away at age eighty-two on August 15, 1957 in Hot Springs, Virginia.

EPILOGUE

The study of family history strengthens our feeling of connection to long ago events that might otherwise seem remote and irrelevant. It gives us a long view of the human condition and its cycle of life, struggle and death.

It is said that a page of history is worth more than a volume of logic. I believe an appreciation of the past is essential to a sense of personal identity and destiny. Making this long journey back in time has inspired in me a deeper reverence for our national and ancestral heritage. If it touches the same chord in others, and encourages similar quests, its purpose is fulfilled.

Captain Moses Guest (1755–1828)

Chapter Notes

1. PHILADELPHIA FREEDOM

1. John W. Jordan, *Colonial and Revolutionary Families of Pennsylvania* (Baltimore: Genealogical Publishing Co., 1978), 52-53.

2. John Thomas Scharf and Thompson Westcott, *History of Philadelphia, 1609-1884* (Philadelphia: L.H. Everts & Co., 1884), Vol. II, 981; *The Pennsylvania Magazine of History and Biography* (Philadelphia: Historical Society of Pennsylvania, 1883), 7:495.

3. William Perrine, "Dock Street," *Philadelphia Evening Bulletin*, 27 January 1919; *The Wilmington Morning Star*, 7 August 1921.

4. *Marriages Authorized by the Philadelphia Monthly Meeting of Friends, 1682-1756*, Pennsylvania State Archives, Second Series, Vol. IX (Harrisburg: 1880), 207.

5. John Guest's grandsons included Henry Guest, a tanner whose home still stands in New Brunswick, New Jersey. Henry was a friend and correspondent of President John Adams and Thomas Paine. One of Henry's sons was Revolutionary War hero Capt. Moses Guest of the Second Middlesex Regiment, New Jersey militia. On the night of October 26, 1779 Captain Guest's company ambushed a clandestine raid led by British Lt. Col. John G. Simcoe commanding some eighty mounted Tory partisans of the Queen's Rangers. Simcoe was widely known for his brutal "no quarter" bayonet attacks on Patriot troops under cover of darkness. That night he planned to capture New Jersey's Governor William Livingston. Instead, Simcoe's horse was shot from under him and he was taken prisoner by Captain Guest, Governor Livingston intervened to save the British colonel from being lynched by the citizenry. After the war Simcoe became the Royal Governor of Upper Canada. He occasionally told American visitors he hoped one day to meet the officer who had captured him, but he was never reunited with Captain Guest. John W. Barber and Henry Howe, *Historical Collections of the State of New Jersey* (New York: S. Tuttle, 1844),455;

Eugene F. McPike, *Tales of Our Forefathers and Biographical Annals of Families Allied to Those of McPike, Guest and Dumont* (Albany: Joel Munsell's Sons, 1898), 9-27

6. *Record of Pennsylvania Marriages, Prior to 1810*, Pennsylvania State Archives, Second Series, Vol. 8 (Harrisburg, 1895), 610.
7. Peter Wilson Coldham, *The Complete Book of Emigrants: 1700-1750* (Baltimore: Genealogical Publishing Co., Inc., 1992), 341.
8. John Marshall, *The Life of George Washington*, 5 vols. (Philadelphia: C.P. Wayne, 1804), I: 373
9. J. Smith Futhey and Gilbert Cope, *History of Chester County, Pennsylvania* (Philadelphia: H. Louis Everts 1881), 336-350.
10. Marshall, op. cit., pp. 378-379.
11. Ibid., pp. 392-393.
12. Sir John St. Clair to Governor William Denny, Pennsylvania Archives, First Series (Philadelphia: Joseph Severns & Co., 1853), 3:267.
13. Futhey & Cope, *op. cit.*, 54.
14. Ibid, 55.
15. Ibid, 54.
16. Ibid.
17. William Clingan of West Caln was a significant figure in Chester County history. He was a Justice of the Peace from 1757 to 1786 and a delegate to the Second Continental Congress during 1777 to 1779. Like many Patriot leaders, his property was ravaged by Redcoat troops during the British occupation of Philadelphia. Futhey & Cope, op. cit., 499.
18. *Pennsylvania Gazette*, 6 July 1758.

2. CAROLINA BOUND

1. Weynette Parks Haun, *North Carolina Court of Claims Record of Patents Granted (Secretary of State Papers) 1740-1755* (Durham, N.C.: W.P. Haun,1996), 35-36; Brent H. Holcomb, *North Carolina Land Grants in South Carolina* (Baltimore: Genealogical Publishing Co., 1986), vi-ix, 115, 142.
2. Gaius Jackson Slosser, ed., *They Seek a Country: The American Presbyterians* (New York: The Macmillan Company, 1955) 6-7.
3. LDS Family History Center Microfilm 214,497, Clarke County, GA, Will Book A, 27.

4. E. Jennifer Monaghan, *Literacy Instruction and Gender in Colonial New England,* American Quarterly, 40(1), 18-41, 1988.

5. Dr. J.B.O. Landrum, *Colonial and Revolutionary History of Upper South Carolina* (Greenville: Shannon & Co., 1897), 1-6.

6. David Ramsay, *History of South Carolina, From its First Settlement in 1670 to the Year 1808*, Vol. II (Newberry, S.C.: W. J. Duffie, 1858), 2:305.

7. Miles S. Philbeck, *Upper Broad River Basin Pioneers,* 1750-1760 (Chapel Hill, N.C.: Miles S. Philbeck, 1984), Appendix B, 812.

8. Alexander Gregg, *History of the Old Cheraws* (New York: Richardson and Company, 1867), 131.

9. Ramsay, op. cit., 1:120.

10. Sam Thomas, *The 1780 Presbyterian Rebellion and the Battle of Huck's Defeat,* Culture & Heritage Commission of York County (1999).

11. Gregg, 128-129.

12. Ramsay, op. cit., 1:122.

13. Ibid., Vol. II, 2:305.

14. Robert M. Weir, *"A Most Important Epocha:" The Coming of the Revolution in South Carolina* (Columbia, S.C.: University of South Carolina Press, 1970), 4.

15. According to local lore the Scape Whore Swamp got its name from a misfortunate woman who escaped into the swamp after being banished from a nearby town for plying her trade.

16. Ramsay, op. cit., 2:292-296, 303.

17. Gregg, 220.

18. Ibid., 221-222.

3. THE SPIRIT OF '76

1. Pension Application, R11877, John Wright, Hall County, Georgia, 6 February 1854, U.S. National Archives.

2. Capt. Robert Ellison organized an independent ranger company in 1775 that was attached to the South Carolina Third Continental Regiment. He was captured at Augusta and paroled by the British. Risking hanging, he violated his parole and rejoined the Patriot militia rising from private to captain in Lt. Col. Jacob Baxter's regiment of Marion's Brigade. Captain Ellison was elected to the state legislature after the war. A.S. Salley, Jr., ed., The South Carolina Historical and

Genealogical Magazine (Charleston, S.C.: The Walker, Evans & Cogswell Co., 1900), 1:195-196; Bobby Gilmer Ross, *Roster of South Carolina Patriots in the American Revolution* (Baltimore: Genealogical Publishing Co., Inc, 1994), 292-293.

3. A.S. Salley, Jr., ed., *Stub Entries to Indents Issued in Payment of Claims Against South Carolina Growing Out of the Revolution,* Books Y-Z (Columbia, S.C.: The Historical Commission of South Carolina, 1927), 129.

4. Moss, op. cit., 436, 908, 1015.

5. Ibid., 1002.

6. Light horse troops traveled mounted and fought on foot. The Carthaginians used lightly armed horsemen as scouts and assault troops when Hannibal invaded the Roman Empire during the Punic Wars. Eight centuries later their Moorish descendants used light cavalry again to invade Europe.

7. Moss, op. cit., 930.

8. Anne Willingham Willis, *A Family History* (Atlanta: Higgins-MacArthur Co., 1946), 114.

9. Bobby Gilmer Ross, *The Patriots at the Cowpens,* (Blacksburg, S.C.: Scotia Press, 1985), 172; J.D.Lewis,www.carolana.com/SC/Revolution/patriot_military_sc_captains_l.html.

10. Moss, *Roster of South Carolina Patriots,* 96, 719; 971; Michael C. Scoggins, *A Brief History of the New Acquisition Militia* (York County Historical Center, 2002).

11. Scoggins, op. cit.

12. Moss, *Roster of South Carolina Patriots,* 570, 1002; Moss, *Patriots at the Cowpens,* 172; J.D. Lewis, www.carolana.com/SC/Revolution/patriots_sc_capt_john_lindsay.html.

13. James Wright, Jr. received three land bounties totaling 615 acres in 1786 from the First Spartan Regiment's former commander, Col. John Thomas, Sr., who became a post-war land commissioner. The extent of James's grants, and the likelihood he used militia pay to buy them, suggests his military service was lengthy. Colonel Thomas also granted William Wright two lots totaling 600 acres in 1784. The properties were located in the Ninety-Six District on the Broad and Saluda Rivers and may have been part of the lands confiscated from Capt. Richard Pearis and other Loyalists after the war. Greenville, S.C. Land Grants, Book A,

107, 153; Book C, 126; Archie Vernon Huff, Jr., *Greenville: The History of the City and County in the South Carolina Piedmont* (Columbia, S.C: University of South Carolina Press, 1995), 38, 40.

14. Moss, *Roster of South Carolina Patriots,* 446, 572, 719; Scoggins, op. cit.

15. Pension Application S26084, Robert Ellis, Morgan County, Tennessee, 10 November 1838, U.S. National Archives; Moss, *Roster of South Carolina Patriots, 1002.* James Wright, Jr. served in Hill's Regiment of Light Dragoons with his future in-laws Daniel, David and John McCall, elder brothers of Mary McCall who married James's oldest son William. Col. Hill's wife, Jane McCall, may have been a member of that family. Moss, *Roster of South Carolina Patriots,* 446, 593-594; Ettie Tidwell McCall, *McCall-Tidwell and Allied Families* (Atlanta: Walter W. Brown Publishing Co., 1931), 14-16, 90, 327, 537, 542.

16. J.E. Hays & John B. Wilson, *Georgia Military Affairs (1775-1793),* (Atlanta, Ga.: WPA Project 5993, 1940), 1:3.

17. Moss, *Roster of South Carolina Patriots,* 547; Scoggins, op. cit.

18. Moss, *Roster of South Carolina Patriots,* 95, 771-772, 925.

19. Ibid., 1015.

20. Salley, *Stub Entries,* Books R-T, 246; Moss, *Roster of South Carolina Patriots,* 1015.

21. Salley, *Stub Entries,* Books L-N, 321; Moss, *Roster of South Carolina Patriots,* 1015.

22. J.D. Lewis, www.carolana.com/SC/Revolution/revolution_SC_troops_1781_5_15_.html.

23. Salley, *Stub Entries,* Books R-T, 246; Moss, *Roster of South Carolina Patriots,* 1016.

24. John Wright Pension Application.

25. Patrick O' Kelley, *Unwaried Patience and Fortitude: Francis Marion's Orderly Book* (West Conshocken, Pa.: Infinity Publishing.com, 2007), 579.

26. David R. Chesnutt, et. al., *The Papers of Henry Laurens* (Columbia, S.C.: University of South Carolina Press, 1994), 14:94.

27. Robert K. Wright, Jr., *The Continental Army* (Washington, D.C.: Center of Military History, United States Army, 1983), 309.

28. William Moultrie, *Memoirs of the American Revolution,* (New York: David Longworth, 1802), 1:223.

29. Chesnutt, op. cit., 94.

30. Moultrie, op. cit., 230-231.

31. Charles C. Jones, Jr., *The History of Georgia,* 2 vols (Cambridge, S.C.: The Riverside Press, 1883, reprint ed. Spartanburg: The Reprint Company, 1965), 269.

32. Moss, *Roster of South Carolina Patriots,* 1002.

33. Col. John F. Grimke to J. Kean, 21 June 1779; Hugh McCall, *The History of Georgia* (Atlanta: A.B. Caldwell, 1909), 420.

34. Gen. Benjamin Lincoln to Gen. William Moultrie, 20 June 1779.

35. Carl P. Borick, *A Gallant Defense* (Columbia, S.C.: University of South Carolina Press, 2003), 120, 252.

36. Moss, *Roster of South Carolina Patriots,* 1002.

37. Borick, *Gallant Defense,* 176-179.

38. Ibid. 220.

39. Moss, *Roster of South Carolina Patriots,* 1002.

40. Benjamin Lincoln, Original Papers Relating to the Siege of Charleston, 1780 (Charleston, S.C.: Walker, Evans & Cogswell Co., 1898), 47.

41. Robert P. Borick, *Relieve Us of This Burthen* (Columbia, S.C.: The University of South Carolina Press, 2012), 48.

42. Ibid., 117.

43. Robert P. Watson, *The Ghost Ship of Brooklyn: An Untold Story of the American Revolution* (New York: Da Capo Press, 2017), 112.

44. Dr. David Ramsay, *The History of the Revolution of South Carolina from a British Province to an Independent State* (Trenton, N.J.: Isaac Collins, 1785), 2:141, 167, 529.

45. Lord Charles Grenville Montagu to General Sir John Dalling, 1 October 1781.

46. Borick, *Relieve Us of This Burthen,* 34, 79.

47. Moss, *Roster of South Carolina Patriots,* 1015.

48. Borick, *Relieve Us of This Burthen,* 79-80.

49. Petition of John Wright, 5 December 1793; A.S. Salley, Jr., ed., *Accounts Audited of Claims Growing out of the Revolution in South Carolina (1775-1856),* File No. 8802 (Microcopy No. 8), South Carolina Department of Archives and History, Columbia, S.C. (1985); Moss, *Roster of South Carolina Patriots, 1015.*

50. Moss, *Roster of South Carolina Patriots,* 39.

51. Affidavit of Jesse Baker, 4 December 1793; Salley, *Accounts Audited,* File No. 8802 (Microcopy No. 8).

52. Pension Application, R11899, Thomas Wright, Surry County, North Carolina, 12 February 1833, U.S. National Archives.

53. Henry Lumpkin, *From Savannah to Yorktown: The American Revolution in the South* (Columbia, S.C.: University of South Carolina Press, 1981), 126; George Hanger (Lord Coleraine), an Address to the Army in Reply to the Strictures by Roderick M'Kenzie (Late Lieut. in the 71st Regmt.) on Tarleton's History of the Campaigns of 1780 and 1781, London, 1789, 82.

54. Melissa Walker, *The Battles of Kings Mountain and Cowpens: The American Revolution in the Southern Backcountry* (New York: Routledge, 2013), 267.

55. A. S. Salley, Jr., ed., *Col. William Hill's Memoirs of The Revolution* (Columbia, S.C.: The Historical Commission of South Carolina, 1921), 9.

56. Moss, *Roster of South Carolina Patriots,* 96.

57. Salley, *Col. William Hill's Memoirs,* 10.

58. M. A. Moore, *The Life of Gen. Edward Lacey* (Spartanburg, S.C.: Douglas, Evins & Co., 1859), 11.

59. Hanger, op. cit., 109-110.

60. Gen. Daniel Morgan to William Snickers, 26 January 1781.

61. Moss, *Roster of South Carolina Patriots,* 570; Moss, *Patriots at the Cowpens,* 172.

62. Moss, *Roster of South Carolina Patriots,* 446, 547; Moss, *Patriots at the Cowpens,* 142, 172; J.D. www.carolana.com/SC/Revolution/Known_Patriots_at_Kings_Mountain.pdf.

63. Moss, *Patriots at the Cowpens,* 338.

64. Robert Ellis Pension Application; Moss, *Roster of South Carolina Patriots,* 1002.

65. Ibid.

66. Robert Ellis Pension Application; Moss, *Roster of South Carolina Patriots,* 292, 1015.

67. Borick, *Gallant Defense,* 240.

68. See note 13, supra.

69. O' Kelley, op. cit., 529.

70. Salley, *Stub Entries,* Books O-Q, 134; *Accounts Audited,* File No. 8808 (Microcopy No. 8).

71. Ibid.

72. Salley, *Stub Entries,* Books R-T, 246; Moss, *Roster of South Carolina Patriots,* 1015-1016.

73. Moss, *Roster of South Carolina Patriots,* 1002.

74. O'Kelley, op. cit., 578.

75. Ibid., 577-578, 707.

76. Ibid., 579.

77. Moss, *Roster of South Carolina Patriots,* 58, 599; Borick, *Gallant Defense,* 120.

4. IN THE LAND OF COTTON

1. Alex M. Hitz, *Georgia Bounty Land Grants,* The Georgia Historical Quarterly, Vol. 38, No. 4 (December, 1954), 341.

2. Ruth Blair, *Revolutionary Soldiers' Receipts for Georgia Bounty Grants* (Atlanta: Forte and Davies, 1928), 47-60.

3. Anne Willingham Willis, *A Family History* (Atlanta: Higgins-McArthur Co., 1946), 114; *Our Wright-Washington Ancestry,* Georgia Archives (Unpublished, 1965), 5.

4. J.E. Hays and John B. Wilson, *Georgia Military Affairs (1775-1793),* Vol. I, (Atlanta: WPA Project 5993, 1940), 3.

5. John Stith was captain of the Columbia County Militia, Second Battalion, in 1801 and promoted to lieutenant colonel, Twelfth Battalion, in 1808. Gordon Burns Smith, *History of the Georgia Militia, 1783-1861* (Milledgeville, Ga.: Boyd Publishing, 2001), 3:210.

6. Willis, *A Family History,* p. 115.

7. Willis, *Our Wright-Washington Ancestry,* pp. 4-5.

8. Hays & Wilson, op. cit.

9. Wrightsboro was a Quaker village founded in 1768 and named for Georgia's last royal governor, Sir James Wright.

10. Edward F. Flint & Gwendolyn S. Flint, *Flint Family History of the Adventuresome Seven* (Baltimore: Gateway Press 1984), 2:1149, 1163.

11. F.M. Newsome & Neil H. Newsome, *Wilkes Co. Cemeteries and a Few Surrounding Counties* (Washington, Ga.: Wilkes Publishing Co., 1970), 150.

12. Smith, op cit. 3:212.

13. 1820 United States Census, Columbia County, Georgia, 44.

14. Dorothy M. Jones, *Wrightsborough 1768* (Thomson, Ga.: Wrightsborough

Quaker Community Foundation, 1979), 70.

15. *Augusta Chronicle,* 17 September 1808, 3, col. 3.

16. Ibid., 27 May 1814, 3, col. 4.

17. Robert W. Fogel and Stanley L. Engerman, *Time on the Cross, The Economics of American Negro Slavery* (Boston: Cliff Brown and Company, 1974), 146.

18. Kenneth M. Stampp, *The Peculiar Institution: Slavery in the Antebellum South* (New York: Alfred A. Knopf, 1956), 192.

19. Charles S. Sydnor, *Slavery in Mississippi* (New York: D. Appleton and Company, 1933), 239.

20. Helen T. Catterall, *Judicial Cases Concerning Slavery and the Negro,* 5 vols. (Wash., D.C.: Carnegie Institution of Washington, 1926) 2:530.

21. William J. Northen, *Men of Mark in Georgia,* 7 vols. (Spartanburg, S.C.: Reprint Co., 1974), 3:327. For an excellent biography of Augustus R. Wright, see David T. Dixon, *Augustus R. Wright and the Loyalty of the Heart,* The Georgia Historical Quarterly, Vol. 94, No. 3 (Fall 2010), 342-371.

22. *Augusta Chronicle,* 24 September 1823.

23. Martha Lou Houston, *Lottery Lists, 1827* (Greenville, S.C.: Southern Historical Press, 1929), 139, 164, 208.

24. 1830 United States Census, Columbia County, Georgia, 363.

25. Robert S. Davis, *The 1833 Land Lottery of Georgia and Other Missing Names of Winners in the Georgia Land Lotteries* (Greenville, S.C.: Southern Historical Press, 1991), 6, 11.

26. Northen, op cit., 125-126.

27. Charles S. Sydnor, *The Development of Southern Sectionalism, 1819-1848* (Baton Rouge: Louisiana State Univ. Press, 1948), 95.

28. 1840 United States Census, Taliaferro County, Georgia, 242.

29. Allen D. Candler & Clement A. Evans, *Cyclopedia of Georgia* (Spartanburg, S.C.: Reprint Co., 1972), 1:111.

30. Ibid., 111-114.

31. Rev. S. Emmett Lucas, *Memoirs of Georgia* (Southern Historical Association, 1895), 2:689; *History of Pike County Georgia* (1990), 337-340.

32. Like many southern boys of his generation Harry was named for Revolutionary War hero Gen. Henry ("Light-Horse Harry") Lee, the

father of Robert E. Lee.

33. 1850 United States Census, Taliaferro County, Georgia, Schedule 1, 669; Schedule 2, 9.

34. The town was named to commemorate General Zachary Taylor's victory at Buena Vista, Mexico in the Mexican War.

35. Nettie Powell, *History of Marion County, Georgia, 1827-1930* (Columbus, Ga.: Historical Pub. Co., 1931), 39, 42.

36. 1860 United States Census, Marion County, Georgia, Schedule 1, 282-283; Schedule 2, 16.

5. SECESSION AND RECONSTRUCTION

1. Nettie Powell, *History of Marion County, Georgia, 1827-1930* (Columbus, Ga.: Historical Pub. Co., 1931), 56-57.

2. Ava Louise Wright, *Sketch of My Grandfather Augustus R. Wright* (undated) 4-5.

3. Richard A. Posner, ed., *The Essential Holmes: Selections From the Letters, Speeches, Judicial Opinions, and Other Writings of Oliver Wendell Holmes, Jr.* (University of Chicago Press, 1992) 80-87.

4. Powell, op cit., 58-60.

5. Atlanta *Southern Confederacy*, 22 March 1862.

6. United States War Department, *The War of the Rebellion: A Compilation of the Official Records of the Union and Confederate Armies* (Washington, D.C.: Govt. Print. Off. 1880-1901), Vol. XIV, 91-92.

7. Ibid., 259.

8. Ibid., 926.

9. Ibid., (1889), Vol. XXIV, Part I, 786.

10. Gen. Clement A. Evans, ed., *Confederate Military History*, 12 vols. (Atlanta: Confederate Publishing Company, 1899), 6:296.

11. *The War of the Rebellion* (1890) Vol. XXX, Part II, 241.

12. Ibid., 245-247.

13. Lillian Henderson, *Roster of the Confederate Soldiers of Georgia*, 6 vols. (Hapeville, Ga.: Longina & Porter, 1959-1964), 4:1007.

14. *War of the Rebellion* (1890), Vol. XXX, Part II, 67.

15. Stanley F. Horn, *The Army of Tennessee: A Military History* (Norman: University of Oklahoma Press, 1941), 291.

16. Joseph H. Crute, Jr., *Units of the Confederate States Army* (Midlothian, Va.: Derwent Books, 1987), 100.

17. *War of the Rebellion* (1891), Vol. XXXVIII, Part III, 716-717.

18. Memoirs of J.H. Booker, Co. E, 46th Georgia Infantry Regiment, Georgia Archives.

19. *Daily Columbus Enquirer,* 26 July 1864, 2.

20. An abatis is a network of cut trees and branches placed in front of an entrenchment to obstruct an attacking force.

21. *War of the Rebellion* (1891), Vol. XXXVIII, Part III, 719-720.

22. Evans, op cit., 6: 339.

23. Augustus R. Wright's home in Rome, Georgia was originally owned by the Cherokee Chief Major Ridge before his tribe's tragic "Trail of Tears" exodus. Today the home is known as the "Chieftain's Museum."

24. Augustus R. Wright's meeting with Gen. William Tecumseh Sherman was reported by Sherman to President Abraham Lincoln in a letter of 17 September 1864.

25. Ava Louise Wright, op cit., 13-15.

26. George M. Battey, Jr., *A History of Rome and Floyd County, Georgia* (Atlanta: The Webb and Vary Company, 1922), 343.

27. Robert W. Banks, *The Battle of Franklin* (New York & Washington: The Neale Publishing Company, 1908), 58-59.

28. *War of the Rebellion* (1894), Vol. XLV, Part I, 736-737.

29. Levi T. Scofield, *The Retreat From Pulaski to Nashville* (Cleveland: Press of the Caxton Co., 1909), 18.

30. *War of the Rebellion* (1894), Vol. XLV, Part I, 737.

31. Samuel R. Watkins, *"Co. Aytch": A Side Show of the Big Show* (New York: MacMillan Publishing Company, 1962), 120, 235.

32. Carey C. Jewell, *Harvest of Death* (Hicksville, N.Y.: Exposition Press, 1976), 51.

33. Banks, op cit., 74.

34. Watkins, op cit., 240-241.

35. Nashville *Republican Banner,* 25 March 1869.

36. *War of the Rebellion* (1894), Vol. XVI, Part II, 757.

37. Benson J. Lossing, *A History of the Civil War* (New York: The War Memorial Association, 1912), 427-428.

38. Powell, op cit., 65.

39. 1870 United States Census, Jacksonville, Marion County, Georgia, 167-168.

6. JOINING CAPTAIN MCNELLY

1. Austin *Democratic Daily Statesman,* 9 February 1876.

2. Walter P. Webb, *The Texas Rangers* (Austin: University of Texas Press, 1987), 224.

3. Austin *Democratic Daily Statesman,* 22 July 1874.

4. Clinton was two miles south of Cuero on the Guadalupe River.

5. *Memoirs of William C. Callicott,* as told to Walter P. Webb (Texas State Archives, 1921), 26-27.

6. Lt. Truxton C. Robinson's works are compiled in Chuck Parsons, *"Pidge:" A Texas Ranger From Virginia* (College Station: Texas A&M University Press, 1985).

7. Austin *Democratic Daily Statesman,* 8 August 1874; quoted in Parsons, *"Pidge,"* 37.

8. Webb, op cit., 298.

9. Capt. L.H. McNelly to Gen. William Steele, 7 August 1874.

10. Ibid., 8 August 1874.

11. San Antonio *Daily Express,* 23 August 1874; quoted in Parsons, *"Pidge,"* 33-34.

12. Capt. L.H. McNelly to Gen. William Steele, 31 August 1874.

13. Ibid., 5 November 1874.

14. George Durham, *On the Trail of 5100 Outlaws: The Inside Story of McNelly's Texas Rangers,* West Magazine, (1937), Part I, 110-111.

15. Gen. William Steele to Capt. L.H. McNelly, 10 March 1875.

16. San Antonio *Daily Express,* 26 March 1875, 2, col. 1.

7. THE BATTLE AT PALO ALTO PRAIRIE

1. Stephen B. Oates, *Rip Ford's Texas* (Austin: University of Texas Press, 1990), 204.

2. Walter P. Webb, *The Texas Rangers: A Century of Frontier Defense* (Austin: University of Texas Press, 1987), 182.

3. A year later Generals Lee and Heintzelman were on opposite sides of the Civil War.

4. On May 13, 1865 Colonel Ford's Confederate regiment fought the last battle of the Civil War defeating a Union force at the Palmito Ranch ten miles east of Brownsville. The news of Lee's surrender a month earlier had not yet reached Ford.
5. *Texas Frontier Troubles,* 44th Congress, 1st Session, House of Representatives Report No. 343 (1876), xviii-xxi.
6. George Durham, *On The Trail of 5100 Outlaws: The Inside Story of McNelly's Texas Rangers,* West Magazine, Parts I-VII (1937), republished by Clyde Wantland as *Taming the Nueces Strip* (Austin: University of Texas Press, 1962); Walter P. Webb, *Memoirs of William C. Callicott* (Texas State Archives, 1921).
7. N.A. Jennings, *A Texas Ranger* (Chicago: R.R. Donelly & Sons Company, 1992).
8. Ibid., 121.
9. Wantland, *Nueces Strip,* 26.
10. *Texas Frontier Troubles,* 11.
11. Durham, *5100 Outlaws,* Part III, 94-95.
12. Ibid., Part I, 113.
13. Durham and Jennings refer to Lawrence Wright as a lieutenant during 1875 events but he did not receive his commission until August 8,1876. Writing many years later they referred to him by his highest rank.
14. Jennings, op cit., 124-125.
15. Durham, *5100 Outlaws,* Part II, 111.
16. *Galveston Daily News,* 20 May 1875, 1, col. 1.
17. Durham, *5100 Outlaws,* Part II, 114.
18. John C. Rayburn & Virginia K. Rayburn, *Century of Conflict, 1821-1913* (New York: Arno Press, 1976), 119.
19. Durham, *5100 Outlaws,* Part II, 115.
20. Webb, *Callicott Memoirs,* 40.
21. Ibid.
22. Ibid., 42.
23. Durham, *5100 Outlaws,* Part II, 116.
24. Ibid., Wantland, *Nueces Strip,* 58-59.

25. Durham, *5100 Outlaws,* Part II, 116.
26. Wantland, *Nueces Strip,* 61.
27. The pistol was kept by Dr. Lawrence B. Wright and said to be the one he used at Palo Alto. Decades later the gun was removed from its resting place in the Wright home by his daughter, Lucile, who tossed it down an outhouse to keep her nephews from playing with it.
28. Webb, *Callicott Memoirs,* 48.
29. Jennings, op cit., 137-138.
30. Wantland, *Nueces Strip,* 61-62.
31. Webb, *Callicott Memoirs,* 44-45.
32. Durham, *5100 Outlaws,* Part II, 117.
33. Capt. L.H. McNelly to Gen. William Steele, 13 June 1875.
34. *Texas Frontier Troubles,* 85.
35. Ibid., 82-83.
36. Webb, *Callicott Memoirs,* 55.
37. Wantland, *Nueces Strip,* 66.
38. *Texas Frontier Troubles,* 79.
39. Ibid., 80.
40. Ibid.
41. Oates, op cit., 413.
42. Alfred, Lord Tennyson, *The Charge of the Light Brigade* (1854).

8. THE RAID ON LAS CUEVAS

1. Capt. L.H. McNelly to Gen. William Steele, 13 August 1875.
2. Wantland, *Nueces Strip,* 89.
3. Austin *Daily State Gazette,* 3 October 1875; quoted in Parsons, *"Pidge,"* 80.
4. Capt. L.H. McNelly to Gen. William Steele, 12 November 1875.
5. Wantland, *Nueces Strip,* 105.
6. Webb, *Callicott Memoirs, 7.*
7. Ibid., 8.
8. Jennings, op. cit., 176.

9. Webb, *Callicott Memoirs,* 8.
10. Wantland, *Nueces Strip,* 110.
11. Durham, *5100 Outlaws,* Part IV, 78.
12. Capt. James Randlett to Lt. Helenus Dodt, 1 December 1875.
13. Webb, *Callicott Memoirs,* 11-12.
14. Austin *Daily State Gazette,* 19 January 1876; quoted in Parsons, *"Pidge,"* 89.
15. Webb, *Callicott Memoirs,* 16.
16. Capt. L.H. McNelly to Gen. William Steele, 20 November 1875.
17. Potter to Alexander, 20 November 1975.
18. Durham, *5100 Outlaws,* Part IV, 80.
19. Ibid., 81.
20. Webb, *Callicott Memoirs,* 25.
21. Ibid., 29-31.
22. Ibid., 27.

9. KEEPING THE PEACE IN NUECES COUNTRY

1. George Durham, *On the Trail of 5100 Outlaws: The Inside Story of McNelly's Texas Rangers,* West Magazine, Part III (1937), 90.
2. *Texas Frontier Troubles,* 44th Congress, 1st Session, House of Reps. Report No. 343 (1876), xvi-xvii.
3. Lawrence B. Wright was the third sergeant according to the company muster roll of 29 February 1876.
4. Austin *Daily State Gazette,* 19 March 1876; quoted in Parsons, *"Pidge,"* 94.
5. Capt. L.H. McNelly to Gen. William Steele, 19 May 1876.
6. Jennings, *Texas Ranger,* 142.
7. Ibid., 227-228.
8. Wantland, *Nueces Strip,* 146-147.
9. Capt. L.H. McNelly to Gen. William Steele, 20 September 1876.
10. Durham, *5,100 Outlaws,* Part VII, 112.
11. Capt. L.H. McNelly to Gen. William Steele, 18 November 1876.
12. Ibid., 24 November 1876.

13. Lt. John B. Armstrong to Gen. William Steele, 9 December 1876; Jennings, op cit., 277.
14. *The* [Nashville] *Tennessean,* 4 July 1877.
15. Harry L. Wright to Farrow, 22 April 1943.
16. Hall to William Steele, 1 February 1878.
17. See, Chuck and Marjorie Parsons, *Bowen and Hardin* (College Station, Tex.: Creative Publishing Company, 1991),
18. Ibid., 111; quoted from Dallas *Weekly Herald,* 25 May 1878.
19. *Lampasas* [Texas] *Dispatch,* 4 April 1878.
20. Austin *Democratic Daily Statesman,* 4 July 1879.
21. Monthly return of Capt. J.L. Hall, 1 October 1878.
22. Galveston *Daily News,* 8 October 1878, 3, col. 3.
23. Harry Lee Wright to Farrow, 22 April 1943.
24. Corpus Christi *Semi-Weekly Ledger,* 13 June 1880, 3, col. 2.
25. Ibid., 27 June 1880, 3, col. 1.

10. GONE TO TEXAS

1. *Galveston Daily News,* 21 September 1875, 1, cols. 1, 8.
2. Ibid.
3. 1880 United States Census, Huntsville, Walker County, Texas, 40.
4. Galveston City Directory (1884-1885).
5. Walter W. Meek to Chuck Parsons, 23 August 1978.
6. Ibid.
7. 1880 United States Census, San Diego, Duval County, Texas, 227, 237.
8. Ibid., Rockdale, Milam County, Texas, 281.
9. 1900 United States Census, Palestine, Anderson County, Texas, 15; 1910 op cit. 3B.
10. Evelyn Wright White to George W. Wright, 2 March 1990.
11. Corpus Christi *Semi-Weekly Ledger,* 17 October 1880, 3, col. 2.
12. Major General C.H. Bridges, Adjutant General, War Department, to the Comptroller of the State of Texas, 2 February, 1932, in re Mrs. Mary Hickey's pension application.
13. 1870 United States Census, Brazoria, Brazoria County, Texas, 2.

14. 1880 United States Census, Corpus Christi, Nueces County, Texas, 8.
15. Frank W. Johnson, *A History of Texas and Texans,* 5 vols. (Chicago and New York: The American Historical Society, 1914), 5:2289-2290.
16. 1880 United States Census, Corpus Christi, Nueces County, Texas, 11.
17. Dermot H. Hardy and Ingham S. Roberts, ed., *Historical Review of South-East Texas,* Vol. II (Chicago: The Lewis Publishing Co.,1910), 757.
18. Corpus Christi *Semi-Weekly Ledger,* 2 February 1881, 3, col. 3.

11. THE SAN DIEGO YEARS

1. Corpus Christi *Semi-Weekly Ledger,* 22 August 1880, 1, col. 3.
2. William R. West, Secretary, Corpus Christi Lodge No. 189, A.F.&A.M., to George W. Wright, 11 April 1990.
3. Masonic Grand Lodge Library and Museum of Texas membership card on L.B. Wright.
4. Corpus Christi *Weekly Caller,* 24 June 1883, col. 3.
5. Ibid., 16 September 1883, 5, col. 3.
6. Ibid., 23 September 1883, 5, col. 4.
7. These anecdotes are related by Philip T. Wright, Jr. and John T. Wright, Jr.
8. Father Peter Bard, a French priest, lived in San Diego from 1877 to 1920. Father Bard baptized and married most of Dr. Lawrence and Mary Wright's children and grandchildren.
9. Corpus Christi *Weekly Caller,* 8 June 1884, 4, col. 6.
10. Ibid., 26 October 1884, 1, col. 4.
11. Ibid., 9 November 1884, 4, col. 6.
12. Ibid., 26 March 1887, 4, col. 6.
13. Ibid., 2 April 1887, 4, col. 6.
14. Ibid., 14 May 1887, 4, col. 5.
15. Walter W. Meek to Chuck Parsons, 23 August 1978.
16. H.H. Puckett to Harry L. Wright, 6 July 1943.
17. Corpus Christi *Weekly Caller,* 11 June, 1887 4, col. 5.
18. Ibid., 18 June 1887, 8, col. 3.
19. Ibid., 28 May 1887, 4, col. 5.

20. Ibid., 2 July 1887, 8, col. 3.

21. Ibid., 9 July 1887, 4, col. 5.

22. Ibid., 25 June 1887, 8, col. 4.

23. Ibid., 27 August 1887, 4, col. 5.

24. Ibid., 22 October 1887, 4, col. 5.

25. Ibid.

26. Ibid., 29 October 1887, 4, col. 5.

27. Ibid., 5 November 1887, 8, col. 5.

28. Ibid., 31 December 1887, 8, col. 6.

29. Ibid., 19 May 1888, 4, col. 3.

30. Ibid., 7 July 1888, 1, col. 5.

31. Ibid., 26 May 1888, 1, col. 6.

32. Ibid., 16 June 1888, 1, col. 6.

33. *New York Times,* 11 August 1888, 2, col. 5.

34. John Bull was a popular nickname for Great Britain.

35. Corpus Christi *Weekly Caller,* 11 August 1888, 1, col. 3.

36. El guarache (sandal) and la bota (boot) denoted the distinction between the Mexican peasant and middle classes.

37. Corpus Christi *Weekly Caller,* 27 October 1888, 1, cols. 4-5.

38. Ibid., 6 February 1889.

39. Ibid., 14 November 1888.

40. Galveston *Daily News,* 29 November 1888, 10.

41. James L. Buckley to Chuck Parsons, 7 May 1979.

42. James L. Buckley to Chuck Parsons, 11 April 1979.

43. The details of the Buckley v. Wright suit are contained in the 123-page handwritten transcript of the Nueces County District Court proceedings and brief filed on behalf of Linton L. Wright in the Texas Supreme Court.

44. Pedro Eznal was the Duval County Deputy Clerk during John Buckley's term as Sheriff. On May 18, 1912, Eznal, Candelario Saenz and Antonio Anguiano were shot to death in San Diego in what appeared to be a politically charged confrontation with Dr. Sam Roberts, Neal Robinson and Charles Gravis. The latter were tried and acquitted by a jury. *Alice Echo,*

22 July 1984, 1-2.

45. Philip T. Wright, Jr. to Chuck Parsons, 16 May 1979.

46. San Antonio *Daily Express,* 11 November 1890, 2, cols. 1-2.

47. Dengue is a viral illness transmitted by mosquitoes causing sudden headaches and severe pain in the muscles and joints.

48. Corpus Christi *Weekly Caller,* 11 April 1891.

49. Ibid., 6 June 1891.

50. Ibid., 18 June 1891.

51. Ibid., 18 June 1891.

52. Thomas C. Lea, *The King Ranch,* 2 vols. (Boston: Little, Brown & Co., 1957), 2:502-503.

53. Corpus Christi *Weekly Caller,* 9 January 1892.

54. Walter P. Webb and Eldon S. Branda, ed., *The Handbook of Texas,* 3 vols (Austin: Texas State Historical Association, 1976), 3:329.

55. W.H. Mabry, *Report of the Adjutant General of the State of Texas for 1892* (Austin: Texas State Library and Archives Commission, 1893), 11.

56. Ibid.; Webb and Branda, op. cit., 329.

57. Mabry, op. cit., 11.

58. San Antonio *Daily Express,* 2 February 1892, 1, col. 7.

59. Ibid., 6 February 1892, 2, cols. 1-2.

60. Corpus Christi *Weekly Caller,* 13 February 1892.

61. Frank H. Bushick, *Glamorous Days* (San Antonio: Naylor Company, 1934), 242.

62. Evelyn Wright White to George W. Wright, 11 September 1989.

63. Corpus Christi *Weekly Caller,* 4 March 1892.

64. San Antonio *Daily Express,* 1 March 1892, 2, col. 3.

65. Erysipelas is a contagious disease of the skin and subcutaneous tissues marked by redness and swelling.

66. Corpus Christi *Weekly Caller,* 11 March 1892, 1, col. 1.

67. Galveston *Daily News,* 11 March 1892, 3, col. 3.

68. 1900 United States Census, San Diego, Duval County, Texas, 915.

69. Ellis A. Davis and Edwin H. Grobe, *The New Encyclopedia of Texas,* 2 vols. (Dallas: Texas Development Bureau, 1929), 2:900.

70. Corpus Christi *Caller Times,* 27 October 1935 and 29 October 1936.
71. Corpus Christi *Caller,* 17 January 1950.
72. Evelyn Wright White to George W. Wright, 31 July 1990.
73. Davis and Grobe, op. cit., 900-901.
74. Ibid.
75. Philip T. Wright, Sr. to U.S. Department of Interior, 31 May 1918.
76. Commissioner G.M. Saltzguber, Army and Navy Division, U.S. War Department, to Mary H. Wright, 31 January 1919.
77. John Nance Garner was Vice-President of the United States from 1933 to 1941.
78. John Nance Garner to General Frank T. Hines, 28 April 1932.
79. E.W. Morgan to John Nance Garner, 10 May 1932.
80. *The Benavides* [Texas] *Facts,* 13 July 1934, 4, col. 3.

12. HARRY LEE WRIGHT AND JOHN W. WRIGHT, JR

1. Palestine, Texas *Daily Herald,* 5 February 1943.
2. 1900 United States Census, Palestine, Anderson County, Texas, 102.
3. Palestine *Herald and Press,* 12 November 1947, 4, cols. 3-4.
4. Edward R. Stanford, Jr. to George W. Wright, 23 July 1990.
5. Palestine *Daily Herald,* 5 February 1943.
6. Palestine *Herald and Press,* 12 November 1947, 4, cols. 3-4.
7. Dallas *Morning News,* 21 January 1929, 1, col. 1.

SELECTED BIBLIOGRAPHY

PUBLIC DOCUMENTS

Busch, Clarence M., State Printer, *Record of Pennsylvania Marriages, Prior to 1810,* Second Series, Vol. 8, Harrisburg: Pennsylvania State Archives, 1895.

Greenville, S.C. Land Grants, Books A and C.

Hart, Lane S., State Printer, *Marriages Authorized by the Philadelphia Monthly Meeting of Friends, 1682-1756,* Second Series, Vol. 9, Harrisburg: Pennsylvania State Archives, 1880.

Mabry, W.H., *Report of the Adjutant General of the State of Texas for 1892,* Austin: Texas State Library and Archives Commission, 1893.

Salley, A.S., Jr., ed., *Accounts Audited of Claims Growing out of the Revolution in South Carolina (1775-1856),* Columbia, S.C.: South Carolina Department of Archives and History, 1985.

______, *Stub Entries to Indents Issued in Payment of Claims Against South Carolina Growing Out of the Revolution,* Columbia, S.C.: The Historical Commission of South Carolina, 1927.

U.S. House, *Texas Frontier Troubles,* 44th Cong., 1st sess., H.Doc. 343, 1876.

U.S. War Dept., *The War of the Rebellion: A Compilation of the Official Records of the Union and Confederate Armies,* Washington, D.C.: GPO, 1880-1901.

MANUSCRIPT SOURCES

Hanger, George (Lord Coleraine), an Address to the Army in Reply to the Strictures by Roderick M'Kenzie (Late Lieut. in the 71st Regmt.) on Tarleton's History of the Campaigns of 1780 and 1781, London, 1789.

Lincoln, Benjamin, Original Papers Relating to the Siege of Charleston, 1780, Charleston, S.C.: Walker, Evans & Cogswell Co., 1898.

Memoirs of J.H. Booker, Co. E, 46th Georgia Infantry Regiment, Georgia Archives.

Memoirs of William C. Callicott, as told to Walter P. Webb, Texas State Archives, 1921.

Salley, A.S., Jr., ed., *Col. William Hill's Memoirs of The Revolution,* Columbia, S.C.: The Historical Commission of South Carolina, 1921.

Willis, Anne Willingham, *Our Wright-Washington Ancestry,* Atlanta: Georgia Archives, 1965.

Wright, Ava Louise, *Sketch of My Grandfather Augustus R. Wright,* Atlanta: Georgia Archives (undated).

BOOKS AND ARTICLES

Alexander Gregg, *History of the Old Cheraws,* New York: Richardson and Company, 1867.

Banks, Robert W., *The Battle of Franklin,* New York & Washington: The Neale Publishing Company, 1908.

Barber, John W. and Henry Howe, *Historical Collections of the State of New Jersey,* New York: S. Tuttle, 1844.

Battey, George M., Jr., *A History of Rome and Floyd County, Georgia,* Atlanta: The Webb and Vary Company, 1922.

Blair, Ruth, *Revolutionary Soldiers' Receipts for Georgia Bounty Grants,* Atlanta: Georgia Archives, Forte and Davies, 1928.

Borick, Carl. P., *A Gallant Defense,* Columbia, S.C.: The University of South Carolina Press, 2003.

_____, *Relieve Us of This Burthen,* Columbia, S.C.: The University of South Carolina Press, 2012.

Bushick, Frank H., *Glamorous Days,* San Antonio: Naylor Company, 1934.

Candler, Allen D. and Clement A. Evans, *Cyclopedia of Georgia,* Spartanburg, S.C.: Reprint Co., 1972.

Catterall, Helen T., *Judicial Cases Concerning Slavery and the Negro,* Wash., D.C.: Carnegie Institution of Washington, 1926.

Chesnutt, David R., et. al., *The Papers of Henry Laurens,* Columbia, S.C.: University of South Carolina Press, 1994.

Coldham, Peter Wilson, *The Complete Book of Emigrants:* 1700-1750, Baltimore: Genealogical Publishing Co., Inc., 1992.

Crute, Joseph H., Jr., *Units of the Confederate States Army,* Midlothian, Va.: Derwent Books, 1987.

Davis, Ellis A. and Edwin H. Grobe, *The New Encyclopedia of Texas,* Dallas: Texas Development Bureau, 1929.

Davis, Robert S., *The 1833 Land Lottery of Georgia and Other Missing Names of Winners in the Georgia Land Lotteries,* Greenville, S.C.: Southern Historical Press, 1991.

Dixon, David T., *Augustus R. Wright and the Loyalty of the Heart,* The Georgia Historical Quarterly, Vol. 94, No. 3 (Fall 2010), 342-371.

Durham, George, *On the Trail of 5100 Outlaws: The Inside Story of McNelly's Texas Rangers,* West Magazine, (1937), Part I, 110-111.

Evans, Gen. Clement A., ed., *Confederate Military History,* 12 vols., Atlanta: Confederate Publishing Company, 1899.

Flint, Edward F. Gwendolyn S. Flint, *Flint Family History of the Adventuresome Seven,* Baltimore: Gateway Press, 1984.

Fogel, Robert W. and Stanley L. Engerman, *Time on the Cross, The Economics of American Negro Slavery,* Boston: Cliff Brown and Company, 1974.

Futhey, J. Smith and Gilbert Cope, *History of Chester County, Pennsylvania,* Philadelphia: H. Louis Everts, 1880.

Hardy, Dermot H. and Ingham S. Roberts, *Historical Review of South-East Texas,* Vol. II, Chicago: The Lewis Publishing Co., 1910.

Haun, Weynette Parks, *North Carolina Court of Claims Record of Patents Granted (Secretary of State Papers) 1740-1755,* Durham, N.C.: W.P. Haun, 1996.

Hays, J.E. and John B. Wilson, *Georgia Military Affairs (1775-1793),* Atlanta: WPA Project 5993, 1940.

Henderson, Lillian, *Roster of the Confederate Soldiers of Georgia,* Hapeville, Ga.: Longina & Porter, 1959-1964.

Hitz, Alex M., *Georgia Bounty Land Grants,* The Georgia Historical Quarterly, Vol. 38, No. 4, December, 1954, 341.

Holcomb, Brent H., *North Carolina Land Grants in South Carolina,* Baltimore: Genealogical Publishing Co., 1986.

Horn, Stanley F., *The Army of Tennessee: A Military History,* Norman: University of Oklahoma Press, 1941.

Houston, Martha Lou, *Lottery Lists, 1827,* Greenville, S.C.: Southern Historical Press, 1929.

Huff, Jr., Archie Vernon, *Greenville: The History of the City and County in the South Carolina Piedmont,* Columbia, S.C: University of South Carolina Press, 1995.

Jennings, N.A., *A Texas Ranger,* Chicago: R.R. Donelly & Sons Company, 1992.

Jewell., Carey C., *Harvest of Death,* Hicksville, NY: Exposition Press, 1976.

Johnson, Frank W., *A History of Texas and Texans,* Chicago and New York: The American Historical Society, 1914.

Jones, Jr., Charles C., *The History of Georgia,* Cambridge, S.C.: The Riverside Press, 1883, reprint ed. Spartanburg: The Reprint Company, 1965.

Jones, Dorothy M., *Wrightsborough 1768,* Thomson, Ga.: Wrightsborough Quaker Community Foundation, 1979.

Jordan, John W., *Colonial and Revolutionary Families of Pennsylvania,* Baltimore: Genealogical Publishing Co., 1978

Landrum, Dr. J.B.O., *Colonial and Revolutionary History of Upper South Carolina,* Greenville: Shannon & Co., 1897.

Lea, Thomas C., *The King Ranch,* Boston: Little, Brown & Co., 1957.

Lossing, Benson J., *A History of the Civil War,* New York: The War Memorial Association, 1912.

Lucas, Rev. S. Emmett, *Memoirs of Georgia,* Atlanta: Southern Historical Association, 1895.

Lumpkin, Henry, *From Savannah to Yorktown: The American Revolution in the South,* Columbia, S.C.: University of South Carolina Press, 1981.

Marshall, John, *The Life of George Washington,* Philadelphia: C.P. Wayne, 1804.

McCall, Ettie Tidwell, *McCall-Tidwell and Allied Families,* Atlanta: Walter W. Brown Publishing Co., 1931.

McCall, Hugh, *The History of Georgia,* Atlanta: A.B. Caldwell, 1909.

McPike, Eugene F., *Tales of Our Forefathers and Biographical Annals of Families Allied to Those of McPike, Guest and Dumont,* Albany: Joel Munsell's Sons, 1898.

Monaghan, E. Jennifer, *Literacy Instruction and Gender in Colonial England,* American Quarterly, 40(I), 1988, 18-41.

Moore, M. A., *The Life of Gen. Edward Lacy,* Spartanburg, S.C.: Douglas, Evins & Co., 1859.

Moultrie, William, *Memoirs of the American Revolution,* New York: David Longworth, 1802.

Newsome, F.M. and Neil H. Newsome, *Wilkes Co. Cemeteries and a Few Surrounding Counties,* Washington, Ga.: Wilkes Publishing Co., 1970.

Northen, William J., *Men of Mark in Georgia,* Spartanburg, S.C.: Reprint Co., 1974.

O'Kelley, Patrick, *Unwaried Patience and Fortitude: Francis Marion's Orderly Book,* West Conshocken, Pa., Infinity Publishing.com, 2007.

Oates, Stephen B., *Rip Ford's Texas,* Austin: University of Texas Press, 1990.

Parks Haun, *North Carolina Court of Claims Record of Patents Granted (Secretay of State Papers) 1740-1755,* Durham, N.C.: W.P. Haun, 1996.

Parsons, Chuck, *"Pidge:" A Texas Ranger From Virginia,* College Station: Texas A&M University Press, 1985.

Parsons, Chuck and Marjorie Parsons, *Bowen and Hardin,* College Station: Texas A&M University Press, 1991.

Philbeck, Miles S., *Upper Broad River Basin Pioneers, 1750-1760,* Chapel Hill, N.C.: Miles S. Philbeck, 1984.

Posner, Richard A., ed., *The Essential Holmes: Selections From the Letters, Speeches, Judicial Opinions, and Other Writings of Oliver Wendell Holmes, Jr.,* University of Chicago Press, 1992.

Powell, Nettie, *History of Marion County, Georgia, 1827-1930,* Columbus, Ga.: Historical Pub. Co., 1931.

Ramsay, David, *History of South Carolina, From its First Settlement in 1670 to the Year 1808,* Newberry, S.C.: W. J. Duffie, 1858.

_____, *The History of the Revolution of South Carolina from a British Province to an Independent State,* Trenton, N.J.: Isaac Collins, 1785.

Rayburn, John C. and Virginia K. Rayburn, *Century of Conflict, 1821-1913,* New York: Arno Press, 1976.

Ross, Bobby Gilmer, *Roster of South Carolina Patriots in the American Revolution,* Baltimore: Genealogical Publishing Co., Inc, 1994.

_____, *The Patriots at the Cowpens,* Blacksburg, S.C.: Scotia Press, 1985.

Salley, A.S., Jr., ed., The South Carolina Historical and Genealogical Magazine, Charleston, S.C.: The Walker, Evans & Cogswell Co., 1900, 195-196.

Scharf, John Thomas and Thompson. Westcott, *History of Philadelphia, 1609-1884,* Philadelphia: L.J. Everts & Co., 1884

Scofield, Levi T., *The Retreat From Pulaski to Nashville,* Cleveland: Press of the Caxton Co., 1909.

Scoggins, Michael C., *A Brief History of the New Acquisition Militia,* York County Historical Center, 2002.

Slosser, Gaius Jackson, ed., *They Seek a Country: The American Presbyterians,* New York: The Macmillan Company, 1955.

Smith, Gordon Burns, *History of the Georgia Militia, 1783-1861,* Milledgeville, Ga.: Boyd Publishing, 2001.

Stampp, Kenneth M., *The Peculiar Institution: Slavery in the Antebellum South,* New York: Alfred A. Knopf, 1956.

Sydnor, Charles S., *Slavery in Mississippi,* New York: D. Appleton and Company, 1933.

_____, *The Development of Southern Sectionalism, 1819-1848,* Baton Rouge: Louisiana State Univ. Press, 1948.

Thomas, Sam, *The 1780 Presbyterian Rebellion and the Battle of Huck's Defeat,* Culture & Heritage Commission of York County, S.C. (1999).

Walker, Melissa, *The Battles of Kings Mountain and Cowpens: The American Revolution in the Southern Backcountry,* New York: Routledge, 2013.

Wantland, Clyde, *Taming the Nueces Strip,* Austin: University of Texas Press, 1962.

Watkins, Samuel R., *"Co. Aytch": A Side Show of the Big Show,* New York: MacMillan Publishing Company, 1962.

Watson, Robert P., *The Ghost Ship of Brooklyn: An Untold Story of the American Revolution,* New York: Da Capo Press, 2017.

Webb, Walter P. , *The Texas Rangers: A Century of Frontier Defense,* Austin: University of Texas Press, 1987.

Webb, Walter P. and Eldon S. Branda, ed., *The Handbook of Texas,* Austin: Texas State Historical Association, 1976.

Weir, Robert M., *"A Most Important Epocha:" The Coming of the Revolution in South Carolina,* Columbia, S.C.: University of South Carolina Press, 1970

Willis, Anne Willingham, *A Family History,* Atlanta: Higgins-McArthur Co., 1946

Wright, Jr., Robert K., *The Continental Army,* Washington, D.C.: Center of Military History, United States Army, 1983.

Index

www.ingramcontent.com/pod-product-compliance
Lightning Source LLC
Chambersburg PA
CBHW070600270326
41926CB00013B/2377

* 9 7 8 0 7 8 8 4 5 8 8 5 9 *